I AM GOD'S CHILD

REBECCA SMITH

Copyright © 2021 Rebecca S. Smith

All rights reserved.

ISBN: 978-0-578-30290-4

DEDICATION

This book is dedicated to Mrs. Rebecca Dozier, Mrs. Sandra Hunter, and to all of God's children along your journey in life.

The LORD is my shepherd;
I shall not want.
He makes me to lie down in green pastures:
he leads me beside the still waters.
He restores my soul:
he leads me in the paths of
righteousness for his name's sake.
Yea, though I walk through the valley of
the shadow of death, I will fear no evil:
for thou art with me;
thy rod and thy staff they comfort me.
Thou prepare a table before me in the
presence of mine enemies:
thou anoint my head with oil;
my cup runs over.
Surely goodness and mercy shall follow me
all the days of my life:
and I will dwell in the
house of the LORD forever.

INTRODUCTION

If someone told me, "Samone, this is your mission in life. *Go!*"

"Well, I am going to decline the offer. I appreciate the offer, but do you have something better?" That is what I would have said, if given the option.

But with God there is no option, there is only *his* way. I have learned there is promise in the pain! It is not about where you *start* in life, but how you *finish* in life. I want you to know you will be tested, and the journey will not be easy. There can be no victory without a test, and the choices you make determine if you pass the test. I want you to know there will be hard times, you might not make the right choices at times, and sometimes life knocks you down. But stand strong, get back up and continue on your journey even when you do not know where you are going. You must learn and grow from your mistakes. You must trust in the process, the process strengthens you, it shapes you and it builds you to be who you truly are.

As you travel along the journey of life, building a connection with God, dealing with circumstances you will endure pain and love. I want you to know not everything will be good, but it will not be all bad either. Learn to lead with *love!* Everything you *do* and *say*, make sure it is coming from a place of *love*. I pray we learn to *love* ourselves, we must learn to see what God sees in us, as the precious children of God that we all are!

Do not let the circumstances or the actions of others change your mind, change your character or change how you treat others. Do not be fooled by circumstance into believing you have already reached your final destination in life. You cannot skip the process of life and then go straight to the destination. To find your purpose in life, you must go through the process of becoming spiritually connected with the holy spirit; becoming the person who God wants you to be and reaching your destination in life.

Remember God is right here with you, but he is waiting for you to take his hand, and to walk *with* him along your spiritual journey.

While you are walking with God, talk to him, get to know him, and listen to him. There is nothing too great for the *almighty God!* We as children sometimes go astray and we become *disobedient!* But it is important you be an *obedient* child. He is a *merciful* and a *gracious God!* He is a jealous God! There is only one God, and we all pray to the same God. God's *love* is *immortal*, and he corrects you because he *loves* you. I encourage you to walk with God and get to know him, so you can find out for yourself how much God loves you!

By *God* you are strengthened! You will come to learn you can handle more than you think you can handle with God. How you navigate through your journey, determines how you finish. There will be naysayers, snakes in the grass and many wicked people wearing disguises. But do not be afraid of the unfamiliar and do not be fooled by any of it.

Remember to walk in faith and to *believe* in *God!*

The Devil wants you to believe you are *not God's Child* and he wants you to believe God does *not* love you! Always remember to look up to your *heavenly father* who is *God* and listen to your *mother* who is *wisdom*. Wisdom guides you through your journey because you *are God's Child!*

Well, traveling along my spiritual journey, I complained a lot, I dealt with many circumstances, and I wanted things to go right for once. I kept asking God *why?* The answer I received was simple; it is because *you* are *God's Child!*

God corrects you, and real *love* is correction. Life is real, and it is a privilege to live life. *Time* and *Death* remind you of the importance of life. Time waits for no one, and you cannot go back in time. *Life* is real, your life is a serious matter between *Life* and *Death*.

In order for us to get to know God, we must become as one with the Holy Spirit. In order to become one with the Holy Spirit we must let go all that is flesh, to become connected with the divine Holy Spirit. As you become connected with the divine Holy Spirit, it is the beginning of a new life, and death to the past life. There is *light* and *love* with the holy divine spirit. Be aware of your enemies, be aware of hidden snakes in the grass, for they are wicked and lurk secretly to put out your light. Know jealousy and envy are what kills.

As *God's children* we all have a purpose in life, and as one of Gods children you must stay with God. You must seek your *purpose* in life. Throughout your journey to fulfill your purpose in life you will complete the mission God placed upon you. Not everyone will understand or agree with your purpose in life and the destiny you must fulfill. The wicked will do whatever it takes to stop you from completing your mission and fulfilling your destiny. The wicked are filled with deceit, jealousy, envy, and hate. The wicked will stop at no means, the wicked will stop at no measure to destroy you and that includes killing you. The devil comes to steal, to kill, and to destroy.

A word for the wise: do not play with snakes and stay far away from the wicked. Those who appear to be your friends may reveal themselves to be foes, betraying you and becoming your enemy. Those who you love, your family, your own flesh and blood may betray you, turning into your foes, and becoming your enemies too.

Know, while traveling along your journey, not everyone is meant to go with you on your journey and you must learn to let them go to reach your destiny. Continually, pray to God, thank God for everyday he allows you to open your eyes and for every day he wakes you up. Always pray to God to keep your spirit strengthened, pray to stay strong mentally, physically, and spiritually. You will need to have strength and courage to travel along your journey.

I believe you can complete your mission in life and fulfill your destiny. As long as you have God with you, you walk in faith, and believe in God to get you there. The devil attacks your mind; be strong and do not fret because God is your *Protector*. There is a spiritual warfare between good and evil. I have come to learn life is about adjustments and change. You have to learn to adjust to life and be open to the changes in life. You will be able to navigate through life easier if you accept change, and life will be harder for you if you are not willing to do it.

I have been traveling my journey of life with God by my side, I had many ups and downs throughout my life. I am here to testify God is real, I believe in God, I serve God, and God is my *protector*. I have experienced love, pain, and betrayal in my life.

Allow me to share some of the stories from my travels, the knowledge and the wisdom I have learned through my walks of life with God.

I pray you seek God; find your purpose in life and fulfill your destiny as <u>*God's Child*</u>.

REBECCA S. SMITH

COMMUNITY

I was born March 23, 1988. My mom gave birth to a baby girl, and my life began the moment I opened my eyes. My mom worked at the local hospital as a nursing assistant and my dad was a cook. My mom already had three children, but I was the only child she had with my dad. I have two older sisters and one older brother. I am the youngest of my siblings and we all have different dads.

I was born and raised in the Sunshine State—Florida. I grew up in Miami, in the part of town called *Overtown*. It is across the other side of the bridge from South Beach. It was not a fancy rich neighborhood with ocean beach views, luxury homes and high-rise condos. It was the total opposite; it was the ghetto. Like every ghetto, it is a poverty-stricken neighborhood where those who are less fortunate live in the poorest conditions struggling to survive and raise a family.

The beautiful thing about Overtown was the *community*. Everybody knew everybody that lived in the neighborhood, and often helped each other out. The neighborhood had *life* back then! I walked up and down the streets by myself or with friends and I felt safe.

When you step outside in the morning people are outside walking around, people cleaning their porches, kids walking to school, elderly folks outside sitting on the porch watching everything and everyone.

I could not walk down the street without one of my parents' friends saying, "Hey, Samone tell your momma and your daddy I said 'Hello'." Sometimes I didn't know who they were, but they knew who I was, and they were around when I was a baby because of my parents. If you needed to borrow some eggs to make corn bread, you can go next door and ask your neighbor for two eggs.

Sometimes, when I found myself locked out of the apartment because I

I AM GOD'S CHILD

forgot my house key, the neighbors let me wait at their house until someone came home. I could trust that adult to watch out for me and do no harm to me while my parents were not around.

The people were kind, they had compassion, love and joy in their hearts back then. I miss that so much! I remember when something so simple like playing kick ball, hide and seek, basketball, red-light green-light, hopscotch and jump rope brought the whole block outside. And before you know it, the whole neighborhood was outside. Adults, children, and everyone just enjoying themselves laughing and playing together having a good time! Those were some of my best memories and moments in my life. Looking back as I write this, I see they are precious, and I took them for granted.

Sometimes we forget about the simple things in life and how happy they made us. I have witnessed different generations of people growing up in Overtown. The elder folks like Ms. Mary, Ms. Grace, and Ms. Unis—just to name a few—that had influence on my life. I witnessed parents, aunties, uncles, and their lifelong friends. I witnessed my sisters, older cousins, and their friends growing up from my neighborhood. And I witnessed my generation of friends and peers that I grew up with. Sadly, a lot of those I have mentioned have passed away and gone on to be with God.

But now the hearts and minds of the community's people are not the same. So many hearts are cold as ice and their minds are in dark places. The times we are living in now have changed drastically. Parents are lost, and the children of today are just left wandering. The community has changed, and the neighborhood is lifeless. It's just dead.

As far back as I can remember—from preschool—I went to St. John Baptist church in Overtown. It was a church, but the preschool was behind the church in another building. The first church sermon that I went to as a child was at this church.

I remember it like yesterday; I spent the weekend over at my mom's best friend's house to play with her daughter. That Sunday morning Nancy came into the room and said, "Alicia. You and Samone get up and get ready, and then come and eat breakfast".

"Yes ma'am." We got up, brushed our teeth, and washed our faces.

I asked Alicia, "Where are we going?"

"Church," she said.

I did not know we were going to church; I did not have any church clothes to wear. Alicia told me to just wear whatever I had. So, I just put on a pair of my jeans with a t-shirt and my sneakers. I felt out of place going to church because I was not wearing the proper clothes; and they were all dressed up. Nancy said it didn't matter, and, "You come to church as you are! It is not about what you are wearing."

We joined her brother Brandon in the kitchen, we ate our bowls of oatmeal as we waited for their mom to get ready. When Nancy finished getting ready, we all walked to church.

I remember sitting there in the third row, just watching the pastor preach and I did not understand what he was talking about. Then it came time to give your offerings, and they passed the offering basket around and at the time I did not have any money. So, when the basket got to me, I just passed it over to Alicia. Nancy saw me when I did it and she asked me why I did not put any money in the basket. I told Nancy I did not have any money, she handed me a dollar, and I had to get up to walk up to the front of the church to put the money in the offering basket.

The best part of the sermon to me was the choir singing. The choir sang the song "Silver and Gold", it was the first time I heard that song. I was so elevated by that whole experience. That weekend I experienced two things for the first time, I said my first prayer before I went to sleep, and I went to church for the first time.

Every night before I went to sleep at Nancy's house that weekend, we all kneeled down on our knees, and we recited *The Lord's Prayer* (Matthew 6:9-13). When I went back home, I told my mom all about my experience I had at church and all about the things I did that weekend. And still, I can see all of it, clear as day, as if it happened yesterday.

Sometimes simple memories like this can put a smile on your face and it can remind you that it was not all bad. I know for me, I am grateful, and I am humbled by my memories. Often at times the bad, the painful and the hurtful memories are the memories that pop up first. The happy and joyful memories are the ones you must dig up. I have so many memories of good and bad experiences that happened in my community with good people who are not famous. But they played a role in my life, so to me they are important, and they matter to me.

The word *Community* is so important! I believe it is especially important for people to start believing in love and for people to start having compassion for others in our hearts.

I remember countless times when my mom and I had to walk to wherever we were going, or we walked to the bus stop to catch the bus because we did not have a car—or my dad had the car at the moment—and we had to get around the best way we could. Sometimes I was so tired from walking long distances, and the sun was extremely hot too. Let me tell you! Those are what we call the 'Hot sunny days in South Florida!'

Sometimes, my mom had to drag me and pull me as we walked down the street. But I thanked God when someone my mom knew saw us walking and offered us a ride to where we were going. The first thing my mom always said was "Thank You".

In my mind, I was saying, "Thank you, Jesus!" Oh, I was quite happy

I AM GOD'S CHILD

for those rides; the back of my shirt was wet and sweaty.

The same way people helped my mom, my mom returned the favor. We all need help from time to time. That was how they looked out for one another back then. That is what love and consideration for others looks like to me. As I look back, I realize how God had his hand over me this entire time! I can honestly say, I am God's child. And I am blessed! And I know that God loves me!

We do not realize God watches over us in so many ways.

I remember as a kid back then when my mom's best friend Nancy was struggling with drugs. This lady showed me how to pray and she took me to church. But Nancy was a drug addict and an alcoholic at the same time. This lady was living out on the streets, and she left her children to fend for themselves.

One day, back then when I was in elementary school, I was outside on the P.E. court sitting down on the ground talking with friends waiting for school to start. When I looked around to scope out the scenery, I suddenly saw her.

I saw Nancy walking down the street along the sidewalk with a beer in her hand heading my way. She seemed to be walking and talking to herself. I saw her, but she did not see me looking at her. So, I waited. As Nancy was passing by, I walked up to the gate, and I yelled, "Hey auntie!"

"Hey boo! How are you doing?"

"I am doing well."

"Hey, let auntie borrow two dollars and I will pay you back."

I knew she was lying, and I knew I was not going to get it back. This was not the first time she borrowed money from me, but I gave it to her anyway. I reached in my pocket to pull out two dollars and I handed her the money through the hole in the fence.

"Thank you, boo! Auntie loves you and be good in school." I let her know that her kids were searching for her. "Ok, thanks boo." Then she walked off as I sat back down.

I have learned that we all have struggles in life, life is hard, and to survive you have to be mentally strong. We also have a battle going on in our minds! You get in bed at night for a good night's rest, but for some reason you just cannot fall asleep. Your mind is racing, thinking about a million things all at once, and you have to pray yourself to sleep.

Have you ever found yourself in this type of situation?

Well, I know I have; *many* times.

You have so much going on in your mind about things that need resolution, and you are searching for answers. You are trying to decide what to do? But there are two voices in your head, and you hear those two voices saying two different things.

In one ear there is God. And in the other ear it is Satan.

You listen to one or the other and you decide! It could turn out to be a good or a bad decision that can change the rest of your life! If you take a look around, sometimes you will see someone walking and talking to themselves. Oh, it looks like they are talking to themselves, but they are talking to voices in their head or a spirit.

On another occasion, my auntie Nia and I were walking to the corner store to get her *Play 3* and lotto numbers. I saw a man walking in our direction, but he was looking to his left and talking. No one was walking next to him.

I remember grabbing her shirt, pointing at the man saying, "Auntie look at this man talking to his self."

The first thing my auntie Nia did when she looked up, was knock my hand down. Then she told me, "Don't point at people." Then she said, "No baby, he is talking to someone, he is talking to a spirit."

That is what talking to God looks like. I talk to God like that a lot!

Remember: the direction your life takes is determined by the decisions you make in your life. If you seek God, pray for guidance and you will make good decisions, then you will help make your life a lot easier. But if you continue to make bad decisions and not seek God's guidance, then you will make things harder for yourself. Some people go through life and seem to never learn from their mistakes. Some people never stop to take the time to wonder why, or to think about the things going on in their life and why things are not going the way they hoped for, and maybe prayed for. Life is about learning lessons, making good choices and doing what is best or right for your peace of mind.

I decided early on in life, that I, Samone, I am going to live my life differently! If I say something, I say what I mean, and I mean what I say. And I do not care what anybody thinks—besides God!

My mom said, "Samone, I raised you to be your own person and to have a mind of your own. To be a leader and not a follower."

I have one life to live; and I can only live for me. Some people choose to fight and to not be defeated, while others become weakened and give up. They go on existing, but not *living* life, and not having an understanding about life.

I believe God is love, and he loves us all. I believe we need to learn to love ourselves more, and love each other as God loves us all.

We can learn to be kind and more respectful to one another as people in this world. This world we live in is so cruel and this cruel world could turn you into a cruel person if you let it. I know there are mean and wicked people in the world. I cannot help but notice how much meaner people have gotten over the years. People are so quick to be mean and to be rude

I AM GOD'S CHILD

to one another. Rather than being nice and kind to one another.

Some people act like it will kill them just to say, "Hello. How are you?"

Just because you do not know someone does not mean you cannot speak to a person and say, "Hello." It is called *manners* people, and we all need to learn to use our manners. We need to learn how to be courteous when speaking to one another.

When someone says, "Hello. How are you?"

Guess what? You say, "Hello. I am fine and you?"

It is not rocket science and it is not hard people!

Doing something as simple as saying "Hello" to a person can start a conversation and lead to communication with one another. I am the kind of person that speaks and says "Hello" to everyone. And if they do not reply back to me, that is ok!

I still speak to people because that is just me and that is how I was raised. Why be mean and why be rude when you can choose to be kind to someone instead? I have had numerous spontaneous conversations with random people I do not know that start just from saying "Hello" to that person. It has led to many friendships and relationships that I have with many people now.

It does not matter what a person's nationality, ethnicity, skin color, age, and gender is for you to speak to them. You will be surprised to find out how much we all have in common and the misconceptions that we have from judging others based off of how someone looks. It is just like the saying, "Do not judge a book by its cover!"

How can we *expect* change and not *be* the change we expect to see? How are we going to lead by an example if we cannot let go of our ignorance? We must be kind to one another, and we must have respect for one another before we can have a conversation to get to know one another. We must come from a place of love and respect in order to get along with one another.

But know this, respect is earned not given, and you have to *give* respect to *get* respect.

• • •

Growing up as a child, I had a lot of people tell me stories about the community of Overtown. How the community was before I was born and how Overtown came to be historic.

History shows the founding of Overtown is a result of the *Jim Crow Laws*, which put segregation into practice in a number of ways, including establishing specific neighborhoods for African American residents.

They say, originally, Overtown was developed by Mr. Henry Morrison

Flagler who was a tycoon from the grain and oil industry. Overtown was initially built to serve as a home to the colored railroad workers employed by Mr. Flagler. The historic Overtown was established in 1869 and it was originally called "Colored Town."

Colored Town was an all-black community, the residents lived in houses called "Shotgun Houses" lined up in rows in a small area and it was the only place coloreds were allowed to be. The colored folks were not allowed to go across to the other side of the railroad tracks, to go downtown, or to go over on the other side of town on South Beach at night after a certain time. The colored folks were only allowed across on the other side of the tracks to work and to perform for the rich white folks. They say, the black community of Overtown was thriving upward, and the town had become famously known as *the place to be* whenever people were in town.

By the 1950s and the early sixties Overtown was a booming black city! People say Overtown of years ago was flourishing with many black owned businesses and they had a community of fifty thousand residents back then.

The community had everything the residents needed right there and none of the residents needed to go across the tracks to pick up anything. The community had businesses such as the cleaners, grocery stores, movie theaters, hotels, and clubs. Basically, it had everything that residents needed to live, work, and to have fun.

In the past, Overtown had become known for the hot nightlife music scene and many black mega celebrities called it home. Overtown was also home to D. A. Dorsey, a famously well known businessman, banker, and philanthropist. He was one of the first black millionaires and D. A. Dorsey did a lot to build up the community of Overtown through purchasing land to build homes for blacks. The house of the Dorsey family still stands in Overtown to this day and remains historic to the city.

They say, when the black performers came to town, they performed on the beach at the top hotels and then they came across the tracks to Overtown to perform at the clubs for free, to party with the residents of the community. When in town the performers stayed at the Sir John Hotel and The Carver Hotel.

During the segregation days, the blacks were not allowed to sleep on the beach and the performers came back across the bay to Overtown. Some say, back in the day, it was nothing to see famous people such as James Brown, Jackie Wilson, Ella Fitzgerald, Aretha Franklin, Lena Horn, Nat King Cole, Josephine Baker, Sam Cook, Sammy Davis Jr., Diana Washington, Joe Louis, Muhammad Ali and many, many more who made Overtown a second home. These famous people were treated like ordinary people; they could walk out of the clubs and walk down the streets at one in the morning with no problem.

They were not seen as superstars, they were perceived and treated as ordinary people. And this small town became home to a lot of big-name celebrities. They say Overtown was the place to be when it came to entertainment and black music. Sadly, Overtown's music never had the chance to become as popular as Harlem's Jazz, or Detroit's Motown music.

In the sixties, though, as the civil rights movement and desegregation began to take place, it was said they were opening things up for blacks. But when I-95 and other freeways were built through the neighborhood, it destroyed hundreds of properties and displaced thousands of people.

The Overtown of then was no more!

The past Overtown more than likely could have still been standing, with those business in town for its black residents with places to go and things for them to do that they liked to do. But the changes that were made came and took all of that away.

The thriving community of Overtown came to an end, and its black residents were left with nothing but stories to tell their children and their children's children about the booming Overtown of the past.

I have heard some of the old stories about Overtown from my family members and my parents. Yeah, they call them the good old days! They happily and proudly speak about the past of Overtown.

Comparing the stories of Overtown from the past, to the Overtown back when my parents were growing up, and when I was growing up in Overtown back in the '90s, Overtown still has not recovered or come close to exemplifying how it once was for the black community back then. The Overtown I grew up in back in the '90s was still a fun place to be, although there was violence and drug dealing just as any poor community.

• • •

The first funeral I attended as a child growing up in Overtown, was of a boy I used to play with. The child's mother had HIV/AIDS and her baby was born HIV positive. The boy was my uncle Joe's nephew and from time to time I played with him. We called him "Scooter"!

Sadly, Scooter died very young. He was only four years old, when he passed. I remember my mom and I walking down the street as she broke the news to me that he died.

I did not know what death was and I did not understand it at the time. I asked my mom, "Where did Scooter go?"

"He went to Heaven to be with God," she replied.

I asked my mom, "Will I ever see him again?"

"No," she replied.

I was sad and I was confused once I heard the news. But I still did not *understand* what was being said to me.

We went to his funeral, and I saw him lying there in the coffin. He was not moving, and his eyes were closed as I walked up with my mom to view his body one last time. I asked my mom, "What is he doing?"

"He is sleeping," she replied.

I asked my mom, "Is he going to wake up?"

"No," she replied. Then tears ran down her face as we took one last look at him before we walked off.

I did not understand why everyone was crying and why everyone was looking so sad. I was told he had gone up to heaven to be with God, he was in a better place, and he no longer had to be in pain or to suffer any longer. I was too young; I did not know, and I did not understand what HIV/AIDS was. I did not understand why they were crying tears if he had gone off to a better place like they said.

The next funeral I attended after that was another child's funeral. This child was my cousin; she was my uncle Robert's illegitimate child, and her name was Remi. My mom took me with her whenever she went over to Remi's mother's house for parties and gatherings. I played with my cousin; we played together in her room with the baby dolls and with the rest of her toys. We had to play inside because it was not safe to play outside in the neighborhood they lived in. There was drug dealing and a lot of shootouts around that area and her mom made her stay inside the house to play.

Well, one year during a Martin Luther King Jr. parade, a shootout took place and Remi was shot in the head. Remi was six years old when she died, and I attended her funeral.

I remember her mother crying tears, she did not want to believe her daughter was dead and gone. My heart ached for her mother, when I overheard my mom saying how Remi's mom still went into her room to wake her up for school in the morning, then reality hits her and she breaks down crying because she had to come to the realization that her child was really dead.

When Remi died, I had the understanding by then to know when you die, you are *not* coming back.

• • •

There were not many jobs in the community of Overtown but it was full of apartment buildings for the residents. It was affordable back then to live in Overtown too. That was one of the main reasons why my parents did not want to leave the hood. I was lucky to have grown up in Overtown where not much really happened daily, it was mainly just crack heads and drunken winos around the neighborhood.

I grew up around people who looked out for one another, and they tried to help each other survive. "You have to take the good with the bad" like they say! I have great fun-filled childhood memories from growing up in Overtown and I met some of my childhood friends from Overtown. I was born in Overtown, and I love my hood! I love all my towners and where I come from!

I am a "Towner for life!"

The violence in the neighborhood was becoming worse, the cost of rent went up for the apartments and it had become unaffordable for my mom financially. I do believe that if it had not been for those circumstances, my parents would have continued to live in Overtown.

We loved Overtown, my family is from Overtown, it is the place where we went to party, to hangout, to have fun with the family. My journey began in Overtown, I am going to tell you all about my journey and take you back to the beginning where it all started for me.

REBECCA S. SMITH

MY CHILDHOOD

The best part of my childhood was living in Overtown. Oh, I loved being around my family as a child. We moved around a lot when I was growing up, home stability was something I did *not* have as a child.

During that time, we lived in an apartment building. They were two-story buildings with ten units; five on the top and five on the bottom. It was two horizontal buildings facing each other. In between them was concrete, we called it *the yard*. The buildings were painted white and brown. To the left of the buildings was an alleyway, to the back of the right building was an open field of grass, and behind the building to the right were single family homes. The residents parked their vehicles in front near their porch, on the side of the building and along the sidewalk.

Growing up under my mom's roof, she had one rule. The rule was: "What happens in this house *stays* in this house. Do not go opening your mouth to speak about what goes on in this house to anyone in the street."

I have broken that rule a couple of times for good reasons. I did not talk to any strangers about what was going on under our roof, I knew the seriousness of certain things, and I also knew I could get in big trouble if I spoke of certain things that would get my parents in trouble. So, I talked to my auntie Nia. And I talked to my uncle Joe; they lived in apartment number five downstairs right next door to us.

Unfortunately, my siblings and I spent most of our childhoods growing up exposed to many family issues: drugs, alcoholism, molestation, and domestic violence. By the time I was born, my family already had problems and they were struggling to survive.

My mom was twenty-seven years old when she gave birth to me. Because my siblings were not my dad's biological children, he did not want to help my mom take care of them while they were together. Instead he took advantage of my siblings by abusing, molesting and mistreating them in all different kinds of ways before I was old enough to understand anything. There was already bad blood between my dad and my mom's side of the family because of the things my mom allowed to go on under her roof and what she subjected her children to because of him.

As it turns out, even before I came along my dad was already physically beating up my mom. My mom left my dad, but she ended up going right back to him. This was not my mom's first violent physical relationship with a man, this was just the most *recent* domestic violence relationship she had. Just about every man my mom was in a relationship with had beaten her except for my oldest sister's father. My mom has an attraction to guys that treat her like crap. I do not know why. My auntie Nia says, "You cannot help people that do not want to help themselves."

The truth is my mom was naïve in love, she was naïve to a lot of situations and decisions that happened back then, and still is. And we, the children, just had to find a way to deal with it. At times I felt like my mom perceived herself as helpless, when she could not see how she was stronger than she thought. My mom has a fear of being alone or ending up lonely and it is still one of her biggest fears. My mom feels like she needs a man, and without a man by her side she does not know what to do. I do not understand her thought process; how she thinks, and the decisions she made used to drive me crazy.

You know, I believe my mom likes dysfunction, it is her normal, and she does not know how to function outside of chaos.

My mom's beauty back in her youthful days was irresistible, and a lot of men wanted her too! She was *gorgeous*! When my oldest sister's father comes around us, he continuously talks about how fine my mom was back in the day.

He says, "Man, back then your mom was shaped like a Coco-Cola bottle!" I cannot help but laugh at him, and then he said, "I don't know what happened to her now."

I had to let him know, "Hey man, this is my mom you talking about!" Then we just bust out laughing.

Mom's smile was gorgeous, with pretty white teeth. My mom stood at five-three, long black hair all the way down the middle of her back. My mom is a light skinned woman, with brown eyes, and she had curves for days! My mom was the life of the party with places to go and people to see. If you are having a party and it starts at noon, she will not get there until two o'clock. I do not know the reason why, but she can never be on time for anything. My mom was the last one to get ready all the time!

My daddy use to say, "Your momma is going to be late to her own funeral." It made me laugh.

As soon as we walk through the door, everybody starts shouting out:

"Go Pam! We arrived two hours late to the party because of her, you know."

My parents were the couple that dressed alike from head to toe and wore matching colors. If my dad was wearing red and white, my mom had on something that was red and white to match him. My mom and my uncle Robert were dancing partners, the two were always on the dance floor doing old school dances. I can see my uncle with a Guinness in his hand, both of them smiling at each other, hyping each other up talking about, "Alright now cuz I see you!"

My family is huge! There are still some family members that I have not met, but I have heard about them. There was always a family relative having a party or a cookout, and just about everyone came over. I know you remember those family cookouts; the women were inside the house in the kitchen or the living room area talking and listening to music. The little kids outside playing, running around the house, and the big kids in the bedroom hanging out. The men were outside posted up doing what they do, talking and listening to their old school music chilling outside.

As a kid, I always tried to get in that room to hang out with my older cousins and siblings, but you know how that goes. They did not let me inside the room, and the answer was *no*! They told me, I was too young, and I need to go play with my younger cousins outside. When it was time to eat, they gathered all the family to come inside to say grace as a family.

As a family we held hands, everyone around the room said what they were thankful for, and we said grace before eating. The elders remind us that we are family, as family we stick together, and family is all we have. We should love one another and help one another. We should not be fighting each other. The elders were happy to see everybody together, they spoke about togetherness encouraging family to spend time with each other and getting to know one another because family is love. We looked at one another to say, "I love you." We all got a dinner plate of food, and we sat down to eat like a family. They turned the music back on, everybody ate, and we went back outside to dance and have dance contests. I know you remember the dance contests. We enjoyed each other for a little while longer, and by the end of the night everybody was packing up getting ready to go home.

• • •

You know, looking back at my childhood, I did not believe my dad loved my mom; I believe he was there because it was convenient for him, and it really was when I think about it. He did not have to pay any bills; it was ok for him to be out all night long drinking, getting high and messing around

I AM GOD'S CHILD

with other women in the streets. Sometimes, my dad came home the next morning after partying all night long, like a fool my mom cooked him a hot meal, gave him loving, and let him rest his head on her pillow in her bed. My mom was in love with my dad, she let everybody know that he was her man, she catered to her man, and he was the love of her life.

My dad was the man of the house, he was a hardworking man with a job, he was allowed to touch her daughter, beat her whenever she got out of line, and she never did anything about it. My dad was a user, he was an abuser, and a liar. He was very mean and nasty at times. He was a pervert, he was a coward, he was rotten to the core, and he was my dad—can you believe it!

My mom was equally as responsible as my dad for her role that she played in all of this mess; my parents were sick in the mind, crazy, dysfunctional individuals that came together and failed at raising children, doing damage, causing more pain!

This is my opinion based on what I witnessed, I know it may sound harsh, but this was my reality, I know people do not like to hear the truth, but like they say the truth hurts! The actions my dad displayed were not of a worthy good man that was in love with a woman, he did not come into our lives to bring any good and I am not sure he wanted to do right by us.

My dad had three bad habits. The first bad habit was his alcohol addiction; he drank beer and liquor. The second bad habit was his drug addiction; his drug of choice was cocaine. He also smoked weed and he popped ecstasy pills. If my dad was not drunk or high, he was not in a good mood or in a happy mood period. Whenever I saw him in a good mood, I knew he was either drunk or high. When my dad was drunk his eyes were very glossy, and when he was high on cocaine his eyes were blood shot red. The third bad habit; he was very abusive verbally, mentally, and physically. And at any given second *the beast* came out.

The beast is what came out whenever he was mad. When the beast came out, the look in his eyes, you can see the coldness and the rage that was inside of him. The beast had no self-control, only rage and a look to kill. I witnessed my mom go through physical, verbal, and mental abuse from my dad most of my life. My grandmother once told me, she was always afraid for my mom, and she prayed for my mom the most because she was afraid that one day my daddy was going to kill her daughter. As a child, I always lived with the fear that one day I was going to come home from school to find out my dad beat my mom to death. While I was at school, I asked God to protect my mom and to keep her alive until I could get home to protect her. My dad liked to put his hands on my mom when no one was around to help her, I knew that was one of his tactics, and I was fearful of it.

One day, as I was walking up in the yard from elementary school my auntie Lena came walking out of her front door. My auntie asked me, if I had my house key because she heard my parents inside the apartment arguing. As we approached the front door, we heard them arguing. When I unlocked the front door, Aunt Lena shouted their names out as she walked toward their bedroom door. The bedroom door was locked, so she shouted their names for them to open the door, "This is Lena! Pam are you alright?"

My dad opened the door; my auntie pushed the door open wider and asked my mom if she was ok. My mom was standing in the corner of the room with tears running down her face. She looked my auntie in the eyes, and she told auntie Lena everything is ok. Lena asked my mom if she was sure, and my mom said everything is ok again.

My auntie looked at my dad, and she said, "Do not put your hands on her. You can argue, but there is no need to hit her."

My mom asked my auntie to take me over to her place, and she will come get me in a couple minutes. My auntie Lena and I left, but she left the front door open because we had a screen door, and she was able to hear what was going on in case my mom might need help.

We walked across the yard to my auntie's apartment; she tried to comfort me, she told me everything was going to be ok. I sat down on the couch as she stood in the doorway looking through her screen door watching our apartment.

Then I heard my auntie yelling "Come on! Run! *Run!*"

I turned around to look out the window and I saw my mom running out of the apartment across the yard with my dad chasing behind her. My auntie held the screen door open for my mom to run directly inside her apartment. But my mom happened to look back as she was running, she ran into the door, and she fell onto the ground.

My dad grabbed my mom by her box braids as he wrapped them around his arm, and he started punching her in the face while her head bounced off of the concrete ground. My auntie Lena ran inside the kitchen to get a heavy skillet frying pan, then she ran outside threatening to knock my dad across the head if he did not stop hitting my mom and let go of her.

My oldest sister—who was pregnant at the time with my niece—walked up in my dad's face shouting, pointing her finger in his face telling him to let my momma go or she was going to punch him.

So, my dad started shouting at my oldest sister calling her everything except the child of God and he threatened to punch her in the stomach. My mom was on the floor begging my dad to stop because he was hurting her, and he was still yanking her braids. My oldest sister punched my dad in the face twice, and then he let my mom go. My dad reacted by punching my oldest sister in the face, and she punched him in the face two more times.

My mom picked herself up off the ground, and my auntie made her get

I AM GOD'S CHILD

inside the apartment to stop my dad from getting to her again. I remember running out of the apartment crying, I bawled my fist up screaming "*Stop!*"

Everybody stopped fighting at that moment.

That day I balled up my fist to my dad, and I had every intention of hitting him as I walked toward him to make him stop. When he looked at me, I looked back at him, and I stared him down. My dad had a shocked look on his face, and it was as if his eyes could not believe what he was seeing in front of him. I remember my mom begging him to leave and telling him he was scaring me. We stared at each other, and then he walked off before my oldest sister's boyfriend came home.

Because of all the horrible things that I have witnessed as a child, my parent's toxic relationship while growing up is exactly why I refuse to be in any toxic relationship, and instead I want to experience real love!

I remember many nights hearing my mom cry herself to sleep with blackened eyes and with bruises on her body. It broke my heart and it made me cry. I made a vow to myself that I will never be with the type of man that was like my dad. If this is what love is then I do not want it! When they thought I was too young to understand what was going on, I *did* understand. When they thought I was not watching or was not paying attention, I was being very observant!

One thing to remember, kids watch you, and kids hear a *lot* more than you think!

I could have never imagined going through what I did as a child and seeing what I saw as a child. But some of us, unfortunately, quickly get a dose of reality and the realness of life.

The truth is we do not get to choose our family, we do not get to choose our parents, the parents do not get to choose the children and we do not get to determine where we begin our journey.

My auntie Nia once said, "I do not understand why we as human beings feel like we are not supposed to experience trials and tribulations in life? Jesus did! Just know that you can handle it through the spirit of Jesus with God by your side. It is ok! Take it to God!" My auntie Nia, told me, to talk to God and that is what I did. When auntie Nia speaks of God, she shouts *God!* Talking to God looks like you are talking to yourself. When I am walking by myself, I talk to God all the time, it does not matter if I am happy, angry, mad or sad.

• • •

One day, I witnessed my dad do something that changed my life forever, and it really opened my eyes to what was going on under my mom's roof that was happening to my oldest sister.

REBECCA S. SMITH

We lived in apartment number five at the time, in a two-bedroom, one bath. During that time, my brother was away at school for the deaf and the hearing impaired up the road in St. Augustine.

My two sisters and I were outside playing in the yard this particular day, while my mom was inside getting ready for work. My mom came outside dressed in her white work uniform and let us know that she was headed off to work. My dad was supposed to have been home to watch us, but my dad had not returned home since he went out the night before. My mom was already late trying to wait for him to get home, and she headed off to work. She gave us permission to stay outside to continue playing as long as we stayed on the porch. Mom told us my dad will soon be home, and she will see us later. I watched my mom as she walked off to head to work until she was no longer in my sight, and I prayed that she made it to work safe.

At the time my parents had no car, we had to get around by public transportation and by foot. About two minutes after my mom walked off, my dad came walking up in the yard.

My dad inquired about my mom's whereabouts, and I told him she went to work. He told us to get inside the apartment, and I told him mom said we could play outside. My dad said, "I do not care what the hell your momma said, and I said get your ass in the house. And since you want to tell me what your momma said, go in the room to lay down to take a nap and do not turn on the TV."

I remember saying to myself, "I cannot stand him, he is so mean! He never lets us outside to play and to have fun." When my dad watched us, we always had to stay in the house, and I could not stand it.

My siblings and I went inside as instructed by my dad, and we laid down in the bed and we did not turn on the TV. I was laying on the right side of the bed by the window. My oldest sister was lying in the middle of the bed and my second oldest sister was laying on the left side of the bed by the closet. After a while both of my sisters fell asleep, and I was still up by myself looking outside the window up at the sky that day. Then I heard the room door open, so I looked out the side of my eye to see who was there, the door was cracked opened a little bit and all I saw was an eyeball. Then the door closed shut. So, I turned on my left side facing my sisters and I pretended to be sleep. The door cracked open again. I pretended to be sleep, but I had one eye cracked open, I saw my dad on the floor on his hands and his knees crawling in the room. Then he gently closed the bedroom door. Then he began crawling on his stomach to the end of the bed carefully and quietly without making noise.

I closed my eyes, but I cracked my eye open again, and I saw him looking to see if any of us were awake. I closed my eye again. Then I felt him lifting up the sheet cover, I cracked my eye open, and saw his head under the covers and his arm moving up between my oldest sister legs.

Both of my sisters were still sleeping, and I was the only one awake. So, I started tossing and turning as if I was starting to wake up. My dad pulled his arm from underneath the sheet cover and he laid down on the floor.

I tossed and I turned again, but this time I started moaning little noises as if I were about wake up and open my eyes. Then my dad started crawling back toward the room door and he crawled out of the room. It was the first time I witnessed my dad doing that as a little girl, and I was shocked. I stayed up the whole-time keeping watch until one of my sisters woke up. When they woke up, I told my two sisters what happened, and we decided to wait until our mom came home to tell her what I witnessed my dad doing. We took turns that night keeping watch because my mom was not coming home until the morning.

I can still hear my mom's keys jingling as she unlocked the front door, because I was sitting in the chair by the door waiting for her. I can still see the tired look on her face as she stepped inside and looked at me.

"What are you doing up so early?" My mom asked.

"I have something to tell you," I said and took her hand as we walked into my bedroom. I wanted to catch my mom before she went into her bedroom, and before my dad woke up. My mom sat on the edge of the bed, and I begin telling her what I saw my dad trying to do.

My mom's mouth opened wide with a shocked look as the tears started running down her face. "Did he see you?" My mom asked me.

"No," I replied. My mom told us to stay in the room, and she walked out of the room.

I decided to follow her, I walked out of the room, I stood with my back against the wall listening and looking through her cracked bedroom door.

My dad was laying down asleep, and she walked up to him shouting his name. "Sam! Sam! Sam! Wake up!"

He woke up. "What the fuck is wrong with you?" My dad said.

"What the fuck are you doing sneaking into my kid's room trying to touch my daughter!"

"What the hell are you talking about? I did not sneak into the room, and I did not touch nobody!"

"You are a liar, Samone saw you!"

"Samone is a liar! I do not know what she is talking about."

My mom called him a pedophile and a pervert!

"I do not play that shit!"

"You do not touch my kids!"

My dad arose out of the bed to grab my mom by the neck, and he threatened to beat her ass. He continued to deny everything. "I do not have time for this shit, you are stupid. I love you and here you are accusing me of this bullshit." My dad proclaimed he was leaving my mom; he began to take his clothes out of the dresser drawers and he threw the clothes on the bed. My mom started begging him to stay, telling him she was sorry for accusing him of doing something like that.

I could not believe it! I just walked back in the room and my heart was broken. I will never forget how my sister cried so hard that day, and the look of fear that was on her face.

My life changed forever and I never trusted my dad after that day. That happened when I was five years old. I knew the one person I could trust was my auntie Nia, and I knew she would believe me if I told her what happened!

When auntie Nia came to pick me up later on that day, I told her about everything and she believed me. After I told my auntie Nia, she called the rest of the family, and she requested everyone to come over to her apartment to have a meeting.

The family came over as requested, we sat down in the living room, my auntie told me to tell everyone what I saw my dad doing, and what my mom did about the situation.

I sat in the living room on the couch, and I explained everything I witnessed that day. I do not know if the family ever confronted my mom or my dad about the situation. I know no one called the police to report it, nothing happened to my dad, and nothing was done about it at all. We still remained under the same roof with this predator! There is no telling, who else touched and might have abused my sister that my mom had around us. I cannot imagine the pain or the hurt my oldest sister was dealing with on the inside emotionally and mentally, and it was my dad doing this to my sister. It was hard for me to love my dad growing up knowing that he was such a wicked person and seeing all the rotten things he did. How can you love a person like this?

I hated my dad growing up, and we had a rocky relationship with one another. My uncle Joe once said to me, "You do not hate your daddy. You hate his ways, and your daddy has to answer to God! Because the man up above sees all, baby, you hear me."

I did not fully comprehend what he meant at that time, but the more and more I thought about it, I finally understood it. And it gave me a different way of looking at the situation. But I was still angry with him, and I did not want to try to understand his wicked ways. Unfortunately, we cannot pick or choose who we want to be our parents or stepparents, and God knows life is hard. We are all prayerfully trying to find our way, and understand the way of life!

It is true like they say, it is not for us to judge, and we can point out the wrong no matter our age. Because one day, we too will be adults, and you will have to answer to God too! We must all be mindful of our actions, and pray for forgiveness for our actions because one day we too will be adults, dealing with life's burdens and making our own mistakes.

As I like to say, the kind of man my dad decided to be is on him. And the kind of woman my mom decided to be is on her. I can only tell you about my experiences, and what pieces they decided to give me. And what I received was exactly that, pieces of them. I can only tell you what I saw that I wish had not happened, but do not get mad at me. Like they say, "Do not shoot the messenger." I am only the messenger in this case.

• • •

Back then in the early '90s, growing up as a little girl, my auntie Nia lived close by us. My mom and her have a close bond as sisters. My grandma used to say, "Them two are thick as thieves!" They beat up boys together, you hear me? They did not play, honey!

My auntie Nia told me a story from back then when they were in high school. They went to a football game together, and both of them had an umbrella just in case it rained, because they did not want to get their hair wet. They were walking up toward the stands, some random guy grabbed my mom's butt, and they beat the guy up with their umbrellas. Still to this day my auntie never leaves home without an umbrella, honey. Because one thing about auntie Nia, you will never see her without her hair done, baby. And she is always dressed up from her head to her toes.

I was my auntie Nia's shopping buddy; she came to get me to take me riding around with her. We went shopping together especially at the thrift stores around the neighborhood. My auntie loves a good bargain, and she knows a good deal when she sees one. Trust and believe what I tell you. There is nothing my auntie cannot do, for real! If my auntie does not know how to do something, trust and believe she will figure it out. Then come back and say, "I told you I can do it." My auntie Nia will tell anyone there is no such thing as 'you do not know', or 'you do not know how to do something'. If you do not know, take the time to use your brain to learn and to figure it out. If you do not try to do it, how do you expect to learn?

If I was not with my mom, then I was with my auntie Nia. Sometimes, it was all three of us together on the weekends early in the morning going shopping together. We shopped downtown at the fabric store, and we were out just about all day. My auntie is really great at sewing, she designs her own curtains, bathroom towels, and she likes to re-decorate her house from time to time. We drove around to some of the local thrift stores that were in the neighborhood, going from thrift store to thrift store. My auntie likes wooden furniture, and she likes to restore it herself. My auntie shopped for nice blouses, pants, all for prices of two dollars, three dollars, four dollars and five dollars to wear for work. My auntie is great at sewing and she resews the clothes with her sewing machine.

The grocery store was the last stop on the route before we went back home. It took my mom and my auntie about two hours to shop in the grocery store. My auntie had a list with the coupons she cut out of the Sunday newspaper for the things she was buying. And my mom just picked up groceries or whatever she saw as we walked around the grocery store. By the time we finished shopping and packed the groceries in the car with everything else, the car was filled with bags in the trunk, the back seat, and in the front seat. There was almost no place for me to sit! And this is what we did just about every other weekend.

When it was just me and my auntie, after we finished shopping we went back to her apartment, and she cooked me dinner. While my auntie was in the kitchen cooking, I was sitting in the living room in one of her antique chairs waiting for dinner to be ready, and we talked about everything. Sometimes my auntie Nia did not have to say anything because I did all of the talking; running my mouth telling her all the things that I needed to get off of my chest.

I was *safe*, I was *comfortable*, and I was *free* to be myself around my auntie. My auntie gave me Words of Wisdom, she encouraged me, and she was my voice of reason. Somehow, when I talked with her I felt so much better. When I had bad news, I called my auntie to talk to her about it because I knew she would not tell me anything wrong. Everything I witnessed as a child growing up, my auntie knows, because she was the one I talked with, or I vented to.

I love my uncle Joe! We call each other nick names; we call one another James Brown every time we see each other, because he is a big James Brown fan. I remember one time, there was a family function at my uncle's house, and the only music he played the entire time was James Brown music. The whole time everybody was sitting down looking around at each other, wondering if he was going to play anything else besides James Brown. Nope, not Uncle Joe. Everybody just kept bobbing their heads to the music and nobody said anything about it to Uncle Joe. My uncle Joe was feeling good, and he was having a good time listening to his music.

I remember my oldest sister saying to me, "What is up with Uncle Joe playing nothing but James Brown music?"

I burst out laughing! I was thinking to myself, "Yeah why don't you go say that to him." Why did I think that?

My uncle is not a mean guy; he is actually a really cool guy. And I can always relate to him. But he does not take crap from anybody, especially in 'his house'! Uncle Joe is what you call a smooth cat! He is a real laid back big, tall guy; he be in the cut chilling, and watching his surroundings. Uncle Joe will tell you really quick, "I do not want any problems." He tells me, I will have fewer problems, if I stay to myself and I do my own thing. Then say, "Be good baby, I love you."

He has a big heart and I love him for it. He is very respectful, and he will help anybody if he can. Uncle Joe always respects his elders, and he is a very straight forward person. So, I suggest you do not ask him anything if you do not want to hear the truth. He lets me know he is proud of me, and he always tells me to keep doing my thing! Uncle Joe does not say much, but he watches everything and when he speaks, I listen. Because I know he is only saying something because he loves me. If he did not care, he would not say anything.

When I was a kid, we hung out in his TV room watching movies, eating food, and talking about anything. My uncle Joe once told me a real man does not put his hands on a woman, and a real woman should not put her hands on a man. "That is not real love," my uncle Joe said. "I love your auntie and I would never put my hands on her. And I will not let anybody else touch her." Trust me when I say he does not play about his wife, my auntie Nia! He will tell you quick, "As long as my wife is good, I am good."

I am free to be myself around him; and I like to make him laugh. After he stops laughing, and he says you are shot out James Brown! I love to make him laugh; it makes me laugh. He advises me to be myself, to speak my mind, and to tell the truth. He says, "Keep it real!"

As a kid growing up, I walked around with him in the neighborhood as he walked his two Rottweiler dogs, and we talked as we walked. My uncle Joe sat outside on the porch with me, and he watched me play around outside keeping a close eye on me. The best part about hanging out with Uncle Joe were the talks we had, he somehow knew exactly what to say. Whenever he saw me sitting outside on the front porch on the milk crate by myself, he sat with me, and he talked with me. I spent so much time with my auntie and uncle as a child.

I remember when my dad told my mom he did not want me going back over to their apartment, saying that when *he* comes home, *I* should be home too. Because *he* is my father and *not* Joe! That really hurt my uncle, and it broke my heart because I did not see them for a while. And I really missed them, and they missed me.

My mom stopped me from going over to their house, and it was back to the chaos for me!

• • •

REBECCA S. SMITH

My daddy coming home drunk and high, sometimes he did not come home at all. But when he was home, everybody was walking around on pins and needles, trying not to do anything that would make him upset. It was like my mom could never do anything right for him. Sometimes he beat her for the littlest things and for talking back to him.

When she finished cooking, she made his plate of food first and she took him his food. My mom opened the TV tray stand, and she placed it in front of him. She had to go back into the kitchen to get his hot sauce, utensils, pour his drink and she took it to him while he sat down watching television in the bedroom. If the food was not hot enough for him when he ate it, he punched her in the face. If she did not iron his clothes the way he liked it, he beat her, and I mean *any* little thing triggered him. If she talked back to him after he told her to do something, he beat her.

We moved from that apartment to a townhouse in Town Park. It had three bedrooms, with two baths. My big brother was still away at school in St. Augustine for the hearing impaired because he is deaf in one ear, but he still had his own bedroom when he came home.

When he was a baby in daycare, they dropped him on the floor and burst his ear drum. The lady babysitting my brother back then did not inform my mom about their dropping her baby on the floor.

Well, my mom did not notice until one day my brother was sitting too close in front of the TV. She kept shouting his name, but he could not hear her; and she had to shake him to get his attention to tell him not to sit so close to the TV. My mom took him to the doctor, and the doctors informed her my brother was deaf in his right ear. And he had to wear a hearing aid in his right ear to hear. My mom decided to send my brother away to school for the deaf and hearing impaired to learn sign language. And to be with other kids that were deaf like himself.

When he came home from school to visit, he taught us sign language to be able to communicate with us. When my brother came home to visit, my dad was on his best behavior, he did not beat my mom, and he did not mistreat my sisters because my brother was home. Sometimes my two sisters informed my brother of the things my dad was doing, but he did not believe them. But once my brother went back to school, the *beast* came back out!

The beatings continued, along with my dad still coming home drunk and high, starting an argument just so he could beat my mom. Sometimes after he finished beating my mom, he came in our bedroom to beat my sisters because they tried to defend our mom. When he was in the bedroom beating my mom, we heard her in the room screaming for him to stop! As he beat her, he shouted, "You are going to learn to listen!" At times, my two sisters ran in the room to try to help my mom, and then he directed his anger toward them.

Well, my mom begged my dad not to put his hands on my sisters. The altercations with him were physical most of the time, and my sisters were down to fight, but they were not strong enough. My mom cried tears with her eyes swollen, and blood running down her nose. For some reason, my mom told my sisters it was ok when they came to her defense, and to go back to our room. Sometimes my dad shoved them out the room, telling us to go back in our bedroom, and then slam the door in our faces! He threatened to beat us, informing us that he was going to beat our ass next! He slammed the room door shut, locked it, and he continued to physically beat our mom. My sisters and I cried together hugging each other listening to my dad beating our mom through the walls.

When he finished beating my mom, he came into our room to beat them with a belt, and then tell us to go to sleep! Some nights we cried ourselves to sleep, other nights we stayed up being angry and talking about running away from home. Sometimes I called their names to check if they were asleep, and they called out my name to check if I was asleep.

I do not know why, but for some reason, my dad did not beat *me*. As a child, I was a crybaby, I stood there watching crying and screaming for the fighting to stop! I was five years old and I did not know what to do!

My dad was a very disgusting man; he pissed in the sink instead of the toilet. And blew his boogers on the bathroom mirror without cleaning it off. He never cleaned up behind himself; we had to clean it up!

• • •

One summer my mom decided to make me stay at my grandmother's house —my dad's mother—for the summer so I could get to know my cousins from that side of my family. I did not want to spend my whole summer over there. I called my mom and begged her to come pick me up almost every day because I wanted to go home.

You know, I told my grandmother about my dad physically beating my mom; and she asked what my *mom* was doing to *make* him beat her. I told her about him peeing in the sink, and how he blows his boogers on the bathroom mirror. And she told me, "That is a lie, he is not like that!" Even after I explained to her that I saw it with my own eyes, that it is true, and he has a side of him that they do not see. My grandmother still did not believe me, she proclaimed her son was a good hard-working man, she believed I was telling her lies and I was instructed to say those things.

I thought I could trust my grandmother, I thought perhaps she would believe me, and somehow make my dad stop doing the things he was doing. I found out later on, when my mom came to pick me up after that summer was over, his sisters tried to fight my mom. They felt like those were lies that my mom told me to say!

Can you believe those fools?

After that situation happened, I was in trouble with my mom, she was mad, and she told me not to go around telling people her business. "What happens in our house, stays in our house." It was amazing to me how naïve my dad's family were when it came to him.

Living in Town Park I remember my dad beating my mom a lot, and him being a very mean man.

• • •

One morning my mom went off to work, she left us home with my dad, and he made us breakfast that morning. The problem came when he called us downstairs to eat, to our surprise it was oatmeal and not all of us liked oatmeal. My dad knew which one of us did not like it, but he gave all three of us a bowl of oatmeal anyway. My oldest sister did not like it. He *knew* she did not like oatmeal because it made her vomit, and she normally ate a bowl of cereal in the mornings instead.

My oldest sister looked at him like he was crazy because she did not eat oatmeal, and she told him that she would eat a bowl of cereal for breakfast instead. He told her *no*; he was tired of her wasting food, and she was going to eat that oatmeal today! I opened my mouth to remind him that oatmeal made my sister sick. He told me to shut my damn mouth before he beat my ass! "Eat damn it!"

My other sister and I started eating our bowls of oatmeal. But my oldest sister sat there looking at her bowl crying. He told my oldest sister to eat the oatmeal, and if she did not eat it, he was going to beat her with his belt. He took off his belt, put it on top of the table and told her to eat it again.

My oldest sister picked up the spoon, scooped up a little bit of the oatmeal, and she put it in her mouth, crying looking at him. He told her to swallow it, and to eat more of it.

My other sister and I stopped eating to watch him. My dad looked at us, and he asked us what the hell were we looking at. We started eating our food again.

My dad continued to make my oldest sister eat her oatmeal, and she swallowed tiny spoonful after tiny spoonful. She slowly dipped the spoon in the bowl and picked up a little bit of oatmeal with the spoon again. "Put some more damn oatmeal on that spoon!" My oldest sister cried tears as she put the bigger spoonful of oatmeal in her mouth, and she started gagging this time when she swallowed it. He told her, she better not vomit, or he was going to beat her if she did. Well, after eating several spoons full of oatmeal, she vomited in the trash can, and he beat her with the belt.

My dad tried to make my oldest sister eat the vomit out of the trash, but she vomited again, and he beat her again. We begged for him to stop, after going back and forth with him verbally. He made all of us go upstairs to our room and stay there until he tell us to come out.

• • •

When my mom left us home with him, he was just so mean to us. He made us stay in our room all day, we had to play very quietly because he did not want to hear noise. Most of the time he made us lay down to take a nap and leave the door open. If he heard us talking to each other, he came into the room and beat us. He did not want to let us go outside, until my mom came home and let us go outside to play.

Mainly, my oldest sister was the one he punished the most, and I suspected he was still molesting her. Sometimes he made my oldest sister stay in the house while me and my second oldest sister went out to play. His excuse for not letting my oldest sister go outside was because she does not listen to what he says, and therefore she was not allowed to go outside.

I caught on to what he was doing, so I started telling him I do not want to go outside to play. Sometimes he *made* me go outside anyway, but I sat outside on the back porch until he unlocked the back door.

We tried our best to protect my sister from the molestation. My mom *should* have believed us and protected her daughter. Honestly, my mom knew it was the truth when we informed her, but she wanted to be with my dad. My mom was selfish, she put herself first. She chose her man over her kids, and we never talked about what was happening under her roof. We went on pretending like nothing ever happened!

My mom does not like to talk about anything and says talking gives her a headache! Whenever, someone tried to talk to her about these things, she starts saying, "I am getting a headache and I do *not* want to talk anymore."

Yeah, this was her response because she does not like to hear the truth. My dad denied everything, and if my mom questioned him about anything, he beat her up. My mom had the black eyes, bruises, and bloody nose to prove it. One thing my mom *never* did was call the police on my dad, even after he physically beat her.

• • •

My mom played cover up, which meant she covered up the bruises by wearing turtleneck shirts, long legged jeans and shades to try to hide her black eyes. My mom made excuses for my dad, after every time he beat her, and they were back together like nothing ever happened. Somehow the blame was placed on her for the physical beatings he gave her because she made him mad, and he lost self-control.

My auntie Nia said, "I do not know how many times your momma is going to let your daddy keep knocking her across her head before she wakes up and smell the roses!"

I prayed for the day when my mom would wake up and smell the roses. I wanted my mom to realize what she considered to be love was not *real* love, I hoped she would realize my dad does not love her and decide to leave him. Then perhaps all of our lives would change for the better, and no more dealing with the craziness.

I guess, I had my hopes up too high, because my mom was *stuck on stupid* when it came to my dad, and she likes crazy love. My dad verbally belittled my mom by calling her stupid, worthless, sorry ass, and then he beat her as if she was a piece of meat. I knew my mom was never serious about leaving my dad, because she continued to take him back, after he beat on her, and after she caught him with another woman, it was the same script every time in the end. It ended with my mom taking my dad back, and him saying sorry to her again for the same thing he apologized for doing the last time.

Yes, I said *stuck on stupid!*

My mom continued to believe my dad was going to change one day, and each time she took him back, she hoped it was the moment he was going to be a changed man forever.

You know what I learned from this situation? Some people do not like change, some people are not going to change, a person has to be willing to change on their own, and it is either take it or leave it. The choice is yours to make because it is *your* life, and *your* time that you are wasting.

My dad continued to clearly show my mom he had no plans to change anything in his life, he was going to do what he wanted to do, and she played the fool for him.

I found it to be rather hilarious when my mom neatly packed my dad's belongings in trash bags, then placed the bags in the living room at the front door, and she waited for him to come home after she caught him with one of his other women.

For some reason, my mom was aware of the fact that she was being a fool for him, but she thought in her mind she was not being played for a fool, and what she had with him is love. My mom complained about being fed up with my dad, she was fed up with his lies, his drinking, the abuse, the infidelity, and she was sick of all his bullshit. Many times, I heard my mom say, "This is the last time, I mean it this time, I am not taking him back, and I am moving on with my life."

Ha! Yeah, that is what she kept on telling herself, but she was still *stuck on stupid* as I used to say.

My mom confessed to her girl friends about my dad cheating on her, how he does not want to pay bills, how he beats her ass, and she still loves him. But she says she will no longer continue to be his fool if he continued to mistreat her, and she can do bad all by her damn self because she does not need him.

But my dad knew exactly what to say, and he knew what to do to get my mom to take him back every time. Yeah, my dad came at her with that sweet talk game, "Baby I am *sorry. B*aby I *love* you. I did not *mean* to do it, let me make it up to you and *prove* it to you." And the main lie was, "I *promise*, I will *not* do it again."

Oh, my mom was a sucker and a fool for those lines all the time. It was like catching a fish on a hook. Yeah, my dad was not too proud to beg when he knew the situation depended on it because he knew it was convenient for him being with my mom.

The funny part to me was after they made up, my dad made my mom unpack all his belongings and put everything back where it was. You know what? She packed his belongings knowing she was going to take him back, but in her crazy mind she thought it was getting her point across and teaching him a lesson.

In the beginning, I forgave my dad, and I accepted his apology when he gave it. Like my mom, I believed my dad when he promised to change, and —like a fool—I also believed his words until those words became broken promises. My dad was not a man of his word, he did not stay true to his word, and he continued to physically beat up my mom.

Well, I am a person who calls it like I see it, some people do not like that about me, but I do not care. So, the next time my dad came to me with an apology or his sob stories, I let my dad know I did not believe him, I did not believe his lies, and I did not care to hear what he had to say. That was the last time he came to me with an apology, and one of his sob stories for a long time. I did not care, and I did not feel bad telling my dad how I felt because he was a liar.

It was auntie Nia who encouraged me as a kid to speak up, to say what was on my mind, and to say how I feel to my parents because I was holding a lot of my emotions inside.

Honestly, I grew up with a lot of hate for my dad, can you blame me? I do not think you can blame me, it stemmed from the horrible things I saw my dad do as a child growing up. I mean, I really, really, really hated my dad! The God's honest truth is I prayed, many times for my dad to die.

Every once in a while, a family member came over to the house to visit us, to check in on my mom, my sisters and I. Whenever family members came over to visit, my dad became Mr. Nice-Guy all of a sudden.

• • •

Sometimes, family members took us places with them to get us out of the house if my mom was not home when they stopped by to visit. By this time now, the relationship between my mom and her immediate family was very rocky because of what was transpiring in our home. Of course, you know that I was still opening my mouth telling my grandmother and my auntie Nia my mom's business. But the family had seen my dad in action for themselves during prior situations, and knew things were not right. So, some family members decided to take a step back to distance themselves from my mom because of her lifestyle choices. My mom was as stubborn as a bull, she is persistent on doing what she wants to do and doing things her way.

The family felt bad for us because we were innocent kids dealing with this whole ordeal. They did their best to try and talk some sense into my mom, but she was not listening to anything they said to her. So, the family became distant. We only saw the family at functions; birthday parties and holidays, if they showed up.

I understood the family's decision and I understood their position to allow my mom—an adult—to live her life the way she wants to. The family did not condone my mom's lifestyle, and they did not want to be around for any of it. They had families of their own and they did not want their children around that mess. At home, my mom did not run a tight ship, her house was not in order, and there was no discipline under her roof. It was the fun house, and I mean a real circus show too.

Sometimes my mom was annoying, she did annoying things at family gatherings when my dad came along with us, and it made family members feel uncomfortable. See my grandfather's first name is Sammie, my dad's first name is Samuel, and both of their nicknames were Sam. So, everyone referred to both of them as Sam, but when both were in the same room, and someone said the name 'Sam' we knew which one of them they were referring to.

Well, my mom took it upon herself to say, "Which Sam? *My* Sam or my *dad* Sam?" She was trying to be funny, knowing they were talking directly to my granddad, but it made my granddad uncomfortable, and he did not like my dad too much.

Why make a situation awkward? Nobody else thought it was funny. I looked around the room to watch everyone's facial expressions, and there was a lot of eye rolling, head shaking, and eye squinting going on, ok.

It was moments like that when I thought to myself, "Now why would you do that? Why?" I knew my granddad did not like that either. You could see from the look on his face it made him uncomfortable, and my grandmother told her to stop doing it. My granddad was not bold to say it himself, he told my grandmother, who spoke to my mom about it, and then my mom apologized to her father. Although my granddad did not like my dad, both of them were cordial with one another, but you could feel the tension. As men they shook hands, they greeted each other, they said a few words to one another and that was it.

My auntie Sandra—who is the firstborn daughter—and my mom did not have a close bond with one another as sisters. My aunt Sandra is a no nonsense type of person, and she is the complete opposite of my mom. I honestly believe once I told her I witnessed my dad trying to touch my oldest sister that day, she was beyond being disgusted and furious with my mom. My aunt Sandra distanced herself from my mom. We saw her at family gatherings and we stopped by to visit her at work sometimes.

Every so often we visited aunt Sandra's house to visit her family, it was always a pleasure to see uncle Larry, my cousins Larry and Jamal too. Aunt Sandra is a soft spoken, kind, spiritual, patient, and sweet woman. She has a smile that lights up the room, if she smiled at you trust me you smiled back. She carried herself in a graceful manner, she was very lady-like, and she had a lovely aura about herself. She demanded respect if you were in her presence, and to be treated like a lady.

My uncle Willie is the first oldest. My mom has a bond and a good relationship with her brother. They have a connection with each other, and a shared closeness that I admire. I love it when they are joking and laughing with one another. They have a special way of greeting one other, my mom addresses her brother by saying, "Hey, heifer!" and he replies saying "Hey, hoe!" They burst out laughing and kiss each other on the cheek. My uncle visited frequently to check in with my mom, my sisters and me. And to get a plate of dinner.

My uncle Willie was a truck driver and spent most of his time on the road. He stopped by to visit once he came off the road from driving. I joked with him, I called him 'playa' because of the many women he juggled and the gold teeth in his mouth.

Yeah, he is a real country boy at heart and loves to dress up like a cowboy wearing fitted denim jeans, collar shirts, cowboy boots, a thick cowboy belt with the big belt buckle, a pair of shades and his cowboy hat too. The whole shebang!

He's also quite the ladies man, he had many women, and a variety of them. Like my mom, he does not make good choices when it comes to choosing the kind of women he deals with; I do not know where he finds these crazy women who use him for money, and then he has a hard time getting rid of them. It was good times, jokes and laughter with him.

My uncle Clifford is the second oldest boy, we called him Cliff for short. He rarely came over to visit us—he and my mom barley get along. In fact, they argued so much, and they worked my grandma's nerves until she told the both of them to shut up! My uncle is an alcoholic too, he drank his beers, and he smoked his cigarettes. He gets drunk every day, he drinks a twenty-four pack of beer by himself, and then acts like a fool. One thing you can count on Uncle Cliff to do is ruin a family function for sure. He looked for the beer to drink, and if there was no beer then it was definitely a problem. He was not going to stick around for long without a can of beer in his hand, but the real problem began once the beer got in his system, and it made him feel bold. He would open his mouth saying things to make others mad, his spoken words cut like a knife, and he did not care what came out of his mouth. Trust and believe it was almost never anything nice.

I do not know why, but for some reason whenever he is drunk, he talked about his childhood growing up. It upset my granddad when my uncle talked about the past, he spoke of the days when my granddad was a drunk coming home physically beating my grandmother and him as a child. The past is something my granddad does not like to speak about, my uncle knew this, but he did it on purpose to make his father mad. My uncle is a great car mechanic, and he is quite smart. He likes to act crazy, and he likes to stir up trouble.

My auntie Coco was away at college, where she attended Howard University. She never moved back to Miami after she went off to college. Upon graduating, she moved to Virginia with her husband and started her own family. We saw Aunt Coco when she and her family came to town to visit. Besides that, we communicated over the telephone, and writing letters because we never took a trip to visit her. I loved it when she came to visit, and I genuinely appreciate the moments I have with her. And the enlightening conversations that we share about life. She was honest with me, she understood me, and I love her sense of humor. She is highly intelligent, she is resourceful, and I think it is because she researches everything, and is willing to learn more. I learn something new after a conversation with auntie Coco; she always encourages me and tells me how proud she is of me. Since I was a little girl, she has told me I am very smart, very mature, and she saw I was different from the rest of my siblings. I appreciate her, I cherish the talks and the moments we share because she noticed me. At times when I thought or I started to feel like I did not matter, she came to encourage me to strive for more because I deserve better, and there is so much more out here in the world for me. But do not be mistaken, she is also a no non-sense person, which means she will put you back in your place if you get out of line.

My Grandmother Rebecca Dozier is an angel! I loved her strength. Since she was a child she had to be strong and grow up fast to become a woman. My Grandma loved God! O, Lord she had faith like no other! I knew from the moments she shared stories of her life as a little girl growing up, the highs and the lowest points of her lifetime. My grandmother says, it is by the grace of God, she made it!

My grandmother was born on December 20th, 1934, in Williamsburg County, South Carolina. Her mother—Mrs. Bertha Isaac—was a housewife and a midwife, and her father—Mr. Willie—was a farmer. Her mother died after giving birth to her youngest sister, when she was a seven-year-old little girl. Her mother barely had any time to raise her own children because she spent most of her time caring for white folks' children, along with cooking and cleaning their houses which did not allow my grandmother the opportunity to really get to know her mother. My grandmother was raised by her father, and her father gave her the responsibility and the duty to help raise her younger siblings, since she was the oldest girl.

While her father worked in the fields, she was inside the house tending to her siblings, and tending to other duties around the house. But seven years later, at fourteen years old, she was given to my grandfather's—Sammie Lee Dozier—family to be married off, and she never finished school. While she was married to my granddad, he treated her terrible, he had awfully bad drinking habits, he was very abusive to her and mean to their children. They had five children together: three girls and two boys. A few years into their marriage, they decided to move to Miami, Florida in hopes of a better life for themselves and their children. But it became tough for the both of them to work and to watch the children at the same time. So, one by one, my granddad took the three eldest children back to South Carolina to live with his mom, while he and my grandma continued to work. My grandparents sent money to South Carolina for the children, and to help fix up his mother's house because they had no water at one point.

My grandmother wrote letters to keep in contact and to communicate with her kids. Not to soon after moving to Miami, my grandmother decided to separate from my granddad because of his constant abuse toward her and the children—made worse by his excessive drinking. My grandmother finally had the strength and the courage to separate from him. My grandmother walked out on faith, a black woman back then with an education span that stopped at seven years old, she was poor, and she had five children to raise.

My granddad was one of those men that had a traditional old school way of thinking. He believed his wife is his property, the man goes out to work, the woman stays at home to clean and to tend to the children. When my grandmother left him she took her two babies and moved to the projects. She remained single for a while, focusing on working to better her future, taking care of her children and paying her bills. My grandmother still remained in contact with her children up the road in South Carolina, and she continued to send money to them. And she continued to work hard while trying to take care of her two youngest children.

Years later, my grandmother met a fellow by the name of Mr. Herbert Sevilla at the Fontainebleau Hotel in Miami Beach. He was a chauffeur at the time to some of the wealthy tenants who lived in the hotel, in what they called the Penthouse Suites. He was bringing the rich folks back and forth to the Fontainebleau during the winter months from places like New York, Chicago, and California. While he waited for his clients to prepare to go back and forth to wherever, he kept himself busy by visiting the different shops in the hotel. One day, while strolling through the halls of the shops, he noticed the 'New Girl' working at the shop for children.

My grandma was quite lovely, and a sight to see back then. She was shapely, with even toned skin, a beautiful smile and long natural flowing hair. Where do you think my mom and my aunts all get their beauty and their curves from? And Herbert was no hunchback himself. He was a tall, slender guy with wavy hair, and with nice toned caramel skin. He was a charming fellow, and he was quite the ladies man too. Well, Mr. Herbert had his sights set on my grandmother, he set out to woo her, and he fell in love with her.

While working at the children's shop, my grandmother practically ran that shop by herself, and after work she cleaned the store owner's house at night. My grandmother cleaned the house for free numerous of times, allowing herself to be taken advantage of over and over.

During those times, my grandmother did not drive, she could not afford a car, and she caught the bus for transportation, or she walked by foot. After cleaning up the store owner's house, my grandmother caught the bus and walked back home at night.

Mr. Herbert was able to get my grandmother to fall for him; she fell in love, and they began their relationship together. After some time, Herb and my grandma began a common law marriage—back then you were declared married after living together for a certain number of years. My grandma and Herb's relationship lasted twenty years; and during that time a baby girl was born before the shop closed down. My grandmother had herself a man, she was in a new relationship, with a new baby girl, and three young daughters she was raising now. But my grandmother was not doing good financially in her life, she still worked at the children's shop in the mall, her annual earnings were ten thousand dollars with no pay raises, and no health benefits. But my grandmother remained stagnant continuing to work at that shop, she was scared, she did not believe in herself, she was afraid to take a risk and to find another job that was better.

As long as my grandmother settled, the store owner continued to take advantage of her, although my grandmother did not see it as being used because she was appreciative of the opportunity and the lady giving her a job. My reasoning for saying my grandmother was being taken advantage of is that the store owner used it to her advantage knowing my grandmother had no work experience and no formal education. I believe the lady preyed on my grandmother's weaknesses, and the lady took advantage of her naïveté the whole time.

My grandmother continued to be loyal to that woman, Herb tried to tell her numerous times the lady was using her, he tried to get her to believe in herself, and to take the risk of finding a new job working somewhere else. Many of my grandmother's girl friends tried to convince her to apply for a job working at the JCPenney store like them, she had the work experience, and she could make more money working at JCPenney.

But my grandmother still did not believe, she was still afraid to take the risk, and afraid of taking risks in life period. She continued to work for that lady making little to no money while living in the projects struggling to make ends meet, and with kids of her own to raise. My grandmother was being overworked, and she did not have time to spend with her kids or time to be a parent to them. My grandmother dealt with problems in her personal relationship with Herb, and it was not easy raising the young child the two shared together with his job consisting of him out traveling on the road.

Well, Mr. Herb was a free-spirited man, and he did the things he wanted to do. During their relationship, my grandmother was not secure with Herb, she did not trust him much, and she was not sure if he was dependable. Although he was a nice man, he was thoughtful, he helped her pay bills, and he helped her out with the children when in town. But Mr. Herb was a ladies man.

My grandmother found out about his other women. She wanted a faithful man; a man she could trust when out of her sight. They broke up a couple of times and got back together. Mr. Herb's great qualities as a man —which had attracted my grandmother to him—were his smarts, his confidence in himself and his abilities. Herb tried to help boost my grandmother confidence, to help her trust and believe in herself because she was capable of doing more. But this led to arguments between them, leaving them angry with each other.

They shared the common habit of gambling. My grandmother likes to play the slots, and the card games. When it came to gambling Herb liked to bet money on horses, his gambling choice was more expensive, and thus worse. And his gambling addiction to betting on horses ultimately led to their break-up.

Herb's father was on his death bed; he lived to be 103 years old. His father left him twenty thousand dollars and ten thousand dollars for his granddaughter Coco's college fund.

Mr. Herb spent his twenty thousand dollars gambling. He bet and bet on horse races until all of his money was gone. Afterwards, he knew that if my grandmother found out he gambled away all of the money she would be upset, he was desperate to win the money back so he took three thousand from his daughter's college fund to win back what he lost gambling.

He took the three thousand dollars, went back to the racetrack, and he gambled the money on horses again. He was able to win back the twenty thousand dollars, the three thousand dollars, and a little bit extra. But when he returned to put the money back before my grandma found out, it was too late, and she realized the money was missing. Although he was able to win the money back, my grandmother was upset, and it was the final straw that broke the camel's back with her trusting him! My grandmother was done tolerating his gambling addiction, his irresponsibility financially, and this situation with him taking the money confirmed her suspicions of not being able to put her trust in him.

Then one day, without any notice, the shop owner showed up to my grandmother's doorstep, gave my grandma a measly thousand dollars, and informed her the shop was closed down. Then told her to have a nice life!

How dare that lady give my grandmother only a thousand dollars, after all the money that shop earned, and the lady was rich. This lady played my grandmother, she did her wrong knowing the shop was going to close down ahead of time, but decided to inform her once it closed down. That lady overworked my grandmother, she underpaid her, not to mention she was a personal maid cleaning this lady's house for free. This lady knew my grandmother was poor, she had bills to pay, and with kids to take care of financially.

Well, the day has arrived for my grandmother to take a risk, to believe there were more opportunities for her, and all she had to do was step out on faith. Luckily, my grandma's friends who worked at JCPenney in the Omni helped her fill out the application; she received the job based off her work experience, her capabilities, and her work ethic. My grandmother began working at JCPenney as a Sales Floor Manager with a starting salary of thirty thousand dollars with pay raises and health benefits. Finally, my grandmother had a job which brought stability to her life, more prosperity financially than she ever had before, and she worked at JCPenney for fifteen years.

Then twenty-five years later, my grandma rekindled her relationship and her love for my grandpa. For my granddad to convince my grandmother to give their love another chance, he apologized for the horrible things he did in the past, and he swore to be a changed man. He begged for the chance to show and prove his love to her if given the chance again.

At the time, he worked at Jackson Memorial Hospital as a janitor. And with both of their incomes put together came more stability in their lives. They renewed their wedding vows, but this time around both of them had a child from their previous relationships. My granddad refused to claim his daughter from his previous relationship, and he denied any involvement with the child's mother.

But then tragedy struck, and the child's mother died when she was a little girl. The family was contacted because there was no guardian for her, and my granddad still would not claim the child as his own. But my grandmother, aunts and uncles wanted to help out with my auntie Vanessa. Living arrangements were made for Vanessa to live and be raised by one of her mother's family members. I remember the weekend aunt Vanessa spent at my aunt Nia's, but she slept at our apartment to play with me. Aunt Vanessa was incredibly quiet, and I understood why, because we were unfamiliar to her, and her mom died.

I cannot imagine what my aunt Vanessa was feeling, and what she was thinking in her mind with her whole world being turned upside down at the moment. She was a little girl trying to understand and trying to deal with the death of her mom. The fear of my mom dying was one of my worst fears back then. So, I tried to make her feel comfortable and at ease. It was hard to get her to talk, and she was sad at night.

When I met my aunt Vanessa for the first time, I could not believe it when they informed me she was my auntie. I thought it was a joke, she was too young to be my auntie, and she was a kid like me. I thought you had to be an adult in order to be someone's auntie or uncle. Vanessa was sent to be raised by *her* auntie. My granddad was an old man, he was not going to raise a kid, and he was not involved with her upbringing.

My grandparents lived in a duplex they rented for ten years, until both of them retired from their jobs and they moved back to Georgetown, South Carolina.

• • •

As a kid, I remember my grandma working at JCPenney in the Omni—the Omni was a mini mall Downtown by the metro rail station next to the Miami Herald building. The Omni mini mall had a cinema, and all the locals shopped at the mall. The locals traveled a short distance to shop, and to see a movie. The Omni was the spot!

I tagged along with my mom and aunt to visit my grandmother working at JCPenney in the Omni. I looked forward to seeing my grandmother, putting a smile on her face, and making her laugh. When I walked off the escalator, I looked around on the sales floor to spot her. When I spotted my grandma, I snuck up on her if she was not with a customer to prank her. Sometimes, I snuck up on her while she put clothes on the rack, I pretended to sound like a man flirting with her. In a man's voice I said, "Hey, sexy lady." I fooled her rather good a couple of times, she put her hands on her hips to turn around thinking I was a man, and then she burst out laughing after realizing it was me pranking her.

Sometimes I spent the night or the weekends with my grandparents while my mom worked double shifts. After school, I walked to the Omni by myself to meet up with my grandma at work, and I waited until her shift ended. Sometimes my grandma allowed me to visit the music store, and some of the toy stores in the mall while I waited.

The music store was my favorite shop to visit, I listened to the music albums with the headphones on display, and I looked around the store for the latest music album released. The kid's toy store was another shop I visited, the rules at the toy store was you can look, but do not touch anything. After walking around the mall visiting the shops, I returned back to the JCPenney store to wait for my grandma's shift to end and we waited for my granddad to pick us up.

Well, I spent plenty of time with my grandparents, although I did not like staying with my grandparents because it was boring at their house. At their house there was not much to do besides taking a nap, watching television, or sitting outside on the porch. There were not many kids in the neighborhood.

There were two options if I watched television, the first option was watching old country westerns with my grandma while she napped because her feet and bones ached from working. The second option was sitting in the living room with my granddad watching the gospel channel, as he check the two-dollar scratch offs and he fell asleep watching television.

My grandparents had one of those couches covered in plastic, I think *everybody's* grandparents had one of these couches, and the plastic sticks to you. It makes you sweat and when you get up off the couch the plastic sticks to your skin, and it feels like ripping off a band-aid. And the *worst* thing you could do is fall asleep on the couch.

But watching television with my granddad meant I had to watch what he was watching; he watched the news and the gospel channel. He fell asleep watching television, but as soon as I changed the channel, he woke up and made me turn the TV back to the channel he was watching. Sometimes my grandma argued with him to let me watch something I wanted to watch, she gave me the remote and allowed me to change the television channel.

I AM GOD'S CHILD

I did not talk to the kids in the neighborhood on my grandparent's block and they did not speak to me. I preferred to stay in the house to myself as usual, but my grandma introduced me to her neighbor's kids, and she thought it would be good for us to hang out together. I tried to get along with those kids, but they did not like me. They pretended to like me, but talked about me among one another behind my back. Those kids passed judgment on me without getting to know me, and prejudged me based on my physical appearance.

So, I decided to stay to myself; it was back to me, myself, and I. This was nothing new to me, I have this problem a lot with people who are intimidated by me. People who do not like me, people who are jealous of me and with people who want to be me! I learned early on, people who do not like you, they like to be around you, and those people get mad when you no longer allow them to be in your presence.

According to those kids, I was a fat girl, they did not like my clothes, I had too much confidence for a fat girl, and they wanted to fight me. But we never fought each other; those kids were cowards, and they were not bold enough to step in my face or fight me. The craziest part is, after I went back to being by myself, those kids came knocking to my grandparent's door wanting to be in my presence again, and every time I had my grandparents tell them I do not want to play with them. Hey, I can respect the fact someone does not like me, but do not think you are still going to be in my presence to be mean or disrespectful to me.

I stayed inside the house with my grandparents and looking back it was not as bad as I thought, but as a kid, it is boring when you are not playing or doing something fun.

The time I spent with my grandparents was actually the peace and quiet I needed back then. We sat in the dining room at the dinner table to eat dinner; eating inside the bedrooms was not allowed. My grandparents cooked the same food dishes consisting of white rice, baked rutabaga, with fried chicken or baked chicken and we ate dessert afterwards. For dessert, we ate ice cream with a slice of peach cobbler or apple pie.

My grandmother lived with diabetes, she took insulin, I assisted with checking her sugar level and I assisted with giving her the insulin injection because of her bad eyesight from dealing with diabetes.

After eating dinner, it was time for us to go to the corner store for my grandparents to play the lotto—the cash three numbers—and get grandma a pack of cigarettes. My family was into playing numbers heavy back then, my grandparents, my parents, my aunts and my uncles too. Each of them kept a notebook with a log of the previous numbers played, and auntie Nia developed a system to determine which numbers to play daily. She came close to hitting the lotto jackpot once, but she was off by one number.

REBECCA S. SMITH

I think my mom has the worst story of almost winning the lottery.

Back in the early nineties when the lottery jackpot was at the highest—one hundred million dollars—my mom had the winning numbers for the lottery jackpot that night. My mom planned on playing the same sequence of numbers she had played for years, and that night those same numbers dropped for the lottery. My mom's numbers dropped, but she decided not to go play her numbers that night after arguing with my dad and she missed an opportunity. And she never came close to winning again. When I heard this story, I could not believe it, and I shook my head in disbelief. Sometimes I tried to imagine it, and I wondered how different our lives could have been if my mom played those numbers that night?

I imagined my mom not walking home alone at night after working double shifts at the hospital, her not coming home too tired to eat, and her not complaining about leg or back pain. I thought about the times my mom walked home, and she walked to work many days. One thing about my mom, she does not have a problem footing it.

I stayed up countless nights praying to God, asking God to watch over my mom, and to protect her. I prayed for my mom to make it to work safely, and for her to make it back home safely. I did not sleep much throughout the night, and I was up early in the morning to see her walk through the front door. I was afraid of the possibility that someone might try to rob my mom or even worse, someone might try to rape and murder her—even though I knew she carried mace, a knife or some sort of object she carried to protect herself with as a weapon.

A woman walking alone late at night carrying a purse; carrying bags? *Come on now*, I watched the local news, and I was not naïve to the world in which we live in. Incidents like that *do* happen in the neighborhood from time to time.

I thought about the times we had no electricity, the power was turned off, and we had to light candles in the nighttime to see our way until morning time. Those were the nights I took cold baths and played with my toys in the tub while my mom sat on top of the toilet seat looking tired, looking stressed out, and looking worried at the same time. We opened the windows for air during the day, we opened the bedroom windows for air at night. Those nights I cried, and I prayed myself to sleep because there was nothing I could do to make things better.

• • •

Sometimes, just to get out of the house, I took a ride with my grandparents to visit their siblings and other family relatives. Especially, if they were going over to auntie Betty's house, she is my grandmother's sister, she was

I AM GOD'S CHILD

a madam at a brothel in an apartment building and she lived upstairs on the second floor with her daughter. When visiting aunt Betty at the brothel, we went upstairs to her apartment to sit down in the kitchen to talk, and the real action involving prostitution was taking place downstairs. Often at times, my grandmother visited her sister to check in on her, and to gamble playing card games. My granddad disapproved of my grandma going to hang out at the brothel with her sister, he did not condone the activities taking place there, and he did not approve of her gambling playing card games.

The prostitutes cooked and they kept the brothel house clean. Aunt Betty bossed the prostitutes around all day, she called the prostitutes hoes, and they responded to being called a hoe as if it was their birth name. I could not believe what I was witnessing, women were being pimped, these women or girls continually performed sexual acts for money daily and were given drugs to cope with the lifestyle. I could see the unhappiness on the prostitutes' faces, although they smiled, and spoke politely.

Overtime the brothel house became old, the place was raggedy, the furniture and the decor inside the house was outdated. The brothel house was no longer a booming place for business, the prostitute workers got old, the number of prostitute workers grew smaller and smaller by the day until the brothel house was closed down. Well, Aunt Betty was a woman up in age, she was a tall lady, she wore glasses, and she kept her hair rolled up in hair curlers. Aunt Betty wore pajama dresses, she walked around in her bedroom slippers, she kept her lighter and a pack of cigarettes in her pocket. This was the kind of things you see in the movies, but I was seeing this in real life.

My grandma and aunt Betty shared habits together, both of them smoked cigarettes, and both liked to gamble. As a kid I watched them play card games of spades, I was the score keeper, and I had fun. I know I was too young to be around grown folks, and too young to be witnessing these kinds of things, but it is life. We are human beings, we are not perfect, and it is called reality. This was nothing new to me, I played card games of spades with my family numerous times as a kid, and I did not get in trouble for it by my parents. While I kept score of the game on the notepad, Aunt Betty kept the money from the winnings in her bra, and she gave me a couple of dollars later on for being the score keeper. My grandma and aunt Betty were partners when playing cards, they were professionals, they won more games than they lost. It was fun to watch them talk trash, slam the cards down on the table, shuffle and deal the cards. It was beautiful to witness, the aroma in the room smelled of cigarettes, and burnt matches, along with the smell of beer on their breaths.

My grandma enjoyed herself playing bingo or gambling period and she found comfort in doing the things she liked. My grandma was willing to take risks gambling, but not willing to take many risks in her life. Even though she had little to no education or certification, she possessed skills combined with a quick learning ability and she mastered her job position! My grandma has been working since she was a kid, she had the tired feet, and aching bones she rubbed down every day from work to prove it. My grandma allowed fear to make her afraid to take more risks, she allowed fear to make her self-doubt, and not believe in herself.

How do you know what you are capable of, if you do not take a risk to try? If you step out on faith, you believe in God, and you pray to God, he will work things out in your favor. The *Book of Psalms* (30:4-5) in the *Holy Bible* it says we may endure God's anger for a moment, but in God's favor we have life. As a woman, my grandmother worked all her life, she struggled to survive, and she tried to do the best with what she had. My grandmother was my confidant, my friend, we joked, and we laughed together. She was a big part of my heart.

My grandma and my mom are two peas in a pod. They cannot be around each other for more than a couple of minutes before they start arguing or disagree about something. Both of them are very stubborn, both think they know it all, and both have a hard time listening. Both complained about the other not listening, they could not agree to disagree, somebody *had* to be right, and somebody *had* to be wrong.

Good Lord, can't we all just get along!?

• • •

My mom is a woman that does not like to speak about the past, she did not speak about her childhood, and the upbringing with her parents. If my mom were to speak of the bad things from her past about my grandparents, it was considered disrespectful to her parents, they called her a liar and they denied the wrongdoings she spoke of. My mom deals with her emotions internally, she did not express herself vocally, and she prefers to listen to music.

My mom loves to listen to music, if she does not want to talk, she will ignore you and listen to some music. My mom takes music with her no matter where she goes, she carried a portable cassette player with a bag of cassette tapes, and extra batteries to listen to her music while walking. My mom loves a variety of music, and her musical library is filled with music from the sixties, seventies, eighties, and nineties classic music. Listening to music is her escape, she drowns everything out around her and all she hears is her music!

My mom's mood swings are determined by the kind of music she wants

I AM GOD'S CHILD

to hear; when she listens to her music she reminisces about things from the past. If she was sad, she listened to a sad song. If she was happy, she listened to a feel-good song. If her heart was broken, she listened to a sad love song. If her love life was good, she listened to a slow jam song. But I remember some nights, my mom went downstairs in the living room to sit down in the dark to listen to sad love songs after a fight with my dad and she cried tears. I followed my mom downstairs to check on her, and to make sure she was alright. Many times, I found my mom with tears running down her face, and she wiped her tears trying to hide them from me because she wanted me to believe everything was ok.

It broke my heart to see her crying, and I started crying because she was hurting. It was almost like I could feel her pain. As a child I stayed by my mom's side when I knew she was hurting or heartbroken about something, I sat with her in the dark listening to music until I fell asleep in her arms as she cradled me like a baby.

I remember when my mom drove a charcoal gray, four door nineteen-ninety Toyota Camry, but someone burglarized the car and stole its stereo system. So, we used my portable cassette boom-box with radio as a way to listen to music when we drove around. While my mom drove, I sat in the back seat with the boom box, a bag of batteries, and the cassettes. I was the back-seat DJ; whatever she requested to hear I played it. We listened to some of the music my mom liked, and some I liked. We rolled down the windows to save on gas—according to my mom riding with the a/c on in the car burns out the gas faster—and we turned the music up loud riding with the wind blowing in our faces.

I am a music lover like my mom, I listen to music to drown out the chaos around me, and the music becomes my escape to clear my head. It is funny how we do not see how we are like our parents in more ways than we think, and most of our habits we picked up from them. There are habits of mine I picked up from my parents as a kid, some good and some bad.

The parent you do not get along with or vow to *not be like*, is the parent you grow up to be like in many ways and not on purpose. Some of our tendencies, some of our habits, we developed from watching our parents, and we cannot see it ourselves. Sometimes, we cannot see past our anger developed from our pain to take a look in the mirror to open our eyes and to check ourselves.

If you carry anger in your heart, anger will lead you to do mean things, causing you to inflict your anger—and your pain—on other people. Now you have caused someone else pain and you have angered someone else. It is not good when you hold onto anger or pain in your heart, and it will lead to your downfall. God does not want you to carry anger in your heart, God wants us to carry love and compassion in our hearts. God knows we cannot carry all of the pain from life's burdens; he wants us to give it all to him. All you have to do is simply talk to God!

All of us have a journey, we all have a story, we all have a purpose, we will have trials and tribulations. It is written. Yes, sometimes in life we will fall flat on our faces, and at times life knocks us down. But what matters is getting back up, after being knocked down, having the courage to keep on going on and having the determination to not give up! How you bounce back! Many people do not know how to get back up, not many people have the will to get back up, many people will not expect you to get back up, and some people will try to stop you from rising up.

Just know the journey will get hard, many times it will feel like you are alone, but you are not alone because God is right there with you. Just because you cannot see God, it does not mean he is not there, but know God is around you and you can feel his presence. If you can learn to sit down, learn to be still to listen, and take deep breaths you will hear God speak to you, I promise.

I am a servant of God, I was sent by God, and I am on a mission to inform all of his children that God is still here! I am God's Child! Our missions is ours to complete, traveling along the journey our commands and our orders come from God whom we serve. This is my journey, the long road I am traveling, and I am here to testify about God, the same God we all pray to!

• • •

As time went on nothing changed in our house, my mom was still naïve when it came to my dad and our living environment, period. My oldest sister began to run away from home by the time she reached middle school, staying at friends' houses, and it became a problem for my mom. My oldest sister kept running away, until my mom decided to allow her to live with my dad's friend's ex-wife because his daughter was friends with my sister. My mom approved of my oldest sister living with their family, and she thought it was the right choice. Instead of my mom being her child's protector, my mom considered this to be the best way of protecting my oldest sister because leaving my dad was not an option. My mom was in love with the man molesting her daughter and not losing him was more important than what was being done to her child.

The plan was my oldest sister continued to attend school, my mom contributed money every month for my sister being under their roof and for her daily necessities.

Now it was my second oldest sister and I left at the house. There was a five-year age gap between us, and she was looking for an escape out of the house herself.

She was doing her own thing, spending time around the neighborhood with friends, and my mom made me tag along with her. She hated it when my mom made me go with her. When she went outside to play with her friends, she complained and had temper tantrums.

My second oldest sister was upset when there was no other option and I had to go with her. She punished me for it even though it was not my fault I had to go with her. As we walked down the street on the sidewalk, she vocally let it be known to me how much she hated my dad, my mom, and how much she hated taking me with her.

It really hurt my feelings to know she hated me and did not want me around her, but everything else I understood.

As a kid I stayed in the house playing, and I was happy to hang out with my second oldest sister. Although she was mean to me, I still loved her, and as her little sister I thought she was cool.

But when we were around her friends, she was strict, and mean to me! I did not have fun hanging out with my sister then, we got in trouble, and my mom spanked our butts for disobeying our curfew many times. When we did not come home at night in time for curfew she came looking for us to get us! It did not matter if my mom had to drive or walk around the neighborhood looking for us, she was coming to find us, and we were in trouble. My mom stopped to ask friends or neighbors for our whereabouts, and she knocked on doors to find us. When we heard our mom was out looking for us, we knew we had to beat her getting home, and more than likely she spanked us, or she put us on punishment.

I hated getting my butt spanked, my mom is heavy handed, she made us pull down our bottoms, bend over on the couch and she beat us butt naked with her belt! Of course, I did not stay still to get a spanking; I ran around the coffee table, I crawled underneath the coffee table, my mom had to catch me to spank me! It is true what they say, "A hard head makes a soft ass!" All my momma had to do was grab her belt and I started crying.

I am not going to lie, I was a crybaby until I toughened up. My mom knew I was a crybaby. If she threatened to beat me, I told the truth because I did not want a spanking, but my sister called it snitching! I did not like being labeled a snitch! So, my second oldest sister broke it down to me, if I wanted to hang out with her then I had to learn to lie!

I was taught *not* to lie, and to tell the *truth* like my parents taught me— until they taught me to lie themselves on their behalf.

As a kid I was not able to be myself, I had to do things other people's way to fit in, and I even had to do this with my own family. I had to prove my loyalty by lying to fit in and to get them to believe I was trustworthy.

But I prefer to be myself and I prefer to do things *my* way. So, I went back to being by myself, and I preferred to be alone because I found myself in bad situations following behind other people. I once heard someone say, "If you teach your child to lie, your child will lie to you."

I decided to stay in the house with my mom, and I played by myself. I wanted to be close to my mom anyway to kept my eyes on her, to make sure she was ok. When my mom suggested I go outside with my second oldest sister, I told her I did not want to go outside. My mom tried to pressure me into going with my sister of course, but I convinced her to let me stay in the house, and my sister was happy! I was happy, and I did not have to worry about getting my butt spanked with a belt for disobeying curfew. I played with my toys, I watched television, and sometimes I went outside to play on the playground in the complex. My mom allowed me to play on the playground by myself. I listened for my mom yelling my name, and when she did I went home. I was with my mom most of the time, I did not want to be around my dad, and I could not hangout with my sisters.

My mom is a lady who lives life on the go, she has places to go, things to do, and people to see. I was right there with my mom as she visited her girl friends, when she went to parties, when she cheated with her side dude, and I was told to keep it a secret. If my dad was not at work, he was hanging out on third avenue with his buddies getting high, getting drunk, and gambling; rolling dice. He spent the rest of his time with other people and with his other women. My dad had another daughter from another woman, I had a half-sister older than me, and he spent some of his time with her too.

There was so much happening, and everybody was busy doing what they do.

• • •

My oldest sister returned home after a couple of months, and she came back pregnant! Yeah, my oldest sister being pregnant was a *big* deal, her pregnancy was a shocker, and there were many questions that needed answering. Who is the father? My mom was in disbelief, and she was unaware of the things my oldest sister was doing; like having sex. My sister was not the same girl, she had a new attitude now, a new demeanor to match, and she was into boys. She was given our brother's room while he was away at school, and *both* my sisters were sneaking boys into the house when my parents were not home. My sisters were talking to boys from school, sneaking the boys inside the house when my parents were gone for hours and I was the lookout for my sisters.

One night, my mom left us home to pick up my dad from work, and my sisters decided to sneak boys into the house that night. My sisters took the boys upstairs to their bedrooms, while I remained downstairs in the living room as the lookout to let them know when my parents pulled up. While I was at my post looking out the window, I had to pee, and I sat there as long as I could, holding it in until I could not hold it anymore.

I was afraid my parents were going to pull up while I was in the bathroom, so I ran upstairs and I tried to go as quick as possible! As soon as I finished, I ran downstairs to look out the window and I saw my parents pull up in the car. So, I ran back upstairs, and I knocked on the doors to let them know my parents were home. There was not much time to spare, we had to move fast because my dad was walking quickly to the front door, and I did *not* want to get caught. One of the boys was able to run out the back the door before my parents made it in the house, but the other boy was afraid to jump out of my oldest sister's bedroom window, and he hid in the closet until we could sneak him out of the house. My parents busted us trying to sneak the boy out of the house, and this was not the first time they snuck boys into the house.

Man! That night my mom spanked our butts like never before with the belt, she placed us on punishment, and we did not go outside for a while. This is another example of how I found myself in some mess because of *other people*. I hated spankings! As a matter of fact, I tried to talk my mom out of beating my butt, but she was not hearing anything I was saying.

A couple of weeks later, my oldest sister found out she was pregnant, and she was having a boy. Listen, we are all human, we all make mistakes, and nobody is perfect. Often times I thought to myself how difficult it must have been for her to be shamed for getting pregnant as a teenager, but yet it was ok for her to be molested as a child by her mother's boyfriend and to have her innocence stolen as a child. It takes a lot of strength to deal with that crazy mess mentally, and the molestation was kept a secret by our mom. My mom *knew* her boyfriend was molesting her daughter, and she did not inform her child's biological father of the things happening to his daughter. My mom admitted the fact she kept the molestation a secret from my oldest sister's father because she knew he would have killed my dad back then if she had told him the truth.

I want you to let that sink in for a moment.

Then one day you make a bad decision that led to a big mistake, now these same adults whom God trusted to care for you are mad at you! They are cowards, not willing to admit they failed you along the way because of their selfishness, foolishness, bad decisions, poor choices and pride!

I am proud of my oldest sister because it takes a lot of strength to deal with that mess, like I said before, to endure ridicule and face it alone with no guidance! She was pregnant by an older boy from the neighborhood, the two of them were not in a relationship together and agreed to co-parenting the child together. But the child's father did not keep his word to help raise their child, and he began to deny being the child's father.

My oldest sister was a single teenage mother now, she was still a young kid and had no clue what she was doing. My mom was right there by her side to support her, to assist her during the pregnancy and for the birth of the baby. She continued to attend school during her pregnancy, and after she gave birth to her baby.

After having the baby, my oldest sister had to attend a school for young teenage mothers to continue completing school and to graduate high school. The school provided day care while my sister went to class to do her work. You know, I commend her for not giving up, and not listening to the doubters or naysayers. I commend her for being strong and focused to graduate high school.

My mom and my sister's mother/daughter relationship had reached its boiling point, and they could not co-exist under the same roof anymore. So, my oldest sister moved out of the house, and moved in with her god parents, and god brother. She was happy to live with her god parents where she and the baby had their own room. My mom contributed money to her god parents' household for my oldest sister living under their roof. Her god mother called my mom's phone all the time, nothing was free, and my mom continuously reimbursed her the money she spent on my sister.

My oldest sister thought the grass was greener on the other side, she did not know her god mother was money hungry, and my mom was paying for her stay under their roof. Her level of disrespect toward my mom was at an all-time high, she had a nasty attitude with my mom, and she did not listen to anything my mom said to her. She began to bluntly disrespect my mom to her face, in front of her god mother, and was publicly disrespectful to my mom in front of others. My oldest sister referred to her god mother as mom, and she proclaimed to have two mothers. She was nice to my mom when she wanted money, when she wanted me to babysit my nephew, and she guilt tripped my mom to get her way. For it is written in *Exodus* (20:12) that we must honor our mothers and fathers for the length of our days shall be long and it pleases God!

We must respect our mothers and fathers even if they wronged us or disrespected us because it is the right thing to do. Being disrespectful toward your parent is not a good thing to do and doing so will block or hinder your blessings. And I fear my God up above! You can be here today, and gone tomorrow. Do not think God will not take you out of this world. It can happen, it happens every day. You are sadly mistaken if you think the Lord will not do it. I do not suggest you test him! I was taught to respect my elders; I spent the majority of my childhood around adults or by myself and you do not bite the hand that feeds you like my grandma said.

My mom was there for my oldest sister despite the disrespect, the bad behavior displayed, and everything else my sister did to her. My mom is an enabler, it is what she does, and I cannot stand it. I hated it. She allowed everything to go on under her roof; there was no structure, no foundation, no order, and no discipline. My mom talks a good game, she says the right things to have other people believe a false perception, to believe she is a woman who has her life together, she appeared to be a responsible woman, and she appeared to have her priorities handled.

You know, I laugh on the inside when I hear my mom talking to other people about their problems or situations. She advises people and has many suggestions for *other* people, but she does not apply any of it to *her* life. My mom does not practice what she preaches, she says one thing, but she does the complete opposite. It is funny, she can see other people's problems, and she knows what they need to do. But she cannot see *her* problems, and she does not know what to do for *herself*.

My mom is a controlling woman; you have to listen to her, and do what she says. But she does whatever she wants to do. She is not going to listen to you, and you cannot stop her from doing what she wants to do. You know what they say about a controlling person who likes to control other people, they are micromanaged, and they lack control in their own life. My mom was being controlled, she had no control, but she wanted to be in control of somebody. She wanted to be a leader, but she was being a follower.

My grandma used to say, I was an angel sent from God to my mom!

● ● ●

Meanwhile back at home, one night we came home to find our townhouse was burglarized and some of our personal belongings were stolen. The burglars broke into the vacant townhouse next door, they knocked a big hole into the wall to get inside our townhouse and were able to steal our belongings without being seen or caught. There were many more townhouses burglarized in the neighborhood, my parents were not happy about the break in, and we moved out of the housing complex.

Well, my mom *decided* to move out the townhouse, but we did not have another place to live, she was not able to find another place quick enough before her lease expired. At the last moment with no place to go, my oldest sister opened up her doors to us, and we moved in with her, all except for my dad.

By this time, my oldest sister lived in a one-bedroom apartment in Overtown with her boyfriend and her son. Her boyfriend was an older man she met while he was locked away in prison. They met over the telephone.

He was locked up with one of her girl friend's boyfriend, the two were bunk mates in prison. Well, my oldest sister was barely a teenager when she began talking to him, and when he was released from prison the two began dating.

At the time, he was in a relationship with the mother of his child, and they were living together. My oldest sister worked as a telemarketer, and was living in her own place; just her and her baby.

When they began a personal relationship he left his girlfriend to be with my oldest sister and he moved into her place. During the beginning of their relationship things were fine, they were getting along good, he was a nice guy, and he treated her good. He stole cars for a living, and did other illegal activities to make money.

Back then, as a kid, I spent a lot of time at my oldest sister's apartment babysitting, and I witnessed some things. My oldest sister's boyfriend had another side to him, the bad side was starting to come out, and things changed quickly.

Her boyfriend was controlling, he was physically abusive, and he was a cheater. The independence my oldest sister had before she met him was gone. He did not want her working, so she stopped working and she depended on him financially. She spent most of her time at home inside the apartment with the kids, cooking, and cleaning. Her boyfriend did not want her going on outings, and he did not want her hanging out with friends. He tried his best to isolate her from family and friends. Sometimes he locked her inside the apartment with the kids, and sometimes he physically beat her up to keep control of her.

My mom made it her business to continuously check in on my oldest sister and my nephew. My mom called her house phone every day to make sure she was ok, and ask if she needed anything. And when my oldest sister did not have a house phone, my mom showed up at her apartment knocking on the front door. She lived in the same apartment buildings we grew up in as children, some of our family members lived over there too, and they kept an eye out for her. My mom was just one phone call away, if my sister needed her for anything or if she was in trouble, and my mom came running once she received a phone call.

One day, my mom and I walked over to my oldest sister's apartment to check in on her. Some days passed by, and my mom did not hear from her. We showed up at her doorstep, knocking and knocking at the front door waiting for someone to open it. We banged on the front door, we knocked on the windows, and we shouted their names. Luckily, my three-year-old nephew heard us knocking and shouting. He climbed up onto the couch, he peeled the aluminum foil off of the window, and he was so happy to see us from the look on his face.

I AM GOD'S CHILD

We talked to him through the window, and we instructed him to get his mother as we looked through the living room window. My nephew came back with his mom, she was in the room sleep, and he woke her up. Her boyfriend left the apartment, locked them inside from the outside, and took the keys to the dead bolt lock with him.

Her boyfriend was not reliable, and he was not a responsible person. He spent most of his time in and out of jail. House arrest is the only thing that kept him in the house, and when he stayed in the house they fought like cats and dogs. In the beginning, my sister did not fight him back, and took the abuse. But as time went on my oldest sister decided to fight back, she began to get the courage, and the strength to fight him, although he may have blackened her eye.

You know what, I admired my oldest sister's courage and her strength to fight him back, although she ended up with a black eye or he knocked her out. My oldest sister was home locked down with her boyfriend when he was on house arrest, but he was back in the streets once the ankle monitor came off, and he was barely home. Let me just say for the record, her boyfriend drove a box Chevy sitting on rims with candy paint and beat out in the trunk. My sister was not allowed to drive that car unless he was in the car with her. He kept getting pulled over by the cops and he kept getting arrested for driving with a suspended license.

Sometimes she swapped car seats with him; she hopped in the driver seat, and he hopped in the passenger seat before pulling over because she had a valid driver license.

Her boyfriend kept getting caught stealing cars, and spent months, and sometimes years locked up for the same things.

My oldest sister was able to work, to hang out with her friends, and do as she pleased when her boyfriend was locked up for long periods of time. She wrote letters to her boyfriend, she put money on his books, and she was there for jail house visits. I tagged along with her and the kids to visit him a couple of times. It seemed like every time her boyfriend was released from jail, my sister was pregnant, and then at the clinic getting an abortion.

Sometimes I tagged along for those visits to the clinic, and I babysat to ensure she got rest to recover physically from the abortion procedure. I saw the sadness on her face, and the pain in her eyes from the procedures because her boyfriend did not want to keep the baby. She was able to keep one of the babies because she was too far along in her pregnancy to get an abortion, and she gave birth to a girl.

My oldest sister had two children now, but only one child from her current boyfriend, and he became more controlling. When my oldest sister found out about his infidelities, he begged her not to leave him, and he took her shopping to buy her things. They continued to fight at times, especially when he came home mad about something.

One day, while I was at my oldest sister's apartment chilling out in the living room watching television, her boyfriend walked inside the apartment with a mad look on his face, and he walked straight to their bedroom. My sister was in the bedroom relaxing watching television, while the baby was sleeping. I do not know what her boyfriend was mad about, but I turned the volume down on the TV because I heard the noise coming from their bedroom. They were in the room arguing, then my sister came walking out heading toward the kitchen. He followed right behind her, now he was mad because she walked away from him, and she did not feel like arguing with him. This fool was so mad at the fact my sister turned her back toward him, he grabbed the Christmas tree and beat her in the back with it.

Honestly, it all happened so fast, so unexpectedly, I was not able to warn her, or shout 'watch out' because I was not expecting him to hit her with a *tree*. I hopped up off the couch, I begged for him to stop, then I ran across the yard to Aunt Lena's apartment to get some help, and she called the police. My sister's boyfriend was not sticking around waiting for the cops to show up to arrest him, and took off running once I ran out the apartment to get help. But my sister did not press charges against him, and the two of them were back together afterwards.

I remember when my oldest sister vowed in my mom's face to be a better woman, a better mother to her children, to love, protect, and raise her children right. She was going to be a better parent than my mom, she was going to lead by example for her children, and as a big sister for us to look up to. She was going to be with a man who loved her, and who treated her good. But those vows did not reflect her reality at the moment, in fact it was the opposite, and she could not realize it.

My little nephew grew up watching his mother get beat up physically and mistreated constantly by her boyfriend. And sometimes her boyfriend mistreated my nephew as a child. He physically beat her, he micromanaged her, and he cheated on her too. Well, it seemed to me, my oldest sister was following along in my mom's footsteps, and she broke her vows.

We must humble ourselves children, if you do not humble yourself, the lord up above will show you why he is called God and he will teach you humility! When you think you are grown, when you do not want to listen, when you think you know it all, God will show you there is more to learn about life, you still have a long way to go, and so much more to learn.

My mom and my oldest sister were two peas in the same pod, and they were alike in more ways than they thought. I have learned you cannot be a good leader if you do not listen, if you cannot take orders, and you do not obey God. You cannot be a good leader if you cannot learn to be a servant, and learn to follow God. It reads in the *Holy Bible*, "The ear that hears the reproof of life abides among the wise." (Proverbs 15:31)

You know God sends a message to you in so many ways, you have to be willing to receive the message sent to you, and do not be concerned with who is the messenger. If you do not listen, then you will not receive the message. My oldest sister did not listen to my mom, although my mom was giving her sensible advice, she was not listening because it was coming from my mom. My sister was being naïve, she was doing things her way, and thought she knew what she was doing. I know my mom is not the best parent, and she did not set forth the best example for us. But my mom has been around the block a few times, as they say, she has done some things, and she has seen some things.

As I look back, I believe things were a lot simpler, there is no shame in you and your family doing what you have to do in order to survive. Because I did not grow up with a gold spoon in mouth, my family struggled together working to survive. All of us lived in my oldest sister's one-bedroom apartment, we made it work, and we survived without killing each other. Although we had some arguments and fights along the way.

Sometimes my mom and my dad fought each other. Sometimes my oldest sister and her boyfriend fought each other. Sometimes my sister's boyfriend fought my dad. He stopped my dad from beating up my mom and threatened to kill my dad. Her boyfriend threatened to dump my dad into a river and tie a concrete block to his ankle to make sure the body stays down at the bottom of the water. My mom begged him not to do it, she begged many people coming to her rescue not to kill or hurt my dad. And sometimes my sister's boyfriend fought my brother. It was chaotic, and fun at times, in a crazy way.

It was jammed up with eight of us living together, sharing a one bedroom, and one bathroom apartment. It was: my oldest sister, her boyfriend, my nephew, my niece, my mom, my brother, my second oldest sister and I all living together.

Some nights my oldest sister allowed my dad to spend the night with my mom, my mom slept on a let-out couch out in the living room. My dad lived a couple of blocks away on fourteenth street, he rented a rooming apartment upstairs from Mr. Benny's store. Some nights my mom and I slept over at his place.

Yes, my mom's bed was the couch in the living room, during the day we sat on the couch, and my mom let her bed out at night. The rest of us slept in the bedroom together, my oldest sister and her boyfriend slept on their queen size bed. My second oldest sister and I shared the bunk bed with the kids. My sister and I slept on the bottom bunk, while the kids slept on the top bunk. My brother made a pallet with some blankets, and he slept on the floor in the bed room or in the living room. Although we shared a tiny, cluttered space together, we were clean people, and we kept the apartment clean. My oldest sister's boyfriend washed dishes, and he mopped the floors every once in a blue moon, which was more than my brother ever did. My second oldest sister and I were assigned chores to do around the apartment.

It was our duty to clean the bathroom, and to wash dishes. My second oldest sister skipped out on doing her chore duties many times, and I became responsible for doing the chores myself. I hated washing the dishes at the end of the day; every bowl, cup, spoon, fork, knife, pot, and pan was in the sink for me to clean. During the day, they used dish after dish, and dropped it in the sink. My name was called constantly, to come wash dishes so dinner can get cooked, and I came into the house to do as I was told. I had to stay on top of my cleaning duties, if they came home to dishes in the sink, and an unclean bathroom then I was in trouble. My mom did not like an unclean house, we had to clean up, and we had to do it right. My mom was not with half cleaning, if you do not clean it right the first time, she will make you do it again until it is done right. I was taught to be a person of cleanliness, I do not like living in filth, and I cleaned up without anyone instructing me to clean. I was six-years-old, I had cleaning duties, and I had babysitting duties.

• • •

Eventually, my oldest sister, the kids, and her boyfriend moved out. They moved across the yard, to an apartment in the second building. My mom took over the lease on the apartment, and we continued to live there. Now, it was my mom, my brother, my second oldest sister, and I. Until my mom approved of my second oldest sister living with her god sister—she spent a lot of time with her god sister, she even spent the weekends at her house. She begged and begged my mom, until she was able to get her way. My sister was happy, and thought the grass was greener on the other side.

As a kid, I tagged along with my mom to visit my second oldest sister at her god sister's place, to check in on her and to make sure she was ok. Well, her living arrangement turned out to be short lived, after she was molested by a relative of her god sister. My mom did not call the police to press charges and to have the guy arrested for what happened.

My brother was home permanently from school now, but his best-friend whom he met at school needed a place to live. My mom opened her doors, and allowed him to live with us in the one-bedroom apartment.

His name is Malcom, he is from Jamaica, and he did not have his citizenship at the time. All of us grew to like him, and we consider him to be family. My sisters and I referred to Malcom as our brother. He was a character, he was a cool guy, and he was hilarious. Malcom is hearing impaired—he is deaf in both ears—his speech is impaired, and he is a good lip reader like my brother. It was not a problem communicating with Malcom. He taught us sign language, and to get his attention we had to tap him on the shoulder or something. To communicate with him, we wrote down what we were saying on a piece of paper for him to read, and he did the same for us too. He always carried a note pad and a pen with him to communicate with others.

As a kid, I had so much fun growing up with my brothers who were complete opposites, both of them were characters and funny in their own ways. I remember when we discovered both of them wore swimming trunks as underwear, we tried to explain the difference to them, but they continued to wear them daily as men's underwear anyway, and we let them do what they do.

My biological brother returned home from school. I have to let it be known he played football while in school, and we traveled to one of the football games to watch him play. My brother, who is deaf in one ear, was a defensive lineman, and I considered that to be an accomplishment.

My brother was home now, but he was a different person than I expected to him to be, and from what I remembered about him. Let me go on the record saying, my biological brother's father was not a part of his life growing up, I do believe he met his father at least once or twice in his life. From what I heard, his father lived in the streets somewhere; he was a drug addict. Now, my brother was a young boy, becoming a man, and the only male figure under our roof was my dad. My dad was not the best male role model for my brother, but they were both men at the end of the day, and he did try to teach him how to be a man. My dad tried to get my brother up off the couch, and out of the house to get a job.

My brother was lazy, my mom enabled his laziness, he depended on her for everything, and she enabled his dependency. My mom treated my brother as if he were a baby, and she made excuses for him. But she also complained about my brother's dependency upon her. My brother was not a dummy, but he liked to play or act like he was dumb. My parents had many arguments pertaining to my brother; his laziness, his dependency, and his bad habits.

My brother stayed home, sitting on the couch watching television and eating up all the food in the refrigerator all day. When my parents went to him about getting a job, he used the excuse of being deaf in one ear as the reason for not working, and my mom fell for that excuse every time. My dad was not a sucker for excuses, and he does not like laziness at all. My dad talked to my brother like he was a man, face to face, and he treated him like a man instead of a boy. My brother's deaf friends were independent individuals, his friends had jobs, they had children, and they lived on their own. My dad saw it as my brother being lazy, he was making excuses, and he did not want to get up off his butt.

If my brother's friends can do it, then so can my brother, he was not completely deaf, and all he had to do was put in his hearing aid to hear. I remember my brother working once, it was a seasonal job working at a toy store for a couple of months.

My brother went back to sitting on the couch and hanging out with friends doing nothing with his time. He sat home collecting his disability check and his food stamps every month. He stayed home on the first of every month to wait for the mailman to bring his disability check, and then he waited for my mom to come home from work to go cash the check.

Once my brother received his cash money, he was gone with his friends and missing in action for days. He was busy hanging out with his friends, partying, doing drugs, and paying women for sex. According to my brother, he thought he was a player and a pimp! That was funny. When it came to women, he was a sucker for love, he let women play him and use him for money. My brother would rather give money to his so-called "girlfriends", before he gave money to his own mother.

Then my brother came back home crying broke to my mom, after he spent all of his money, and he had no food to eat. He expected my mom to be there every time, to help clean up his mess and to make everything better for him.

At times, I wanted my mom to give him tough love, and I did not want her to help him. Because there he was not learning his lesson, and he went out to do the same thing every month. Sometimes my brother had a temper tantrum like a little child, and he said disrespectful things to my mom if she did not help him. Sometimes I wished I were old enough to punch him in the face. I did not think that was cool, because that is not how you treat your mother!

My brother was a mean, selfish, lazy, rude, and disrespectful son. His first serious relationship was with an older woman with three kids and no job; a cocaine junkie and a whore. He moved this woman and her children into his apartment with him twice. My brother was turned out in a bad way being in a relationship with this woman, he became a drug addict and a cocaine junkie too. That woman left him home with her children, while she took his money every month to go on a cocaine binge in the streets, sleeping around with men and then came back home once the money ran out. This is sad to say, but my brother has been a drug addict for most of his life, and my mom's enabling has handicapped him.

To parents I say, your child will not remain a child forever, a child grows up to become an adult as time goes on. How you raise your children is on you, but if you do not raise your children with morality, principles, respect, integrity, dignity, discipline, respect, faith, love and to fear God then you will create a monster.

That monster will be *your* creation, you are responsible for your creation, you will have to deal with the monster you created. You cannot be mad with anyone but yourself because you only have yourself to blame!

As the parent, you are to raise the child with love, while teaching and preparing the child about life. As the children reflect you, your teachings and your actions. Do not deceive the children from the reality of life and coddle them like babies forever. You are not in control; the child is not under your command and your control because you are not God!

God is in control, and we are his children. You are to prepare the child for their journey, as they seek God to find their purpose in life and complete their mission. God is your child's protector; children are a blessing from God, they are not a burden. We were his children before he blessed you with his children.

● ● ●

My brother Malcom was the opposite of my brother, he was not lazy, or disrespectful. He was a thoughtful and caring person. And funny too. He was respectful, he was reliable, he was a go-getter, he was good with his hands, and he used his hands to make money.

He was very good at fixing things like bicycles, televisions, and electronics. He took things apart, put it back together and like magic, Abracadabra it was fixed. He fixed things for people in the neighborhood, he fixed things for free to help out, and sometimes he was paid cash for his services or given something in exchange like a bike. If he received cash, it did not matter how much he earned, if it was twenty dollars or five dollars, he came home to give it to my mom to help out. My mom did not open her hands to take any money from him, instead she told him to keep his earnings for himself. He catered to my mom, and he was there to do anything she needed him to do. He fixed things around the house, he cooked, but only spaghetti, and he helped keep the apartment clean.

My brother Malcom was also a person of cleanliness, he cared about his personal hygiene, and he showered daily. He cared about his appearance, he kept himself groomed, he ate healthy foods, and he worked out for fitness. He was quite the ladies man, he was a gentleman, and he was charming. His smile was gorgeous, he had beautiful white teeth, he brushed and flossed his teeth daily. That smile was his bread and butter when it came to the ladies. The ladies could not resist his charm and his smile. Whenever women complemented his smile, he smiled even more showing those beautiful teeth to seal the deal of getting their phone numbers.

Look, my brother Malcom was deaf, he had game as a deaf boy, he rode a bicycle, and he got a lot of action from women if you know what I mean. My oldest sister's girl friends loved him, all of them flirted with him, and he flirted back. He did not talk to any kind of girls, he did not like dirty and unclean women. He liked girls of all different shapes and sizes. I remember him hooking up with one of my oldest sister's friends for the holidays, and we caught them by surprise.

My brother Malcom was a tall guy, he was slim and muscular with an eight pack for a stomach. Every night before bed, he did sit-ups, and push-ups. And for fun, sometimes he lifted me up when doing push-ups. When it was time for him to get ready to go out, he picked out his outfit and his shoes making sure everything matched. He pulled out the ironing board, to iron and spray starch his clothes making sure they were properly creased. He laid his clothes out on the bed, grabbed his soap, wash cloth, towel, and his grooming kit and headed to the bathroom. If you had to use the bathroom guess what? It was going to be a two-hour waiting period, that is how long it took him in the bathroom to take a shower and groom himself. There was only one bathroom, if somebody needed to use the bathroom while he was in there you had to get a piece of paper and slide it under the door to get his attention. While taking a shower, he liked to sing or rap while showering and you hear the sounds of a bah, bah, bah, bah!

I do not know what songs he sang or rapped, only he knows because the music was in his head, and I thought it was the funniest thing. Then he moved to the bathroom mirror singing and rapping again using his grooming brush as a microphone. All you heard again was a bah, bah, bah, bah as he sang or rapped and checked himself out in the mirror. That boy was fresh, he got dressed, dabbed on some cologne, and he put a rag in his back pocket.

He rode a bicycle, it was a tandem bike, I saw this kind of bike on TV before, but it was the first time I rode that kind of bike. He rode me around the neighborhood and to the corner store on his bike. I liked to lift my feet up on the handlebars, I let him pedal the bike for both of us and he pedaled too fast anyway. He also had a tricycle before, we popped wheelies and we did doughnuts on that bike to make it lean on one side. It was fun around my neighborhood, when everybody came outside to take turns riding the bike around the block and I was right there for it all. My brother Malcom lived with us, until he was deported back to his country, Jamaica, and the last time, I saw him I was a little girl.

As a little girl, I struggled with my emotions and my anger. I felt alone, unloved and forgotten many times. Often at times I felt as though I did not belong with my family, I felt like I was destined for greater things in life. I was the lone one, but somehow, I was awakened, and it is God who was right there with me every step of the way. My God protected me, guided me and it is because of God's mercy and grace that I still have life. They say it takes a village to raise a child, I believe it is true because it sure took a lot of people like my grandma, aunties, and uncles to help raise me.

I thought I was alone, I thought I was forgotten, but God will not forget, nor forsake his children who love him. Although I may have felt that way at times, God never left my side, God loves me, I am blessed, and I love God! I am precious to God, he planted me here like a seed to grow and sprout. I am thankful, I am humbled, I am gracious for the lord God Almighty's mercy and the favor he has upon my life. I give all my glory to God, my father who sits high and sees all!

I believe in God; I believe in the unproven which thou cannot see because my faith comes by hearing and not by sight. I call the devil a liar, I am strengthened through Christ Jesus, there is nothing too mighty for God and all things are possible with God!

As a child, I sensed the presence of God around me, I felt the energy and sometimes I turned around to see if someone was behind me. As I turned to look back, I saw nothing, but I felt the presence of God and he came to me as I walked by myself most of the time. I thought I was being paranoid, and it felt like I was being followed. As I calmed myself, I began to feel the energy of the presence surrounding me, a tingling feeling ran through my whole body and a sense of peace came over my entire body. It was a feeling of assurance, a relief of peace came to my mind, I knew in my heart I was safe, and I knew God was with me at that moment. From that moment on I began a relationship with Christ Jesus, we walked, we talked, and we talked from day to night. Like I said before, I talk to God no matter how I am feeling, and no matter what I am going through because he protects me in so many unimaginable ways. God sends me a message letting me know, he is right by side, and if I am on the correct path along my journey.

My God loves me unconditionally; he has loved me like no one has and I am grateful for his love! Among all the drama and chaos going on under our roof, I was blessed to have angels that God sent to watch over me. Besides my Aunt Nia and Uncle Joe living in the apartment next door to us, I had my aunt Lena who lived across the yard in the other apartment building. I love my Aunt Lena, technically she is my cousin, but I consider her to be my auntie.

• • •

Aunt Lena was a single mother raising two boys, and she worked as a probation officer. I was her riding partner, she took me with her to make house visits, and I watched her with the probation parolees. Aunt Lena was straight up, she talked to the parolees with respect, and she was not with the tricks or games they tried to play. I liked being her riding partner, anytime she was going somewhere, she walked across the yard to come get me. I hopped up to get dressed, to put on my shoes and my clothes to leave with her rather than sitting home doing nothing. I enjoyed our car rides, I enjoyed her company, I enjoyed being in her presence, it was loving, fun, and peaceful. The car rides were long, she was afraid to drive on the highway, and she took the local roads to get to where we were going. As aunt Lena drove, I looked out the window at the surroundings, she put on some music, her favorite is jazz music, she loves music and her favorite instrument is the saxophone.

If we were not on a car ride, we were back home sitting on her front porch chilling outside, talking with some of the neighbors, and watching the neighborhood. Sometimes, Aunt Lena did her hair and nails while we sat on the porch. Aunt Lena was a person of cleanliness, she kept up with herself, her hygiene, and her appearance. As we sat on the porch, she washed her hair, hot combed it, and then rolled it up with hair rollers. Her hair was beautiful, it was long, soft, and silky. She gave herself a manicure and a pedicure. Sometimes, we sat on the porch from day to night.

My auntie Lena was a very bold woman, she was straight forward, and she opened her mouth to say what is on her mind! She was a beautiful woman, she had personality, and she gave love a try a couple of times, but she was not so lucky when it came to her love life. I love her, I admired her boldness, the moments we shared together were filled with jokes, laughter, encouragement, and genuine love between the two of us.

My aunt Lena cracked jokes on everybody, including me, and I laughed at the jokes myself because they were funny. I remember her cracking jokes about one of my favorite outfits I was attached to as a kid, she teased me for wearing that outfit over and over. As a matter of fact, it was my favorite pink and white polka dot outfit I absolutely loved as a child. My mom brought it from one of the clothing shops downtown, and I think she paid five dollars for it. It had two different bottoms, pink pants with white polka dots, and a pink flair skirt with white polka dots. The top was a pink sleeveless button-down blouse, with a white collar, and white polka dots. I was not listening, and I was not hearing nothing my family had to say about me wearing my polka dots. I made sure my mom washed it, so it was clean, and I preferred to wear my outfit with my sandals.

My family was fed up, my mom began hiding my outfit, and I found it no matter where she tried to hide it! One day, my mom decided to finally get rid of my outfit, and she threw it away without me knowing. I searched all over the apartment for my outfit, I checked everything and every place where I thought she may possibly have hid it and I had no luck finding it. I literally cried looking for my polka dot outfit; I mean I cried like a baby because I could not find it anywhere.

I remember those days I sat on the porch with my mom, Aunt Lena, Aunt Nia, and other neighbors. While my mom greased my hair and scalp with aloe, and her concoction of hair grease mixed together. I was tender headed; I gave my mom a hard time when she combed out my hair after she washed my hair. My mom popped me with the comb for not being still, she pulled and yanked my head combing out my hair. I sat there on a milk crate, while getting my hair done, I listened to them talk without opening my mouth to speak without permission. I was taught to stay in a child's place, and out of grown folk's business. My mom was quick with her hands, she would slap me in my mouth so fast making me bite my tongue —and let me tell you that mess hurt. You know how you bite your tongue, that one tear rolls down your face, and you cannot cry because it hurt to cry. If there was something they did not want me to hear, I was told to put two fingers in my ears, and not to remove them until I was told. They checked to make sure my fingers were in my ears before they whispered to each other, although I was still able to hear sometimes, and I pretended as if I did not hear anything.

I spent a lot of time at my aunt Lena's apartment when my parents argued and fought. Aunt Lena walked across the yard to come get me, when she heard the commotion, and she took me back with her. She tried her best to distract me, and to keep me from seeing my parents fighting. She made me watch TV in her room, she gave me snacks to eat, and she instructed me not to come out. During physical altercations, I did not listen, I still came out of the room anyway, and sometimes my cousins had to stand by the door to block me from getting out. I remember crying many times and praying—asking God to please let my mom be ok! My dad had threatened to kill my mom before, I believed him, and I was afraid for that day to come.

I witnessed a lot as a child, it was a lot to deal with emotionally between watching my parents argue and fight. And then watching my oldest sister go through the same thing with her boyfriend. As a kid, I was surrounded by chaos, I thought they were crazy people, and I could not get used to any of that drama.

You know, I thought to myself, "I think my mom has a mental issue," I started to believe that perhaps my dad had knocked my mom across her head to many times, and the blows to the head shook her brain lose like my auntie once said before. Because I could not understand in my right mind, why my mom put us through all of this drama and misery over a man! How can you love a man with a perverted eye? How can you be ok with your boyfriend molesting your daughter? I did not understand, he was my dad, and I hated him for what he did to my oldest sister.

How can you say "I love this man" when he beats you up, disrespects you, belittles you, and cheats on you? My dad used to beat my mom really bad, I mean it was horrible, and he spit in her face before. I had so many thoughts and questions in my mind, but not enough answers. None of this made any sense to me, dysfunction was not about to become my norm, and I cannot function in dysfunction anyway! A lot of bad examples were being shown to me, but I knew I did not want to travel down the same road as my mom or my oldest sister and end up like them.

• • •

I attended, Phillis Wheatley Elementary school from the first grade to the sixth grade, and we lived across the street from my school. I arrived at school late more days than I arrived on time, even though we lived across the street. Yeah, I know it is ridiculous! But it is true. I was not a morning person, I stayed up late night watching TV and someone had to wake me up in the morning for school. Waking me up in the morning was a hassle, my mom poked me, she popped me on my thighs, she shook me, and she poured a pot of cold water on me to wake me up. The pot of cold water, and the popping me on my thigh definitely made me get up. But I was still halfway sleep, at times I sat up on the edge of the bed and I fell asleep sitting up. Until my mom came back in the room to make sure I was up and getting ready for school. I pretended to be awake, sometimes she caught me sleeping on the edge of the bed, and then started yelling at me. So, I went into the bathroom to brush my teeth, wash my face, then I fell asleep on the toilet, and my mom caught me sleeping again. I was late for school, and both of my parents had to be at work.

For me, school was an escape from the chaos at home, I wanted to play around with my friends and I had to go to school. I behaved myself in school sometimes, I did my class work, and I did my homework. I was a good student, my teachers complemented me on my intelligence, and I was an honor roll student when I decided to do my work. But other times I got myself into trouble doing stupid things with my friends and my classmates.

I was a hallway patrol monitor once, I allowed some of my friends to hangout on my post with me and roam the halls. But someone snitched on me, and I was no longer allowed to be a hallway patrol monitor. I was on the chess team; I did not take it seriously and I quit the team. I was on the dance team once, but I quit that too. I tried out for the basketball team, I did not make the team, but I was the score keeper. I dipped and dabbed in different school extracurricular activities because my mom asked me too.

You know I really enjoyed myself at school when I did go to school, and I loved my teachers at school. Most of the teachers, janitors, and cafeteria workers at the school were from the community, some of them grew up in the community.

My favorite teacher was Ms. Troy, who was my third-grade teacher, she taught reading and writing. I loved Ms. Troy, she was the best, she was kind, and she was patient with me. She was a great teacher, I always enjoyed her class, and I excelled in it.

My problem in class was my mouth, I could not keep my mouth shut, I am a talkative person, I like to make people laugh and I was a class clown. Yeah, my mom had to show up to the schoolhouse many times for parent, student, and teacher conference meetings about me keeping mouth shut in class when my teacher told me too. I was the magnet for noise in the classroom, when I was in class with my friends, we sat next to each other and ran our mouths. There were five of us girls busy talking instead of doing our classwork and paying attention. My friends were from the community, we grew up in the neighborhood together, we lived on different blocks, but we all went to the same school.

I liked to make my friends laugh, I liked to make my teachers laugh, but sometimes the teacher had to tell us to keep the noise level down in our area. Sometimes, the teacher assigned us different seats to separate us, to stop us from being so loud in the class because we were talking, laughing, and joking. I was the culprit behind the loud noise in the classroom, the teacher knew it, I had to stand in the corner of the classroom many times, and sometimes the teacher moved my desk to the front of the classroom next to their desk. My desk faced the classroom for my classmates to look at me, and all of that still did not stop me from not keeping my mouth shut.

Until my mom was contacted about my behavior, and my mom was the one who showed up to the schoolhouse wearing a bath robe. Her bath robe was pink with a flower on it, and it had holes in it. My mom came to school, to sit in the back of the classroom to monitor me, and my behavior. I was not acting out, at least I do not think I was, and I did not tell my teachers or my friends about my personal life at home. Like I said before school was my escape from home, I wanted to have fun and try to find some peace in my life.

You know, back then my mom was an involved parent in my school life, she chaperoned on field trips, she surprised me at school on my birthdays with cake and ice cream allowing me to share it with my friends, and with my teachers at school. She attended the open house at school to get to know my teachers, to see what I was learning in school, and to check on my grades in class. All of my teachers were acquainted with my mom, my friends thought she was cool, and I really appreciate her!

My most embarrassing memory from elementary was a field trip to the Everglades. My mom was not able to get the days off to chaperone for the trip, and it was horrible. It was my fault, I did not listen, and I did not follow the guidelines on the trip. We were informed to not take showers, to wash off instead, and to not spray on any bug repellent. I did not listen. I was not about to go three days without a shower, I took a shower anyway, and used the skin so soft oil my mom gave me to use for the mosquitoes. I should have listened, and I should have followed the guidelines like everyone else.

"Why, Samone?" That is all I kept saying to myself, over, and over after what happened to me next.

I do not remember the activity they had us doing that day, but I do remember the mosquitoes biting me like crazy in my face! I must have been really juicy that day, I must have had like thirty mosquito bites on my face, and my face swelled up like a pumpkin! I could not stop scratching my face, the bites turned into dark spots on my face, the swelling went down on my face, and I was ugly. I had a polka dot face! My friends tried to make me feel better, by sugar coating things saying it was not as bad as it looks and then laughing behind my back. I did not care, I was mad with myself, and I had myself to blame for my face being ugly at that moment. Afterwards I laughed about it once my face was back to normal, and I laugh about it now, but I was not laughing then when it happened to me. I learned my lesson that day, I made sure, I followed the guidelines on the next camping trip.

• • •

Early on I learned the hard way you cannot trust everybody, not everybody is your friend, and not everybody means you well. And sometimes you cannot trust your family either. I was a loner, and I stayed to myself most of the time if I was not hanging out with my four girl friends in school. I was not popular, but I spoke to everybody, and I got along with most of my peers. I stayed to myself, and I did not brother people. Some of my peers did not like me, they pretended to like me, and they came around me because I was funny. This applies to my childhood, my adulthood, and my life in general because people can be so wicked!

If you are a person with a good heart protect it, wicked people prey on your heart, and they seek to destroy your heart! A wicked person will be so nice to you, they do not like you, and yet befriend you to destroy you secretly. You have to beware of the snakes in the grass, stay away from them, do not play with snakes and keep them far away from you.

I AM GOD'S CHILD

You know I grew up with my siblings having animosity for me, it was nothing I did to them that brought it about, I think it was because of who my dad was and that I was his daughter. And my mom was a more involved parent in my life when I was a child, she did things with me that she did not do for my siblings when they were children. Along with our mom still being in a relationship with my dad, him molesting my oldest sister, and all of the other drama that came along with him growing up in our lives.

Back then my sibling's fathers were not involved in their lives, and they were not around to help my mom support them financially. My mom did not have the money financially to provide my siblings with the things they wanted, and my dad did not help her support my siblings. But my dad was a part of my life growing up, he did support me financially, I had birthday parties, he brought me things and he brought me gifts. My siblings considered me to be spoiled by my dad, I felt like they were jealous, and they hated me for it. I think it was misdirected anger and misplaced hate toward me instead of it going toward the persons it was intended for like my mom, my dad, or their fathers too. I was a kid, I am not responsible for the things that transpired in their lives growing up, and I am not the person who did those bad things to them. At a point in time somewhere my mom neglected my second oldest sister, she stop paying attention to my sister and the things she was doing.

My second oldest sister was in middle school, she was doing her own thing and she was skipping school. I think it was her way of acting out to get attention from my mom, who knows what else she was dealing with mentally and emotionally alone. My mom allowed her to do whatever she wanted to do, and my mom put her off on others.

She had a teenage boyfriend, and as a young teenager she was in an abusive teenage relationship with him. Her boyfriend was from the neighborhood, and his family lived in the building. I overheard my mom discussing my second oldest sister, she was skipping school, and she was failing in her classes. My sister was not listening to my mom, she was out of control, and she was being rebellious. My mom found out she was being physically hit by her boyfriend, she was skipping and failing in school, so my mom sent her away to live with Aunt Coco in Virginia for a change of scenery. My mom asked Aunt Coco for help, she agreed to allow my second oldest sister to move in with her family and to continue her schooling up the road. That arrangement only lasted a couple of months, before she was sent back home to Miami for skipping school and continuing to be rebellious.

My sister was back home, and began hanging out with our oldest sister. Their sisterly bond began to grow with the more and more time they spent together. My oldest sister shared her wardrobe with my second oldest sister, she brought her things, and she took her out places. You know, it used to hurt my feelings overhearing my sisters complaining about the things my dad brought me, all the things he did for me, and how he spoiled me. They talked about being there for one another and having each other's back because there was no one else they could trust or depend on. I was a kid hearing these conversations among them, I thought it was something I was doing wrong, and it was my fault.

    As a kid, I shared with my siblings, and I gave them my money. I shared my clothes, my shoes, my food, and I had no choice but to share with them. I am not saying I did not want to share with them, although it did get to that point, and it became a problem for me. I saved up the money given to me by my grandmother, my parents, and whoever else gave me money. The amount of money given to me did not matter, I saved up all the bills, and the coins too because it is all considered currency at the end of the day. When my siblings knew I had money, they asked to borrow money from me time after time and they never paid it back to me. But I could not borrow any money from them, I could not wear their clothes or borrow any of their belongings, and the answer was *no* when I asked to borrow their things.

    My mom preached the importance of family to me, the importance of sharing the things my dad brought me, with my siblings to not make them feel left out. My mom like to say, "Family is all we have, and we must stick together!"

    I used to wonder if my mom was preaching this same thing to my siblings. And if she did, I did not see it. I felt like my siblings were selfish, it was all about them and they only liked to use me for my things or to do things for them.

    My mom put me off on my oldest sister to go off places or to be with her boyfriend, and my sister used me as a babysitter all the time. I was seven years old, babysitting my three-year-old nephew for my oldest sister. I babysat her friend's children too. I babysat for my oldest sister when she went out with her boyfriend, and her friends. I was taught how to change diapers, how to prepare baby bottles, how to feed and to burp a baby. I was trustworthy, I knew what I was doing, and she had nothing to worry about.

    I stayed inside the house to myself most of the time, I was younger than the other kids living in my building, my mom arranged play dates for me with my cousins or others on the weekends sometimes. Sometimes I went outside to play with my cousins and the kids from the neighborhood. I played hide and seek, hopscotch, kick ball, basketball, jump rope, red light-green light and all the other games we played growing up. There were things the older kids were into that was too advance for my age range, I did not really get along with the other kids. I preferred to be by myself, I did a lot of thinking, daydreaming, and most importantly talking to God.

Only God knows me, he knows my heart, he knows my pain, he knows my thoughts, and I only felt at peace when I talked with him. But I had some fun growing up, we had fun times, and it was not all bad times or bad memories for me. We had fun around the way in my neighborhood for the holidays, and during the summertime.

• • •

During the summer, my cousins Cindy and April came over to spend the summers with us. I love my cousins! Listen, we lived in that small apartment, when my cousins came over to stay, we made it work, we shared beds together and we made palates to sleep on the floor because it did not matter as long as we were together to have some fun. I remember some nights when my mom allowed a friend of my oldest sister and her little brother to sleep at our apartment at night when they had no place to sleep, and she feed them something to eat.

My cousins were the same age as my sisters, I was a git back then; I was not allowed to hang out with them, but I did go certain places with them, and we played in the yard together. My cousin April did not come over frequently for the summers, but my cousin Cindy came over a lot to hang out with my second oldest sister. April hung out with my oldest sister and her friends sometimes. April was laid-back, quiet, shy, and stayed to herself most of the time. She was cool, she has to trust you to be her true self and to open up to people. She was in the military, which was the reason she stop coming over, but she did come to visit us, and she was wearing her military uniform. Yeah, we walked to the corner store for snacks, and we watched TV together.

My cousin Cindy is awesome, we shared a connection although she was older than me, and I love her spirit. She is genuine, she is funny, and she has a great personality. She is very smart, she is a human music jukebox, we had fun together, and I loved it when she came over for the weekend or summertime. She carried herself differently from my sisters, she was nicer to me than my second oldest sister; we talked to one another, and we shared heart felt conversations together.

Sometimes we stayed inside the apartment making sandwiches, watching movies or music videos together, and she did the dance routines from the videos while I hyped her up. We were pranksters, and when all of us were together we pranked one another. Nobody was off limits, including myself, and the first of us to fall asleep at night definitely woke up the next morning with toothpaste on their face!

Cindy vouched for me to go to the movie cinema with them at the Omni, and if she did not vouch for me the answer was no from my second oldest sister. We walked through the graveyard to take a shortcut, it was scary walking through the graveyard at night, and we ran as fast as we could to make it to the other side.

We went outside to play in the yard, when we were bored with nothing to do, we played freeze tag, red light-green light, kick ball, hide and seek together. But my second oldest sister and Cindy used to hangout on the street corner by the building with our boy cousins, and their friends from the neighborhood while my mom worked the night shift at the hospital.

We had many family outings to the Miami-Dade County Youth Fair during the beginning of the year, Santa's Enchanted Forrest during the winter, and to Bayside. It was a group of us packed up in two or three cars, we squeezed in and sat on each other's laps. The car rides were sort of fun, we argued over who gets the window seats going and coming back home. We had to duck our heads down in the car every time we saw the police to not get pulled over, we were not wearing our seat belts, and we did not want to get any tickets.

It was my mom, my aunties, my sisters, my cousins, other people from the neighborhood and me of course. As a family these were some of the festivals, and places we looked forward to year-round to attend to enjoy ourselves.

We went to the Goombay Festival every year, it was my mom and Aunt Lena's favorite event to attend. The Goombay Festival was a Bahamian event festival. It was a costumes parade, with live instruments, and there was food vendors serving Bahamian dishes. I love the conch fritters, the conch salad, and the best part of the parade to me was the Junkanoos. As the Junkanoos start getting closer and closer the crowd began dancing alongside with them!

I remember the Pack Jams in Overtown. The pack jams were in different neighborhoods on random days and at any given time. They were like a block party minus food and drinks. The DJ's set up the speakers to play music, the people in the neighborhood came outside to listen and to dance to the music. Well, as you look around you see more and more people walking up, listening and dancing to the music. The crowds consist of adults, teenagers, kids, the winos and the DJ jammed music until the cops came to shut it down.

When I was not old enough to attend the pack jams with my sisters, I sat on the porch by myself, and I listened to the music the DJs played. Sometimes, I was able to go to the pack jam if there was an adult with me for supervision. I went with my mom or Aunt Lena, and we stood back on the corner jamming to the music watching the crowds dancing over by the

DJ speakers.

Sometimes I went with my sisters and their friends. Once my sisters and I stayed past our curfew time, and our mom came to the pack jam looking for us! Yes, my mom was the parent to grace the DJ microphone saying our names out loud and telling us to get our butts home ASAP!

For birthdays, we had birthday parties and birthday bashes in the middle of the yard for everyone to celebrate including our neighbors. Sometimes—well most of the time—it was cake and ice cream at home with the family. I am not one who likes birthday parties, I prefer the cake and ice cream at home with the family. I was sort of a loner, I was shy as a kid, and I did not have many friends besides the friends at school.

My mom had a birthday party for me once as a kid, and she invited all the kids around the neighborhood to the party, most of the kids I did not know, and some of the kids I did not get along with. My mom tried her best, and I appreciated it.

My second oldest sister had a sweet sixteen birthday bash outside in the yard. It was a birthday party for my sister and her boyfriend at the time. The DJ was setup in the yard playing music, we had drinks, soda, water, wine coolers, and liquor, their two birthday cakes, and a lot of food to go around. We celebrated with more of our family, friends, neighbors and whoever we knew that all showed up to the party that night to celebrate.

We celebrated Independence Day, my family brought a *lot* of fireworks. Sometimes we celebrated the holiday home in the neighborhood lighting fireworks in the middle of the streets. And other times we celebrated at other family members houses with more of the family. We wore our holiday outfits and shoes to match.

To me the best part came at nighttime, when the real fireworks show began and everyone lit fireworks at night. After there were no more fireworks to light, my mom brought out the wire hanger, and the SOS pads. We straightened out the wire hanger, then hooked the pad on the end ensuring it was on tightly and then we set fire to the pad. Everyone took a turn standing in the middle of the street swinging the hanger around in circles and everyone else stood far away. That was the grand finale for the night, and we used all the pads until there was no more left.

Sometimes growing up as a kid we celebrated Christmas together as a family, the cozy feel, and the cold temperatures along with the smell of fresh pine tree made it feel like holiday season. We went together as a family to pick out a pine tree, we looked for a nice size pine tree with thick branches so the tree looked full. I loved it, especially the smell of fresh pine tree. I was excited to get back home to decorate the tree, and we tied the pine tree down on top of the roof of the car. We had to get it through our small doorway, then stand it up, and I crawled under the tree to tighten the screws on the pot underneath the tree to keep it straight. My mom brought out the Christmas lights, the ornaments, and more decorations in the closet. We untangled the lights, we checked to make sure they were properly working, and we wrapped them around the tree. We put up the ornaments, the candy canes, and we put the star on top of the tree. We put more lights up in the window, along with Christmas stickers on the window and I sprayed the "snow" on the window. Lastly, we plugged everything in and turned off all the lights to see how everything looked. It looked really good.

As a kid Christmas was fun for me, I enjoyed the holiday season, the days leading up to Christmas day, and I felt the spirit of Christmas. My mom is a festive person, and she likes to celebrate the different holidays which made me enjoy celebrating the holiday. I enjoyed spending time with my family, I enjoyed sitting on the couch with my blanket watching television and drinking hot cocoa late nights by myself.

On Christmas mornings I woke up to presents underneath the tree with my name on it, I made lists for the gifts I wanted, and I gave it to my mom, then she gave the list to my dad. My Christmas outfit was a sweat suit and a brand-new pair of sneakers because my mom was only able to afford to buy us something new for a special occasion.

My Christmas list was a long list filled with things, and I had to narrow it a couple of times after my mom laughed once she looked at the number of things I wrote down. My parents had a budget, and I wrote down a list of at least five things I wanted because I wanted way more than my parents could afford. Sometimes I received at least one or two of the things I wrote down on my list, and I was surprised to see what gifts my parents decided to get me. And sometimes I did not receive anything I wrote down on my list, but I was thankful for the gifts I did receive from my parents on Christmas. You know, I do have some memorable Christmas stories about some good and some not so good times that I remember.

Once for Christmas I received a pair of roller blades, I did not know how to skate, I did not own a pair of skates before, and my mom helped me learn how to skate a little bit that day.

I used to go to the skating rink with my sisters a lot when I was young, I stood around watching them skate with their friends having fun. My oldest sister tried to teach me how to skate, but it was not a success, and I was tired of busting my butt on the ground.

So, I was gifted my first pair of roller blades for Christmas, I skated up and down on the porch before I tried to skate in the middle of the yard on that concrete. I fell on my butt a couple of times, and I scratched my elbows up too. I was determined to learn how to skate in roller blades, day after day I went outside in my roller blades. I skated up and down on the porch. I skated up and down on the sidewalk. And I skated around in the middle of the yard. Well, I learned how to skate in my roller blades, I got better the more I continued to get back up every time I fell on my butt.

Next year, I received a bike for Christmas—which I had on my Christmas list—and it was a ten-speed Huffy bike for a girl. I was not able to ride around the neighbor with the kids because I did not have a bike, but that changed once I received my bike that year. Well, I had my bike for a week before someone stole it off the porch, and I was sick to my stomach because I could not believe someone stole my brand new bike.

This Christmas is one I will never forget because something horrific and tragic almost happened to me as a little girl. On Christmas day, my mom let me go ride my bike around the neighborhood with my friends. As we were riding through Town Park Village, my back wheel slipped, and I fell off. I rode on top of a sand patch as I was turning, causing me to fall off of the bike, everyone kept on riding though and left me behind by myself.

I scrapped my elbows and my knees pretty bad. As I got up to dust the sand off of me, I tried to get back on my bike to catch up with my friends, a young dude stepped out of the shadows walking toward me, insisting on kidnapping me to rape me and then kill me.

The young dude said to another guy, "A little mama is thick. Let's take her inside to rape her and then toss her body."

I was afraid! I was trying to hurry up and hop on my bike to take off. Luckily, for me the other guy came off the porch to stop him from approaching me.

The other guy told me to hurry up and go as he tried to hold off the young dude who wanted to snatch me. I did exactly as I was told; I was trying to hurry up to get far away as possible. I pedaled so fast, I did not look back and I rode my bike straight home. I was afraid, my adrenaline was rushing, the palms of my hands were sweaty, and I no longer felt the pain from my scrapes.

Once I made it home, I did not utter a word to anyone, I put my bike in the house, I cleaned my scrapes from falling off my bike, and I sat on the porch by myself thinking about what just happened. I was eight years old; I was almost raped and killed like my life meant nothing. There was no one else around to help protect me, Christmas day could have been the last time I opened my eyes, I could have been dead with my lifeless corpse lying somewhere, and no one would have known what happened to me until my body was found. I knew in my spirit, I was supposed to have been dead that day, but my angels were watching over me. I must say, "Thank You God!" I often think about that day when I reflect on my life, and I thank God for his protection over me.

• • •

Well, my mom followed right behind my oldest sister again, and we moved across the yard into my oldest sister's two-bedroom apartment once the lease expired for our apartment. We were all crammed back up in an apartment together, and it was chaos all over again.

My oldest sister was still fighting with her boyfriend, they had many issues in their relationship and her boyfriend continued to be in and out of jail. After a while, my oldest sister, her boyfriend and the kids moved out again into an apartment upstairs. My dad moved out of his rooming apartment and moved into the apartment with us. It was my parents, my brother, my Jamaican brother, my second oldest sister, and me all living together. This time we had a little bit more space because this apartment had two bedrooms instead of one bedroom and this apartment was larger.

It was the same thing all over again with my parents and their drama filled crazy dysfunctional relationship. My mom worked double shifts at the hospital most of the time, trying to make ends meet to pay the bills and keep the lights on in the apartment.

My dad worked as a chief in the kitchen of a well-known franchise restaurant, he spent most of his time at work, and chilling out on the avenue with his friends. Once my dad came home from work, he went onto Third Avenue to hang out with his buddies drinking, gambling, doing drugs and whatever else they did together. My dad stayed out on the avenue all night long, then he came home late-night hours drunk and high. My parents had issues in their relationship, and my dad was still physically beating my mom. It was chaos almost every day.

I spent a lot of time home by myself, while my mom worked double shifts at the hospital and my dad was wherever he used to be at. At the time, my mom had a car, and my dad played nice with my mom when he wanted to use the car. Sometimes, my mom let my dad drive the car, he dropped her off to work and he kept the car. My dad drove around in the car drunk, he went out on the avenue to hangout, at times he did not pick my mom up from work and she had to walk home.

Yeah, my dad had a pager, my mom paged him 911 over and over. My dad did not respond to the 911 pages, knowing he was supposed to pick her up from work and he did not come home with the car until he was ready to. My mom made it convenient for my dad, he used my mom for the car to go be with his other women. My dad powered his cellphone off, and he did not respond to his pager when he used the car. My mom had to chase my dad down for her car, he showed up later on with a crappy excuse and lied through his teeth about his whereabouts. Back then all my dad was good for was lying and broken promises if you ask me.

Well, my dad did nothing but break promises he made to me, and I remember him not being around that much. He promised to take me to the cinema to see a movie, and he never showed up to take me to the movies. Instead, my mom and I went to the movie cinema together without him. I cannot tell you how many times it hurt me when he broke his promises and I eventually I stop believing in his word.

Some nights my dad did not come home, and he did not come home for days. I cleaned up the apartment without being told what to do, I cooked food for myself, and I cared for my mom. If I did not clean up, no one else was going to clean up without my mom saying something, and I took it upon myself to do it. Although, my mom never noticed I cleaned up without me bringing it to her attention.

Well, being home alone most of the time I learned to cook for myself, I ate sandwiches, and I made grilled cheese sandwiches because it was all we had to eat at times. Some nights my mom came home hungry from work, I cooked her grilled cheese sandwiches, I ironed her work uniform, and I woke her up late at night to go work her double shift at the hospital.

Everybody was busy doing their own thing, my brother decided to go steal cars with my oldest sister's boyfriend and his friends. My foolish brother is deaf in one ear, he cannot hear out of his left ear without his hearing aid and this idiot did not have the hearing aid in while he tried to steal cars. He broke into someone's car, he did not hear the car alarm going off, and he did not hear the police sirens coming.

My brother led the police on a car chase driving back home in the stolen car trying to get to my mom and the police caught him. He jumped out of the moving car as he got closer to the apartment, the police officer hopped out of his patrol car to give chase on foot when my brother ran. My brother ran down the porch shouting for my mom, with the policeman gaining on him running on foot.

My mom was cooking with the kitchen back door open, she heard him shouting, she opened the screen door for him to run inside and the police officer tackled him to the floor in the living room. He was on the floor screaming "Momma help me!"

The police arrested him and took him to jail that day. How do you go out to steal a car when you cannot hear! Where do they do that? That was a stupid decision. I am not going to lie, we laughed at him, and I made fun of my brother when he came home.

• • •

One day, we unexpectedly came home to all of my dad's belongings gone, he packed up his things and he moved out of the apartment while we were not there. I can never forget that day, my dad left like a coward, he did it in a sneaky way and it was something he planned on doing anyway.

My dad was home that morning, I saw him before I left for school, he waited for my mom, my second oldest sister and I to leave the apartment. He left without saying goodbye, he did not leave behind a written letter explaining anything, or his whereabouts, and there was no way of getting in contact with him. His cellphone had no minutes, and his pager was off.

My mom was shocked, she was hurt, she was embarrassed, and she was heartbroken that day he left her to be with another woman.

I was happy, I thought the lord had finally answered my prayers and he was gone out of our lives.

If my dad left my mom, I knew she was not going to leave him. We did not see my dad, and we did not hear from him in days. My dad had multiple women, and he tricked with multiple women paying for sex, and he left my mom to be with the mother of his oldest daughter.

My mom was aware of my dad's infidelities with other women, both of my parents were cheating on each other, but she stayed with him, and she still wanted to be with him. My mom pretended to be ok, and acted like she was not sweating him anymore. It was good! But I knew she was embarrassed, and she felt heartbroken because she loved him.

As soon as I started getting comfortable thinking he was not coming back, guess who pops back in the picture? My dad! I was hoping my mom would be strong enough not to fall for his lies or any of his sweet talk and not take him back this time.

My dad showed up at the hospital to speak with my mom, to apologize about leaving her, and to weasel his way back around to use her. Well, I guess my dad thought the grass was greener on the other side, but that other woman was no fool like my mom, and she was not willing to put up with his drama or mess!

My parents played games with one another, they liked to toy with each other, and my mom considered this to be a competition for my dad with this other woman. His other woman did not have a car, and she did not know how to drive a car. I watched my parents secretly creep around with one another and we pretended to still be a happy family.

My mom and I woke up earlier than usual in the mornings to drive across town to pick my dad up to drop him off to work. He waited on the street corner a couple of blocks down from his other woman's house, to make sure no one saw him getting picked up by mom. Well, we picked him up from work at night and dropped him back off on the street corner. We went on family outings, the three of us went to dinner and to the movie theaters like a family. I thought my mom was being a complete fool for my dad, and this entire situation with them was foolish. This was something my dad barely did when he lived with us, he was ghost most of the time, and he was the king of broken promises.

Then my dad began to inquire about me coming over to spend the weekend with him and getting to know my half-sister. Honestly, I did not have a relationship with my half-sister, I knew she was my sister, we never developed a bond with one another, and I did not know much about her although she did attend some of our dad's family functions. You know, we were cordial with each other, we acknowledged one another, and we spoke to each other, but that is it. When I was younger my half-sister spent the night at our house maybe once or twice and that was about it. I never really cared about getting to know my half-sister, to be honest I did not like her snobby mean and bossy attitude.

Truthfully, I did not want to spend the night with my dad at this woman's house because I did not want to be around people I do not know. And I did not want to see my dad with his other woman knowing my parents were creeping around together at the time. Well, my mom made me go spend a weekend with my dad anyway; I had no choice in the matter. It was awkward. I was a shy kid and seeing my dad interacting with his new family was uncomfortable for me. I was quiet, I did not say much, and I was respectful to everyone. I met his girlfriend, and my dad introduced me to more of her family members that lived in the project buildings nearby.

It was shocking to see my dad interacting with his girlfriend differently than he treated my mom, he washed dishes, swept the floor and cleaned the bathroom that weekend. My dad was nice to his girlfriend, he was patient with her, he catered to her, and he talked to her respectfully with a peaceful tone. His girlfriend was gone during the day for my dad and I to have some alone time together. His girlfriend spoke to me, she was nice to me, and I did not have a problem with her. I spent some time hanging out with my half-sister, and her sister, that weekend before I went back home. I spent one weekend with my dad at his girlfriend's house, but I enjoyed myself and the time I spent with their family.

Of course, my mom questioned me once I arrived back home to find out what took place during the weekend I spent with my dad, and to find out if his girlfriend was around me. I overheard my mom telling her girl friend everything I informed her about that weekend with my dad, and how she told my dad not to have his girlfriend around me or there was going to be a problem if he did. At that moment, I understood why his girlfriend was so distant that weekend, and like I said before I did not have a problem with his girlfriend. That was grown folk's business and drama.

But my parents continued to creep around with each other, until my mom gave my dad an ultimatum and he had to choose between the two of them. I do not know what all the deciding factors were for my dad, and what led to him making the choice he made, but I am quite sure I was one deciding factor based on his decision. One thing I can say about my mom during the situation, she never talked bad about my dad to me, she tried to encourage me to spend time with him and told me he loves me very much!

Truth be told, I did not care, I wanted away from the drama and the chaos around me. But my dad choose to be with my mom, he packed up his belongings and he came back to live with us. I guess my mom won the game! My mom was happy to have my dad back with us, he was on his best behavior for about a week, and then it was back to his same old tricks as usual. It was chaos all over again with the drugs, drinking, and fighting as usual.

Over time things started changing, but some things stayed the same. One issue continued to worry me, and I prayed to God constantly for his protection over my mom. My dad continued to drive around in the car doing what he did, while my mom walked to work and walked back home by herself day or night. I worried about something bad happening to my mom walking by herself with a purse and other work bags she carried with her. I prayed myself to sleep at night, and I prayed for God's protection over my mom. Sometimes Aunt Nia walked my mom halfway to work at night, but she walked to work at night most of the time alone. My mom carried a can of mace in her purse, sometimes she carried a knife with her for protection and anything else she could use as a weapon just in case something happened.

One time we put a couple of pens together, took the tops off the pens and then wrapped the pens together with a rubber band for my mom to use as a weapon walking to work. I prayed to God; I asked the Lord in Jesus' name to protect my mom from all evil, and all wickedness. "Lord, can you please make sure my mom gets to work safely, and make sure she gets back home safely in one piece." I thanked the Lord every night and morning my mom went to work and came back home. I am forever grateful for God's mercy, his love, his grace, and his protection because he keeps us in so many ways.

• • •

Well, as time went on, everyone's paths began to go in different directions, and things began to change as the times changed. My cousin Cindy's mother no longer allowed her to come back over to our house for the weekends or during summertime, after someone stole six hundred dollars out of her bag.

It was a big ordeal; the two suspects were my dad and my brother because they were the only people inside the apartment when she went inside to put money in her bag. But my dad left the scene, and my brother accused my dad of stealing the money. My mom made up excuses for my dad about the ordeal, and she tried to make it seem as if my brother might have stolen the money. All I know is the money was gone, and my dad was missing from the scene. That was the last time I saw my cousin Cindy for a long time, we lost contact with one another, and there were other contributing factors that led to her mother stopping her from visiting us anymore like there being no order under my mom's roof.

My Jamaican brother Malcom was denied citizenship, he was deported back to his country and we lost contact with him too. Then my oldest sister's boyfriend was arrested, he caught a case, and he was sentenced to serve a long period of time. My oldest sister and the kids moved back into the apartment with us.

Then surprise, surprise, it was not long before we moved out of the apartment, the family split up, we went our separate ways and we lived different places.

My oldest sister and her kids moved back in with her god parents. My mom helped my brother get an apartment living around senior citizens with government assistance through a program that helped the disabled. But it was not long before my brother was back to being a drug addict, and he moved his crack head friends into the apartment with him causing many disturbances in the complex.

If I am not mistaken, I think my second oldest sister was allowed to go live with her god sister again momentarily. I remained with my parents, our belongings were packed up in a moving truck, and we lived in a motel for a couple of months. Luckily, my grandparents were retired, they purchased a house in South Carolina, and they moved out of town.

When my grandparents moved out of town, we moved into the duplex they were living in. Once we moved into the duplex, my second oldest sister had to come live with us although she did not want to come. I was attending middle school now, and my second oldest sister was attending high school. She was skipping high school, she was failing and continued to be disobedient not listening to my mom. She did not want to clean up and do any of her chores around the house.

My mom had her hands full, and a lot on her plate—figuratively speaking—dealing with my siblings and my dad because she was trying to do everything for everybody else.

My oldest sister and the kids moved into the duplex with us also. The duplex was more spacious, and there were two bedrooms, so it was all good. But with all of us living under the same roof again, the past history of all the altercations along with the harsh words said to one another, the energy in the house was bad! Especially between my sisters, my mom, and my dad because my dad was seen as the villain. My mom was caught up between trying to be there for my siblings, trying to please them and trying to please my dad. Because my siblings were busy living life, making their own choices and decisions doing all the things they wanted to do. But whenever they found themselves in a jam or in a mess from a bad decision, they all called momma to come clean up their mess and help them.

My mom was still chasing behind my dad, and she was busy trying to please him too. And she was creeping around doing her own thing on the side with other dudes.

As for me, I was not a problem, I was cool being by myself, and staying to myself, but I was around watching.

Yeah, my mom took me along with her to visit her married boyfriend's house, and sometimes her married boyfriend brought his child along with him when visiting my mom. Look my mom does not have any shame in her game, and I am not here to judge, but it is what it is. At the end of the day, I understand my mom was still a woman, although she is my mom.

Anyway, my oldest sister was running wild now, her boyfriend was locked up, she was not waiting for him to be free, and she no longer wanted to be with him. She was in her twenties, but she was busy out in the streets being a party girl, not home caring for her children.

At one point my oldest sister became a stripper, and she was up in the club stripping at night. She was busy chasing after men with money, she slept around with men for money, and she did other things in return for money. My sister put her kids off on other people, and then she put her kids off on my mom while running around in the streets. She was acting like a single woman with no children!

My oldest sister was flying free as a bird in the sky, and she was going from man to man. Every time she came over to the house or when I saw her, she was with a different dude, it was never the same guy twice. She came to the house when she wanted some money from my mom, and to drop her children off or more like ditch the children to be with men. Sometimes, my oldest sister spent days away, weeks away from her children without a phone call notifying anybody of her whereabouts, and no phone number to get in touch with her. My nephew and niece were both still little children. Occasionally, my oldest sister randomly showed up to the house with a dude, with some gifts sometimes, and then she was gone again until she came back.

Most of the time my oldest sister showed up to the house when she knew my mom was at work on purpose to not deal with my mom being in her ear complaining or talking. I helped my mom out with the kids, and I babysat them. I helped bathe the children, and I helped get them ready for daycare in the morning. I did not mind babysitting, but it was tough when the kids asked questions about their mom. I did not have answers to their questions, and I had to tell them I do not know.

The kids asked me, "Auntie, where is mommy? Auntie when is mommy coming back to get us?"

Then there was my brother, he was a drug addict, he was strung out on drugs really bad. He was in jeopardy of getting evicted from his apartment in the senior citizen complex, and he continuously called on my mom to come help him.

The senior citizens complained about the noise disturbances coming from his apartment at night, they complained about his crackhead friends fighting over drugs. A couple of times, my brother had physical altercations with his so-called crackhead girlfriends and so-called friends, then my mom was contacted by the police. My brother allowed his crackhead friends to live with him, he was busy getting high with his disability check and not paying his rent. He also traded his food stamps for cash, so him and his friends could get high. He called my mom for money when he had no more and needed food to eat after going days without eating. My brother was a follower and a fool that allowed other people to use him all the time. But when my brother called, my mom went running over to help him, to do all she could for him, and she gave the little bit of cash she had to him. It was sad to see my brother strung out on drugs, but she continued to enable him, and he continued to do the same thing every time getting high!

Then comes my mom chasing behind my dad, and their crazy chaotic personal relationship. My dad kind of eased up on the physical abuse, although every once in a while, he had an episode and things did get physical. I do not know what to call my parents' relationship, but they were still together, pretending for others as if they were happy and loved one another.

We no longer lived in Overtown. We lived in Little Haiti, but it did not stop my parents from going to Overtown to hang out with their friends. Yeah, my dad still went to Overtown on a daily basis after work to hang out with his buddies gambling shooting dice, getting drunk and high before he came home at night. My dad began to drive home drunk night after night coming home from Overtown or wherever he was coming from.

Sometimes my mom went with my dad to hangout in Overtown to drive the car back to ensure he did not drive home drunk. And to make sure he did not get into a car accident killing himself or someone else driving on the road. Sometimes my dad argued with mom to drive home drunk insisting he was not intoxicated, and he was ok to drive the car. Not only was my dad driving intoxicated, but he was also high on cocaine, pills, and weed! Our only means of transportation was my mom's car and she was still making car note payments for that car. My mom lost sleep at night worrying about my dad when he did not come home throughout the night, and she needed her rest for work in the mornings. My dad continued to be selfish, careless and reckless doing whatever he wanted to do anyway.

One night, my dad gave my mom a scare, he came home bloody, beaten up badly with his face and body covered with his blood. My dad proclaimed he was in Overtown hanging out that night, he made a stop on his way home, someone pistol whipped him, he was robbed for his jewelry and his money. Instead of my dad driving to the hospital, he drove himself all the way home for my mom to clean up his wounds. My dad drove home with a broken arm, his face swollen, eyes swollen and one of his eyes closed shut. My mom cleaned my dad up as best she could, and then she took him to the hospital. I thought this incident might have taught my dad a lesson and slowed him down. But once he healed up, he was back in Overtown hanging out, up to the same shenanigans and driving drunk again. This fool was still coming home drunk trying to argue and fight with my mom just about every weekend. My dad continued to be a fool, playing with the devil and playing with his life.

Until, one night my mom's fear of my dad driving home drunk and getting into an accident in the car happened! It was only a matter of time before something like this happened, drinking and driving is what my dad did all the time. Thankfully, no one involved in the car accident was hurt, only the cars were damaged, the accident was my dad's fault, and his life was spared. My dad slammed into the back of another car waiting at a red light, but he hit the car and then drove home. This fool committed a hit and run leaving the accident scene. My dad was jacked all the way up off those drugs and liquor. My dad was so messed up, he could not stand up to walk, and I do not know how he made it home that day.

But the person's vehicle my dad hit, that person followed him home, and called the police. My dad was so wasted, he did not know the person followed him home, but he knew he was in a car accident. My mom's car was smashed in the front, and was considered totaled. My mom only had one more car payment to make on the car before she owned it, and then this situation happened with my dad. My mom prevented my dad from getting arrested that day, she lied for him to the cops, and hid him in the closet inside my bedroom.

Now, we were without a vehicle for transportation, and we had to catch the bus to get around or foot it wherever we had to go. My mom could not afford to get another car at the moment, my dad was not remorseful for any of the things he has done, and the thought of getting another car was not in his mind because he did not care! As far as my dad was concerned, it was my mom's car, it was not his car, and he did not care because he was not responsible for it.

You know, my dad went on acting like that situation never happened, he never apologized to my mom for wrecking her car, and he did not thank her for keeping him out of jail.

I can tell you right now, I would *not* have lied for him.

First of all, he would not have been able to get my car keys to get behind the wheel of the car to drive drunk anyway. Prior to this incident happening, sometimes my dad did not come home, my mom and I had to walk or catch the bus in the mornings to get on with our day. Sometimes my dad came home too jacked up, and drunk in the mornings to drop me off to school. So, I had to get up to catch the bus, if I had the money to catch the bus, and other times I walked to school in the mornings. I always walked home by myself after school, and I was used to this type of thing happening most of the time. My mom and my dad caught the bus to work.

To catch the bus, I had to pay a fare of sixty cents, and most days I did not have money for the bus fare. So, I woke up earlier than usual to walk fourteen blocks to school to make it on time. I set the alarm on my phone to wake me up every morning so I could get dressed and ready for school.

You know, I learned how to do things on my own, I learned self-sufficiency, I had to learn to survive, and it taught me independence. Sometimes my parents gave me money to budget for the week, I took the five dollars or ten dollars they gave me, I used the money for bus fare and for food to eat. I had to pay for school lunch, there was nothing to eat at home, so I went to the local supermarket around the corner from the house to get food to eat once I got home.

While at school I sipped from the water fountain for the gas pains in my stomach from not having food to eat. I watched my friends eat their food, I did not ask them for any, and I kept my business to myself. To save money, I walked to school, and I walked back home. But every now and then I caught the bus home from school instead of walking back home.

Sometimes I did not have any money for the week to eat lunch or to catch the bus because my parents did not have any and I had to do without. So, I walked to school, and I walked back home from school because it did not matter to me.

• • •

It was the start of middle school for me, I was growing up, and I was no longer in elementary school. All of my girl friends from elementary and I attended the same middle school, but we did not share many classes or lunch periods together. We shared maybe two classes and one lunch period. When my friends and I *did* hangout together in school, it was like old times filled with fun and laughter.

While in school, I participated in class, and I did my work. I paid attention to my teachers, and I wrote down my notes sometimes. But I did not do my homework, and I did not do my class projects. Honestly, I did not care about school that much, but I did the work in school to get average grades for my parents satisfactory because my mom checked to see my report cards.

I was the kid who went to class and sat in the back of the classroom. I stayed to myself most of the time, I spoke to other kids I knew from my old neighborhood and yet I still came across other kids having a problem with me. But I did not care because *they* were the ones with the problem, not *me*. I know what it is like to have somebody not like you for no reason, and they do not even know you. I preferred to stay to myself to have less drama and less problems because a lot of people are haters.

My parents were not paying any attention to me, I spent most of my time home alone. When not at work, my mom was busy chasing behind my dad trying to keep up with him and hanging out with her friends. I was home by myself during the day, until my parents came home at night. I cleaned up the house, I feed myself, I watched movies, I played my video games, and I listened to my music to pass the time by. I made myself something to eat with whatever was in the kitchen, I ate sandwiches and noodle soups most of the time.

Sometimes, my parents came home to cook dinner, they invited their friends over to the house to play card games of spades, enjoying themselves drinking, eating food, getting high together and then going back to their friends' place to party some more. Sometimes, I worried about my parents, and I tried to stay up waiting for them to get home.

Over the weekends, my parents allowed my best friend from school to stay over with me. Sometimes I spent the weekends over at my best friend's house with her and her family.

Sometimes I felt unloved, I did not know how to feel, my emotions and my thoughts were all over the place. I became an emotional eater trying to cope with my emotions and my thoughts. I was a chubby kid, I was overweight, and self-consciously I did not believe I was beautiful.

As a kid growing up, I could not stand it when my granddad picked at my weight; he had to mention something about my weight every time. My granddad looked at me, he did not see a kid, he did not care about my feelings emotionally, and all he saw was my body size. I did not like my granddad, I thought my granddad did not like me, and I never understood why he said such mean things to me as a child.

I had low self-esteem, although I did not say it and I wore a jacket over my clothes to cover my body. I tried to dress like my second oldest sister—she was a tomboy, I liked her style, and I dressed like a tomboy to be like her. But there was one problem, my parents continuously claimed to have no money, when I asked them to buy me some clothes or shoes and they hollered broke to me. My parents brought me new clothes or shoes for special occasions and the start of the school year.

Honestly, my mom was not a responsible parent to go shopping to buy me the necessary things I needed like underwear, socks, a training bra, clothes and shoes. But I was a clean person, and I kept myself clean. I kept the clothes and the shoes I did have clean. I wore hand me downs, my sisters' hand me downs and other people's hand me downs my mom brought home for me to wear. Honestly, I mixed and matched my clothes throughout the week wearing the same clothes and two pairs of sneakers for the entire school year. It is all good, I managed with what I had, and I survived it.

• • •

After a while, my oldest sister decided to come back home, she had to stop living in the streets to tend to her kids, and the kids missed their mom. Well, she was no longer in the streets living a fast lifestyle, but she was still a party girl, she was being a whore, and she was tricking, which saddens me to say, but it is the truth.

My oldest sister cleaned up her life a little bit, she found a job doing telemarketing, and she was able to save up enough money to buy her first car. Her first car was an '87 white Cutlass, with blue interior, and she named the car "Old Betsy". My sisters drove around in the car all day, up and down the street trying to find somewhere to go or find something to do.

During that time, my sisters and I used to hang out together a lot. We went to the beaches together with the kids to have some fun and relax. I went with my sisters to the beaches for Memorial Day holidays, and I saw some things that was too grown for my young eyes. But my oldest sister was on a mission to find a man with money to spend on her and to take care of her. She had multiple men, past boyfriends from high school, recent men she met, and she neglected her kids to go out on dates or to hang out with men. My oldest sister loves to party, and she loved going out to the club to "find her kids a daddy" as I once heard her say to the kids.

My oldest sister was successful finding a man who was willing to pay for it, he appeared to have money, he showered her with gifts, and he took her out on dates night after night. But do not get it twisted, my oldest sister messed around with dudes on the side, on the low, and she was caught a couple of times.

My second oldest sister followed behind my oldest sister a lot, she was hooked up with the friend or the brother of the guy dating my oldest sister. But it was not long before my oldest sister was pregnant from this new man, she had abortions, and she had a miscarriage once.

But it was too good to be true and there was a *big* secret.

This man was married with a family; a wife and three kids that he went home to at night. But hey, my oldest sister was ok with him being a married man, she continued to date him, he continued to spend money on her. Her married boyfriend moved her and the kids out of my mom's place, and into a condominium apartment. Then my mom agreed to let my second oldest sister go live with my oldest sister, My mom did not know what to do about my second oldest sister and she asked for help from my oldest sister.

But my second oldest sister continued to do the same thing; she was failing in school because she was cutting class and skipping school most of the time to hang out with a boy. Yeah, she had a boyfriend now, and she was sneaking out of the apartment to be with him. After a while, my oldest sister got fed up, my second oldest sister was not listening to her, her mind was wrapped up on her boyfriend and she was sent back home to live with us again.

My second oldest sister did not want to live with us again, she was well acquainted with her boyfriend's family, she wanted to go live with her boyfriend and his family. She did not care about anything, she had no idea as to what she wanted to do with her life, and she was caught up in her boyfriend like he was Prince Charming in a fairy tale story. For some reason—I do not know why—my mom agreed to allow my second oldest sister to go live with her boyfriend and his family. Well, she was supposed to continue going to school, she and her boyfriend attended the same high school. My mom really believed she was attending school, and she believed the lies my second oldest told her.

This time, my second oldest sister completely stopped going to school, she dropped out of school with her boyfriend, and she followed him around. Yeah, she dropped out of school, and she was pregnant too. To be honest, I was not shocked nor surprised when I heard the news, it was bound to happen, and I do not know what my mom expected to happen.

Firstly, she did not care about school, she was already cutting class and skipping school before this. It was only a matter of time before she was pregnant, she was sexually active, and she was allowed to live with her boyfriend. *Hello!*

My oldest sister and aunt Nia tried to convince my mom, it would be a bad decision to allow my second oldest sister to move in with this boy and his family. At the time, I had never met him, and I did not know him, I just heard of him. Until she and her boyfriend began randomly showing up to the house to hangout.

When my second oldest left home, I was home alone with my parents, and I was afraid to be home alone with my dad. I felt safe when my sisters lived at the house, and we shared a room together. I was afraid of my dad one day, perhaps sneaking into my room trying to touch me or waiting until we were home alone.

I did not trust my dad, after I witnessed him sneaking into the room trying to touch my oldest sister in the past, and I never trusted him since. Why would I think otherwise, my dad molested my oldest sister? I stayed in my room to myself, and I kept my room door locked. My mom suggested, I use one of the baseball bats in the closet to protect myself if my dad ever did try to do something to me. Although my dad never gave me that kind of indication, and he never tried anything with me. I made sure my dad felt my energy, I showed him I did not trust him, and I did not care how he felt about it one bit because I was protecting myself.

When I met my second oldest sister's boyfriend, he seemed like a cool guy, he was playful, we joked around and laughed most of the time I was around him. I minded my own business, I did not have a problem with him, and I was still getting to know him. He was a tall, big guy like a basketball player. He had played basketball in high school, but he quit the basketball team, before dropping out of school.

I rode around in the car with them as they drove around town visiting his friends, other family members and going out places. But I quickly saw a glimpse of reality, it was not good, he was no Prince Charming, it was all a façade.

After my second oldest sister's boyfriend had a family dispute with his older brother, he was kicked out of the house, and they came to live with us for a while—during her pregnancy—before going back home.

He had a bad temper, he was quick tempered, and he had a beast that came out like my dad. He was verbally and physically abusive to her while she was pregnant. At any given moment, he embarrassed her, he flipped out on her in public and talked to her like she was a kid not caring who was around watching.

Oh, this fool flipped out on her many times, especially when my second oldest sister upset him, or she did not listen to him, and he snapped quick like the snap of a finger. He belittled my sister, she behaved like a kid in his presence, and did as instructed before he physically beat her. He threatened to punch her the face, and sometimes he punched her in the face anyway without saying a word.

My second oldest sister's boyfriend dominated her, and he completely controlled her. She tried to hide the fact her boyfriend was beating her, she tried to cover up the bruises, and she did not open her mouth to say something or to ask for help. I remember when her boyfriend punched her in the face one day, and she was still pregnant with my nephew at the time. He punched her in the face so hard, he knocked her into the kitchen window, her nose began bleeding, and she went to the bathroom to clean herself up like nothing ever happened. The abuse continued on once they moved back to her boyfriend's family's house, and her boyfriend went as far as to put voodoo on her.

One day, while my second oldest sister was putting away the folded clothes in the dresser drawer, there laid a picture of her with her name written on the back, and a liquid substance swirling around in a pack. I overheard my mom talking about the incident, and she presumed the voodoo was reason why my second oldest was fool-hearted for her boyfriend, along with tolerating the physical abuse. The physical abuse continued after the birth of the baby, my second oldest sister called my mom for help sometimes, and my mom continuously checked in on her to make sure she was ok. My sister's relationship with her child's father reminded me of my parents' relationship with the abusiveness. But I was happy for the birth of my nephew, and I was happy to be an auntie again.

I AM GOD'S CHILD

MY TEENAGE YEARS

Summer was coming to an end, I was beginning high school now, and the start of the school year was approaching. I spent my summer at my oldest sister's house, she was pregnant, and she gave birth to a baby boy. She needed help with the kids, her boyfriend was busy working and I decided to spend the entire summer helping them out. She had a child with her married boyfriend, and they were officially together now in a personal relationship living together.

My oldest sister's married boyfriend's wife showed up on her doorstep one day, a big ordeal took place, and her married boyfriend decided to leave his wife to be with my sister. By the end of the summer, I wanted to stay at my sister's house, I enjoyed spending time with them, and I did not want to go back home with my parents. They asked me if I wanted to live with them. I said *yes* of course. So, they agreed to allow me to come live with them, they were ok with shouldering the responsibility of taking care of me. But I had to get permission from my parents to come live with them, after sitting down to talk with my parents they gave me permission to go live with my oldest sister. I thought the grass was greener on the other side and I should have known better looking back at their prior relationship issues. I went from one bad situation, into another bad situation.

It was the start of my freshman year of high school, I attended Carol City High School and I was new to the school. Our friend Alicia lived with my sister at the time also, and it was her senior year of high school. We were acquainted with the neighbors next door, we caught rides to school in the mornings and rides home after school sometimes with their family.

While attending school I stayed to myself most of the time, I did not speak to anyone, I did not bother anyone, and I did not have any friends. I was not a mean person, I did not trust people, and I was not friendly. I like to mind my own business, and I had less problems staying to myself. If someone asked me to borrow a pen, pencil or paper, I lent it to them. I participated in class, I did my classwork, and I received good grades. I still had my self-insecurities, I still dressed liked a tomboy until I slowly came out of my shell. I began to dress more like a young lady, and I began to love myself the way God has made me. Since I shared the same lunch period with Alicia sometimes, I sat with her and some of her friends to eat.

My oldest sister continuously tried to get me to hang out with Alicia and her friends to get out of the house. Then she tried to get me to hang out with her girl friend's daughter, her girl friend and her daughter lived with us for a short period of time when they needed a place to stay. I hated it when my oldest sister tried to force me to socialize with other people, to hang out with other people, to go places and do things I did not want to do.

I did not like her girl friend's daughter, that girl was a liar and a thief like her mother! That girl stole my money, and then lied when I confronted her about it. I preferred to be home relaxing comfortably, being among my family, playing with my little niece and nephews. I played video games and watched movies with the kids. You know, I wanted to be where I had peace, among people I trust, and I know.

I did not want to hang out with Alicia either, I already knew how she get down and the type of company she kept around her. Alicia's thing was sneaking off to meet up with boys, lying about her whereabouts and sometimes sneaking boys over to the house. I did not play those types of games, I knew better than to do those type of things, and I did not want to rain on her parade or intervene. That is why I declined to go anywhere with Alicia, when my oldest sister suggested I go hangout with her if she was going someplace.

On one occasion, my oldest sister forced me to tag along with Alicia, and things went wrong. I used to hang out with Alicia before, she was doing the same thing back then, sneaking off to hang out with a boy and I was not with that mess. Alicia and her girl friend were supposed to be going to the mall to the cinema to watch a movie. My oldest sister imposed me on Alicia and her friend in their hang out night together. I declined to go to the movie cinema with them, I was home chilling out by myself, but my oldest sister forced me to join them.

My oldest sister's boyfriend dropped us off to the bus stop, we were going to catch the bus to the mall and then call her boyfriend to pick us back up at the end of the night. Well, once we arrived at the bus stop, and my sister's boyfriend was out of sight these two fools were on the phone calling some boys. They never planned on going to the movie cinema, Alicia lied to my oldest sister to get out of the house to be with her girl friend and meet up with some boys. They were calling the boys to tell them our location, so they could come pick us up. Well, those plans did not sit well with me, I did not want to be a part of those plans, and I was not going along with those plans.

The driver pulled up like a maniac in a black car with two dudes sitting in the front seat, the guy sitting in the passenger seat opened the back door and he told us to get in. I looked at the both of them like they were crazy, and I told Alicia I am not getting in that car with them! I did not know these guys.

Her friend hopped in the back seat of the car. Alicia insisted that it was safe for me to get in the car with these guys and she told me to get in. But I told Alicia I am not getting inside of that car. Alicia's girl friend insisted she get inside of the car with them and leave me behind. These were guys Alicia and her girl friend was talking to, but I did not know these boys and I was not with it. Alicia tried to beg me to get inside of the car, but I told her no and I began walking away.

Alicia and her girl friend decided to get out of the car, then the car pulled off speeding like a bat out of hell. They were mad at me because I did not get in the car with those boys after they drove all the way over here to come pick them up.

But I did not care! I listened to my spirit and my spirit kept telling me no! I did not like being put in this kind of situation, I was mad at my sister because I wanted to stay home, and I was placed in this predicament dealing with this foolishness.

I began walking away, I was going to walk back home, but Alicia begged me not to go back home right away. She did not want to get in trouble with my oldest sister, and if I showed up home my sister was going to ask questions. And the first question was going to be, "What happened?"

Alicia wanted to kill some time walking around the shopping plaza for her to come up with a believable lie to tell my oldest sister, I was not going to snitch on Alicia, but I was not going to lie to my sister. After walking around for a couple of hours my patience worn thin and I was ready to go home at this point.

Night fall was approaching, we decided to walk home to kill more time and it was not that long of a walk back to the house anyway. Well, the lie Alicia and her girl friend came up with did not make any sense to me, and I knew my sister was not going to fall for a lie that made no sense. As we were walking down the street along the sidewalk, my oldest sister and her boyfriend pulled up on the side of us in the car. We hopped into the car.

Immediately my oldest sister questioned us, she wanted to know why we were not at the movie cinema watching a movie?

Well, nobody responded to my oldest sister's questions, and I left the questions for Alicia to answer because I was not going to snitch. My sister was getting upset receiving no answers. Once we arrived at the house, and pulled in the driveway things went downhill fast.

My oldest sister questioned Alicia again, but she refused to talk, and she was giving my sister a hard time. Well, my sister asked Alicia to step out of the car, which she did not want to do and then my sister snatched her up out of the car.

Once we were inside of the house Alicia told my oldest sister a lie first, and then she came clean telling the truth. At this point my sister was terribly upset, and Alicia was in a lot of trouble for trying to be sneaky.

Well, Alicia decided to be brave that night, she got beside herself and my oldest sister beat her up. My sister decided to take Alicia's friend home to speak with her parents about this stunt they tried to pull. Alicia and I had to go with them to take her girl friend home, but Alicia refused to get in the car when told to do so. She walked away from the car. She yanked her arms away from my sister and my sister punched her in the face.

It was not a good sight to see, and the more Alicia resisted the more my oldest sister punched her. My sister's boyfriend and I had to run to break it up. Alicia still refused to get inside of the car again, she bawled up her fist at my sister, and my sister threatened to hit her again.

Well, to make a long story short my oldest sister drove to Overtown to take Alicia back home to her mom and took the rest of her belongings back to her later on.

• • •

Living under my oldest sister's roof I shared a room with my niece. I love my niece for the record, but she wet the bed at night, and sharing a room with her was a bad experience for me.

My niece did not like to keep the room clean; she did not like to make up her bed in the morning, and she was lazy. When my niece wet the bed, she laid in the wet bed trying to cover up the fact she wet the bed, and she hid the wet clothes in her dresser drawer. I found the wet clothes she tried to hide in her drawer when I cleaned up the room, I cleaned up behind her and I checked her dresser drawer.

Instead of my niece getting up in the middle of the night to use the restroom, for some reason she rather wet the bed, and then try to cover it up. My oldest sister allowed her to continuously wet the bed, until I complained because I shared a room with her, I cleaned up behind her and I had to smell the odor. Honestly, my niece was being lazy, my oldest sister did not want to believe my niece was being lazy, and we disagreed continuously.

To prove to my oldest sister my niece was being lazy, I woke my niece up in the middle of the night twice to make her use the bathroom to pee for two weeks, and she did not wet the bed at night for those two weeks. My niece was being lazy, and if I threatened to spank her for wetting the bed, she did not wet the bed. I am a person of cleanliness; I like to keep my space clean, I do not like dirt, and I do not like odors.

I had to be patient with my niece, although sometimes I had to spank her butt because she really like to test my patience over and over. I tried talking to my niece, I tried to teach her how to be a clean person and how to clean up.

My mom had me cleaning up since the age of five, my mom kept a clean house, she made us clean up the house and after ourselves. My mom had me washing dishes, sweeping, moping, dusting the furniture, cooking, cleaning my room, and the house. On Saturday mornings, my mom woke us up to clean the house, and to go to the laundromat to wash our dirty clothes. Saturday was cleanup day, we cleaned up as a family, and going to the laundromat was considered a family outing, I enjoyed doing it. My mom showed me how to use an iron, she taught me how to iron clothes and she made us iron our school clothes for the week. I find cleaning to be therapeutic and I like to talk to God when I am cleaning. They say, "Cleanliness is next to Godliness." Hey, it is what they say.

My oldest sister and her boyfriend had a blended family. Both of them had two children from previous relationships, and all of the children got along fine. They were kids, the boys shared a room together. One minute they were playing with one another and the next minute they were fighting one another. Her boyfriend's sons came over for weekends and during the summertime.

They played house together pretending to be happy, they were supposedly madly in love during the beginning of their relationship. But that happiness and love sure went away rather quick. My oldest sister thought she found her Prince Charming and knight in shining armor all in one package. But I knew enough to know that nothing is never ever what it appears to be, and it is all an illusion.

Well, I say people will trick you if you let them, people will deceive you, and they will lie to get what they want from you. Yeah, my oldest sister was bamboozled if you ask me, and she was a fool too chasing behind the wrong things in life, she was fooling nobody but herself.

Once my oldest sister's boyfriend moved her into a condominium apartment, it was a struggle for him to keep up with those bills financially trying to take care of two households at the same time back then. My oldest sister and the kids moved from place to place. While her boyfriend was busy working to make his money, after work some nights he came over to her place to get some—if you know what I mean—and then getting up to leave afterwards.

They argued about the bills not being paid, her wanting to get out of the house to do things. My sister and the kids stayed in the house most of the time. Her boyfriend was lying about paying bills, and he was living out of his means if you ask me. He was a controlling and possessive man, but not physically aggressive. He wanted to know where she was going, what was the reason for going, and how long she would be gone.

They had plenty of break ups and make ups. Their arguments and fights were not a pretty sight to see. Well, both of them played tit-for-tat with one another, and when they broke up her boyfriend wanted everything back that he paid for.

Once he helped her get a car, they had an argument on the way home that same night, so he took the paperwork to the car, and he put it in his mother's name before my oldest sister could sign the paperwork. A couple of times her boyfriend got her fired from her jobs, and he did horrible things to hurt her when he was upset or if she broke up with him.

Oh, my sister's boyfriend used profanity, and he spoke derogatorily. Yeah, he used to tell her she was not shit, she does not have shit and she will not be shit without him. Her boyfriend talked macho talk, afterwards he begged my sister to take him back and to forgive him. Once he pretended as if he shot himself because she did not want to be with him. The supposed blood on his shirt was ketchup!

My oldest sister moved into a house with government assistance for housing to have some stability in her and the kid's life. This fresh start was going well, and with the new baby they seemed happy.

When it came to the kids, my oldest sister and her boyfriend were not disciplining parents, there was no order and no structure when it came to the kids. When I moved in, automatically I became the in-house babysitter and maid. I spent my time home babysitting the kids and cleaning up the house. I cleaned up the living room, the family room, the bathroom and the kitchen every day. Man, I hated washing dishes throughout the day, and all the dishes in the sink at the end of the night before I went to bed. I cleaned the counter tops, the stove top, I swept the floors, and I mopped the floors before going to bed.

My oldest sister complained about the kids being too young to clean up behind themselves or wash dishes, but she was not the one cleaning up behind them and cleaning up the house. Those were excuses coming out of her mouth to me, the kids were not too young, and they needed to get in the habit of cleaning up anyway. So, I put the kids to work, I taught the kids how to wash out their dish, I made them clean up their rooms and I made them clean up the bathroom sometimes as I stood there to watch them clean. My oldest sister did not clean up the house daily, and neither did her boyfriend "because he paid the bills" according to him.

My oldest sister and her boyfriend were gone most of the time. The kids spent most of their time inside the house watching movies, playing video games, playing with the dog and outside playing with one another or with friends. Yeah, my oldest sister had a dog name Coco, an American Husky with a white fur coat, and black eyes. But Coco did not last long. It was not long before her fur coat turned beige, she kept running away from the house, and my oldest sister decided to get rid the dog because she did not want her anymore.

Over the weekend, sometimes we had a house full of kids including one of my nephew's friends along with my oldest sister's god son who came over for the weekend. Sometimes I went over to my parents' place for the weekend when they had a house full of kids, I needed a break from it all, I was tired of babysitting, and I needed peace of mind.

My parents moved back to Overtown in our old neighborhood, in the same apartment buildings in a two-bedroom apartment and my second oldest sister lived with them. I spent time with her and the baby on those weekends. But it was back home for the rest of the week, and back to school for me. My oldest sister's boyfriend spent most of his time working, going to the gym, and hanging out with his friends. My oldest sister spent most of her time out shopping, hanging out with her friends, but with the newborn baby she stayed home for a while.

My oldest sister's boyfriend worked in the printing industry, he worked as a press man on the press machine, and he made good money doing it. Her boyfriend's problem was prioritizing, budgeting, and paying bills. He continued to blow money and he was struggling to pay the bills. He wasted his money renting exotic cars and going out clubbing with his friends. He worked hard for two weeks, put in long hours at work to go spend thousands of dollars renting cars for the weekend or for the week and barely had money for gas.

My oldest sister and her boyfriend were both party animals. My oldest sister along with her girl friends partied with her boyfriend and his guy friends. They partied every weekend and sometimes they had parties at the house. I was home babysitting the kids, and sometimes I babysat their friend's children while they went out to party. My sister's boyfriend spent money on her too, she did not work, he brought her the things she wanted, and he took her out to the places she wanted to go.

Meanwhile, they switched from one personal vehicle after another and struggled to keep the bills paid in the house. The vehicles kept getting repossessed, my mom put vehicles in her name for them and those vehicles were repossessed too.

My oldest sister and her boyfriend began to have trust and infidelity issues in their personal relationship, along with her boyfriend's control issues too. My sister did not like a couple of her boyfriend's friends, she thought they were whore mongers—which they were from what I saw—and she accused her boyfriend of cheating on her. One of her boyfriend's friends had the balls to bring another woman to a surprise birthday party she had for him at the house and tried to hook the woman up with my sister's boyfriend at the party.

Her boyfriend rented those exotic cars to go to the club, to a party, and sometimes for no reason at all. He drove around in car rentals pretending as if he was someone rich, pretended to have more than he did, and pretended to be someone he was not. He had places to go when he had a car rental, he drove around going places for no reason and to make sure people he knew saw him in that vehicle. Sometimes he lied to people telling them it was his personal vehicle, and he was a professional boxer. His friends were fake pretend ballers too, they cheated on their wives or girlfriends and sometimes they asked him to use the car rentals to go out or to take out other women.

My oldest sister accused her boyfriend of being unfaithful, she did not trust him, and he denied being unfaithful at the time. Well, she was not sure if he was being unfaithful, and she was unsure about putting her trust into him after prior relationship issues. I thought my oldest sister did not trust her boyfriend because she knew his ways, and she knew the kind of things he did, because it was the same way her boyfriend hooked her like bait on a hook to catch a fish.

My sister assumed when her boyfriend was around his friends and out of her sight he fooled around with other women. He did have a wandering eye and he was a flirt. But he was very controlling, he did not want her to go out with her girl friends or going out to parties.

Sometimes her boyfriend started an argument to make her mad, sometimes he begged her not to go out, sometimes he left in the car and then stopped answering his cellphone to make her stay home. They had a problem sharing one vehicle, neither one of them wanted to be home that much and both of them wanted to ride around in the car all day. Well, most of the time if they went somewhere, it was together when her boyfriend was off from work, and if my oldest sister went somewhere by herself in the car it was not long before he was calling for her to come back home. Sometimes, my sister powered her cellphone off while she left the house to go shopping and to run some errands leaving him home with the kids.

There was definitely a problem when they had two vehicles at one time, my oldest sister convinced her boyfriend to get another vehicle. Most of the time when they had one vehicle, her boyfriend drove the car to work depending on his work hours, sometimes my oldest sister dropped him off to work and picked him back up later on. Sometimes her boyfriend worked late night hours till the rise of morning, he worked long hours and he traveled long distances driving to work. Well, one thing I can say about her boyfriend, the man did get up to go to work to make his money, and sometimes he worked two jobs at a time.

There were a few problems when it came to her boyfriend trusting her, he did not trust her when she was out of his sight or at home with the car because he knew she was going to find somewhere to go in the vehicle. He tried to keep tabs on her while he was at work, her boyfriend called the house phone, and her cellphone to make sure she was home with the car. He did not like some of her girl friends, he thought most of them were whores, and he did not want her to hang out with them, so he said.

Well, yes some of them were whores, her friends were no different from his friends and they were her friends before she met him. He thought she was fooling around with other men or up in another man's face, and he was trying to keep her on a short leash because he knew her wild side.

My oldest sister had a wandering eye, she was a flirt also, she loved to be the center of attention and she did things for attention. If you ask me, I think her boyfriend thought she was a whore, he was quick to call her a whore when he was upset, he was paying for her and he was buying her love trying to keep her happy.

It looked like my oldest sister and her boyfriend partying together turned out to be a bad thing, once her boyfriend was drunk, he flirted with other women in her face, and she found phone numbers in his pants pockets. Those incidents in the club, along with her boyfriend's actions was conformation for my sister to believe she could not trust him, and he was being unfaithful. Well, my oldest sister was upset, and it was game on from that moment forward to her.

It became a tit-for-tat game among them. My sister did things to get back at her boyfriend and her boyfriend did things to get back at her. Things were so bad between them, my sister stopped speaking to him, she completely gave him the silent treatment around the house, and she gave him attitude. Her boyfriend did not like being ignored, and he begged her to speak to him. I was caught in between a rock and a hard place as they say, they came asking me my thoughts about their situation and what I think they should do.

Honestly, I did *not* want to be caught up in the middle of whatever they had going on, I have been caught up in the middle of their mess before a couple of times, and it was an uncomfortable position to be in. My oldest sister put me in some uncomfortable situations to lie for her and to keep her dirty secrets.

My advice was talk things out with one another, communicate with one another to figure out if they wanted to be with one another and to cut out all of the foolishness they had going on. They decided to reconcile their relationship.

• • •

Then my drug addict brother moved in with us, and he slept in the room with my nephew. My brother was a lazy bulldog, he sat home all day eating, sleeping, and sitting on the couch watching television. He did not work, he did not want a job, and he continued to wait on that disability check faithfully every month.

My brother's hygiene was horrible, he was twenty-seven-years-old, he did not want to shower daily, he wore the same pair of dirty clothes over and over without washing them. He did not want to brush his teeth, his breath smelled horrible. I argued with him about brushing his yellow stained teeth, taking a shower, and wearing clean clothes. I could not stand it when my brother randomly walked up in my face and started talking to me because he spits when he talks sometimes. I had to back up, then put my shirt over my mouth and nose because I could not take the smell. The smell made my stomach hurt, and I felt like vomiting.

According to my brother, his breath did not stink, he did not stink, and he did not need to take a shower daily, only once a week. He did not groom himself and he did not get haircuts—which he needed badly. I argued with my brother a lot, I was not going to condone him living and smelling like a bum living on the street when there was no reason for any of that mess.

I did not get along with my brother very well. I got up in his face, and I was not afraid to tell him to wash his butt! My oldest sister and her boyfriend left him alone and let him be. But I could not do it, they wanted me to condone it and not say anything to him about his hygiene.

I did not trust my brother, he was a drug addict, I thought he was a pervert, and a pedophile. I thought he was an unsanitary person, he was mean, and he did not care about himself, or anything. My brother was addicted to porn since I was a kid. I caught him watching it a couple of times. He tried to get me to watch porn with him before, I told him no and I told my mom on him, but he denied it. My brother flirted with any girl or woman with a vagina and breasts.

I hated it when my oldest sister sent my brother to pick me up after school, he came early before school let out, and he sexually harassed the teenage girls walking pass as he stood outside of the car. My sister ignored my request to not send him to pick me up. I had to make it a point of emphasis he will get arrested by the police if he keep doing it, and then she stopped sending him to pick me up.

I was happy, my brother was disgusting, and he was embarrassing me.

I AM GOD'S CHILD

• • •

In the middle of the school year, my oldest sister and her boyfriend decided they wanted to purchase a bigger house. During the weekends, we woke up bright and early to drive around looking at different homes, until they found the home they wanted. My sister gave up her house, and she lost the housing assistance provided from the government. She was hesitant to let go of her house, she still wanted to have a place to come back to in case things did not work out with her boyfriend and if he was not able to pay the bills at the new house.

But her boyfriend convinced her he was able to earn enough money to afford to pay the bills for this new house, which was more expensive. She trusted him, and she let go of her house. Honestly, I questioned her boyfriend's motive for wanting to move, my mom tried to convince my oldest sister not to trust her boyfriend, he had already proven to be untrustworthy and an unreliable person. So, why believe him and trust him, again.

When my oldest sister asked for my opinion, I gave her my honest opinion, I told her she needs to find a job, and I did not see anything wrong with the place she was living in. I did not want to rain on my oldest sister's parade, she was excited about the move and the new house, so I did not press the issue.

We moved into a large two-story home with four bedrooms, three baths, a huge kitchen, dining room area, living room area, three car garage, two family rooms with one upstairs and one downstairs. The house sat on a cul-de-sac, big front yard and a big backyard.

Things were going well, my oldest sister and her boyfriend had a lot of plans for that house. First, they needed to get some furniture, they planned on decorating, painting the walls, and doing some upgrades to the house, like building a pool in the backyard. The house was empty, we barely had furniture besides our belongings, and the bedroom furniture sets in the rooms. They were trying to keep up with the Joneses, and they made it appear to others on the outside looking in like everything was all good.

This time I had my own bedroom, with my own bathroom and it felt so good to have my own privacy. I did not have any bedroom furniture, I did not have a bed to sleep on, they planned on getting it for me later on. I made a pallet with blankets, and slept on the floor.

The kids were taken out of their previous elementary school and transferred to the elementary school near the new house. I was taken out of Carol City high school, but there was a problem with me transferring to the high school near the house and I remained out of school the remainder of the school year.

My oldest sister's boyfriend spent his days working, coming home to get some sleep, and then going back to work again. My sister spent her days home with me, my brother, and tending to the baby.

I spent my days cleaning the house, in my room to myself reading the *Bible*, praying, cleaning, and fasting. I woke up early in the morning to hear the birds chirping first thing in the morning. "The early bird gets the worm" like the old folks say! I recited my favorite scripture PSALMS (23-song) over and over. I took deep breaths and I sat down with my sliding door open for fresh air. I sat in silence waiting to hear from God and I talked to him asking him to show me the way. And I prayed for his continued strength upon me. I needed it! I felt unappreciated, I felt unloved, I prayed for peace of mind. I prayed for a better life filled with happiness and I prayed for love. I began fasting, I ate apples, and I only drank water. I did not eat or drink anything else besides an apple and water. I continued to fast for a month straight.

Until I heard the message from my spirit, God is still with me, and I needed to keep going! I continued to wake up early in the morning to hear the birds chirping while I get some peace and quiet before everyone in the house woke up. I continued to pray, and I talked to God throughout the day as I cleaned up the house.

• • •

In the meantime, my brother found himself in some trouble because of his perverted ways and being up to no good! I knew he was up to no good when I noticed him sneaking out of the house around midnight every night. I was suspicious of his behavior because I knew my brother could not be trusted.

One night he left the house around the same time to go for one of his walks and he returned back home sitting in the back of a cop car that night.

Apparently, my brother was walking around the neighborhood being a peeping tom, he watched a woman walk around her house naked and she spotted him outside peeking through the window. The lady called the police and the cops caught him. Luckily for my brother, the cops came to the house with the woman to speak to someone because he was deaf, and he told them he lived in the community.

I remember being downstairs in my room and hearing a loud bang at the front door. I walked to the door, I looked through the peep hole and saw two cops with a woman standing on the porch. I shouted my oldest sister's name and I told her the cops were at the front door. I opened the door to greet the cops and they asked to speak with the owners of the house.

My oldest sister came walking down the stairs to greet them and she asked the officers what the problem is. The officer pointed toward the police car and asked my sister does she recognize the person sitting in the backseat of the car. And when we looked, we saw this fool with his head hanging out the window of the cop car.

My oldest sister said, "Yes, I recognize him. That is my brother." The officer began to explain the situation to her and the officer walked back to the car to get my brother to bring him over toward us. When he brought my brother over, my sister said, "What the hell is wrong with you! Why are you peeping in peoples windows, you know better than that!"

I knew he was up to no good! I felt it. My brother had a scared look on his face, and he began to explain himself. He proclaimed, he was walking down the street, he happened to noticed all the lights on in the lady's house, and he noticed the lady walking around naked. He claimed to only be looking, and he was not going to harm anyone. He apologized to the woman, and he repeatedly said, "Sorry." He began to cry tears when the cops said he might be going to jail. Now, he wants to start crying like a baby because he got caught and he did not want to go to jail.

The woman was undecided on pressing charges against him, and she wanted to know to if he was a dangerous person. My oldest sister assured the cops and the woman that our brother was not a dangerous person and nothing like this will ever happen again, and they had nothing to worry about because he will not be a problem again. The woman decided to not press charges, the officers warned him about doing anything else and the officer took off the handcuffs.

• • •

Meanwhile, my oldest sister and her boyfriend were beginning to have problems in their relationship again. The happiness was starting to fade away really quick and the finances were becoming too much for her boyfriend to handle. I figured this was going to become an issue sooner or later and now they came to the realization they were in over their heads.

My oldest sister was walking around looking stressed and unhappy. She began getting drunk and she drank herself to sleep at night. She spent most of her time upstairs in the bedroom sleeping, watching television, and drinking.

Her boyfriend was barely home, he was busy working, and he was becoming tired of doing nothing but working all the time. He worked two jobs at the time, and he drove himself from one job to the next. He was busy working, but he was not keeping up the bills and was lying about it. They were living paycheck to paycheck and barely breaking even every month. We were living off of her boyfriend's income only, my oldest sister and my brother both used their food stamps to put food in the house. Her boyfriend was back up to his old tricks again, he was lying about paying some of the bills and hiding the truth from my sister.

One day while we were home, a tow truck showed up to the house to repossess one of the vehicles, and my oldest sister called her boyfriend while he was at work. She was on the phone arguing with him and fussing at him. He was on the other end of the phone, pretending and playing dumb telling her there must be some sort of mistake.

The repo man had the proper paperwork to verify everything, and my oldest sister gave them the keys to the vehicle. Well, her boyfriend stopped paying the monthly truck payment and he was behind on the payments by three months. Most of the money went to paying the mortgage, which was three thousand dollars, they had two vehicles, which meant two car payments and two car insurance bills a month. Also, the utility bills, cable bill, other daily expense like gas money, and there was no extra money to save or spend. That was the beginning of the end.

We lived in this house for three months before we moved out. By wintertime we downsized to renting a smaller home.

We moved to Broward County, where they rented a home with three bedrooms, one bath, and I attended Hallandale High School. It was my sophomore year of high school; I was behind on my class credits from being out of school and I had to catch up. I knew no one at this school and I stayed to myself as usual. I did not speak to anyone in class, I sat by myself for lunch, and I walked home by myself.

I was not trying to get comfortable, and I was not trying to make any new friends because I knew my living situation was temporary. They were looking to purchase another house with more space and renting this house was temporary because we had to move out in a hurry from the previous house.

I woke up early in the mornings to get dressed and walk a couple of blocks to the bus stop where I caught the school bus. I needed to get out of the house on time to make it to school every day because I could not miss any days from school.

I went to school; I did the work necessary in class and I caught up with my class credits to no longer be behind or be at risk of being held back. I attended school and I came straight home afterwards.

I spent most of the time home—with my brother and the kids in the house—to myself chilling out. I was back to sharing a room with my niece and right back to smelling pee again.

My brother and my nephew spent their time in the bedroom playing video games or in the living room watching television. My niece spent her time watching cartoons while coloring and drawing in her writing tablet.

Sometimes, I went in the living room to watch television and hangout with the kids. But I mainly stayed in the room to myself listening to music while daydreaming and praying to God.

The neighborhood was boring, there was nothing to do, and there were no kids playing outside, only elderly people sitting on their porch. There were not many kids in the neighborhood, there were no kids living on my block, and there were not many kids at the school bus stop with me in the mornings either.

My oldest sister and her boyfriend were not on the best of terms when it came to their relationship at the time. My sister was able to get a job, which lasted momentarily, after her boyfriend was able to get another vehicle because it was repossessed again.

My oldest sister and her boyfriend were barely home once they were able to get another vehicle after the last one was repossessed. Her boyfriend was back to his old ways, and he began spending his money on exotic car rentals for the weekends again. Besides going to work, he was at the gym and in the streets driving around all day.

My sister spent most of her time riding around in the streets all day with her friends until nightfall. She proclaimed she was out trying to find ways to get money to get things for us because it was almost Christmas season, and they were trying to save up money to get another house. She did not have a job, which meant she was doing something illegal, hanging out with her girl friend who was a thief and a scammer. She was out shoplifting and committing fraud to get things.

But I did not care about Christmas gifts, I was bored of being home all-day babysitting, and cleaning up the house. I received a mini boom box stereo for Christmas, I did not waste any time putting it to use, and I used it every day to listen to music in the room by myself.

My oldest sister and her boyfriend were still playing house, but they were not happy in their relationship and cheating on each other.

By summertime next year, my oldest sister's boyfriend saved up enough money to put down for a house, and we moved into another place. But my brother did not move in with us to the next house, he moved to Overtown living in the apartment my parents were living in, and my parents along with my second oldest sister moved into a rental property home.

Well, we moved into a nice and more spacious home, in a housing community where her boyfriend once lived previously with his ex-wife and children. He also financed the rental property my parents were living in now, and he put the property in his stepfather's name. They rented the house out to my parents and my parents paid the rent money directly to her boyfriend every month.

We moved into a house with three bedrooms, two baths, family room, and a pool. The neighborhood was nice, it was quiet, and the neighbors were nice people. We spoke to our neighbors, the neighbors spoke to us, and we never had any problems. The kids' elementary school was within walking distance of the house, there was a public park near the house, and my school was a much longer walk from the house. Sometimes I walked to school in the morning, but most of the time I was dropped off, and I walked home from school sometimes.

This was our third time moving and the third different school I attended in three years. It was my junior year, and I was attending Miramar High school. I knew no one at the school, I was quite used to being by myself and—you know the routine—I stayed to myself.

There were a couple of classes and teachers I enjoyed while attending school. Some of my teachers recognized how smart I am when I did attend class, during the times I participated in class activities, and from my work I turned in at the end of class. Most of the time my teachers left a positive message written on my paperwork or they pulled me to the side to have a personal conversation with me speaking about my intellect and trying to encourage me to do more in school.

My teachers recommended other opportunities to place me in other classes at a higher level of learning where they believed I should be placed. I had one of my teachers ask me, what were my plans after high school, and if I had considered attending college because I was too smart not to go to college.

At one point I aspired to be a lawyer, I wanted to go to college, and I wanted to go to law school. But I changed my mind when I researched how many years of my life I may have to spend in school again, and then the price of tuition to attend a university made me change mind about those dreams. I needed money now, I did not have that kind of time, and I was focused on finding a way to make my own money once I graduated high school.

Back at home, my oldest sister and her boyfriend were back to playing house once again while still trying to repair their relationship. I shared a room with my niece, and she still continued to wet the bed at night. I had to constantly get on my niece about cleaning up the room, making up her bed and taking off her bed sheets after wetting the bed. Honestly, the bedroom had an odor, my niece's pee had a strong smell. It smelled strong like cat pee, and the smell continuously gave me a headache.

Look, sometimes I spanked my niece's butt for being lazy, I showed her how to take the sheets off of the bed, and to put the wet sheets in the laundry room dirty clothes basket so it can get washed. Then I told my niece to take a shower to clean her body off after wetting the bed, and to put the wet clothes in the laundry dirty clothes basket too.

Instead, my niece did the complete opposite, she laid in the bed in the pee, and continuously lied about wetting the bed. My niece was hardheaded, and the little girl did not listen. Sometimes, I caught her rolling her eyes at me, and cutting her eyes at me like she was a grown little woman. But I had to check her, I let her know I do not play with kids, and I will not tolerate disrespect from her.

My sister's boyfriend did not believe how sneaky my niece could be, until he caught her crawling on the floor in their bedroom one morning trying to steal money out of his pants pocket and he spanked her butt.

My two nephews shared a bedroom together and with her boyfriend's sons when they came over on the weekends. I had to continuously make the boys clean up their bedroom and stop them from fighting. Most of the time I was home watching the kids while my oldest sister and her boyfriend were out somewhere. I let the kids go outside to play, get in the pool, play their video games, watch television and have fun playing with another. But I made sure I kept my eyes on them, I monitored them to make sure they were safe and making sure they were not being sneaky or up to no good knowing them because they were sneaky.

I spent my time around the house cleaning up, I cleaned the living room, the family room, the kitchen, washed the dishes and I mopped the floors. I kept the house clean, I cleaned up behind everyone and sometimes I cleaned up my sister's bedroom for her when she asked me. But I had time to myself, I took naps, I read a book, I watched television, I listened to my music, and sometimes I played video games with the kids. I did not have any friends, I did not have places to go to hangout and I spent my time home, with family, where I preferred to be.

My oldest sister and her boyfriend did nice things for me to show their appreciation from time to time. They brought me tickets to go to music concerts, and sometimes I went on outings with them. I did not ask for much and I did not want much. I enjoyed myself going to music concerts with my sister and we had such good times together.

● ● ●

I still had a problem with my oldest sister when it came to getting me out of the house to hang out with other people and it was becoming annoying.

Once again, she forced me to go out with Alicia and some of her friends for Memorial Day weekend. Alicia was in town during college school break, and she was staying at our house. She had plans to hang out with some of her girl friends on the beach, my oldest sister suggested I tag along with her, and hounded me until I got dressed to go.

That day, I was in the house chilling comfortably on the sofa watching television and eating some snacks to myself peacefully. And safely at home might I add too.

My oldest sister drove Alicia and I to her girl friend's house, where we then hopped into the car her girl friend borrowed from her sister and we headed to the beach. There were four of us riding in the car, Alicia, two of her girl friends and me. We made it to the beach that day, but honestly, I do not remember much about what we did on the beach, besides one of her girl friends being annoying and I was ready to go back home.

But leaving from the beach that night to go home is a time I can never forget, and I often think about *what if*!

On our way leaving the beach that night, we were involved in a car accident, I could have lost my life and I am lucky to be alive. The same annoying girl friend was the designated driver, while driving she was clearly not paying attention to the road, she was talking on her cellphone and speeding at the same time. It bothered me, I kept telling her she needed to get off of the phone and pay attention to the road. This girl was not obeying the stop signs, and she ran a red light going across the intersection. There were a couple of times we almost had an accident on our way to the beach because this girl did not know how to drive. I was in the back seat watching the road like I was the driver, she kept on insisting everything was under control and I had nothing to worry about. But I felt like it was only a matter of time before we *did* have an accident with the way this girl was driving, and I was praying that I made it back home safely.

This girl was still talking on the phone as she was approaching a red light, there was another car waiting at the light on the other side to go across the intersection in a different direction.

Everything happened so fast.

Before I could say anything, the light turned green for the other car to go across the intersection, this girl never stopped at the red light and simultaneously the cars collided as the other car took off once the light changed green to go. Alicia and I were sitting on the right side of the car, she was in the passenger seat; I was sitting behind her in the back seat. The cars collided on the right side of the car where we were sitting, and the last thing I remember seeing were the headlights from the other vehicle as I tried to brace myself for the impact of the cars colliding together.

The right side of the vehicle where Alicia and I sat crushed inward. The collision was really bad, the car we were riding in was pushed across the street onto the sidewalk near the fire hydrant and I do not remember how I got out of the car.

Oh, my God!

Man, I am telling you right now there was one of God's angels with us, watching over us because we could have died. The impact of the crash was so strong it jerked our bodies so hard it could have snapped my neck as the cars collided. I remember opening my eyes to see Alicia having a panic attack on the street corner, and the paramedics being called as pedestrians stood around watching, asking if we were ok.

There were no fatalities, no major injuries, including the two male passengers in the other vehicle. They were checked out by the paramedics, the driver had soreness in his neck with a minor headache and the passenger had minor head trauma from hitting his head on the dashboard.

But everyone was ok, and alive, so I was thankful.

I did not get checked out by the paramedics, the paramedics insisted that I let them check me and I refused the care. I think I was still in shock from the accident, but I did not feel anything, and I was able to walk.

I was upset, I paced up and down the sidewalk to calm myself down. I was upset with Alicia's girl friend who was driving the car. I really felt like punching her in the face and I was not trying to hear anything she had to say to me. Because she was careless and reckless with my life that night.

Alicia called one of her guy friends to pick us up and drop me off home because I was not getting back in a car with that girl driving again. Once I made it home that night, I took a shower and went to sleep. It was late night hours when I made it home and everyone was in bed sleeping. I laid down in the bed that night replaying what happened over and over in my mind. I knew in my spirit that one was a close call and I had to pray myself to sleep. I laid in the bed that night looking up at the ceiling thanking God and thanking Jesus Christ my savior until I fell asleep. Then I opened my eyes up the next morning to live and see another day. I did not mention anything about the car accident, my body was sore the next morning, and I had a headache for about two days.

• • •

We were living in a nice home, in a nice neighborhood, with nice cars sitting outside in the driveway and everything seemed to be going well. My oldest sister and her boyfriend seemed to be happy in their relationship because the money was right at the time. They had some extra money thrown back their way from the house purchase, they were having parties for people to see the house, the cars, the motorcycles, the four-wheeler and pretended like they were living the good life. They began going out clubbing again with some friends. And her boyfriend was back to renting exotic cars for no reason.

My oldest sister was enrolled in school for criminal justice, her boyfriend bought her schoolbooks and everything else she needed for her class course. She was so excited to start school, she could not stop smiling or talking about it and I was happy for her. She had evening and night classes on different days of the week. In the beginning, she was going to all of her classes and doing her class work. But coming home to do her homework became a problem for her and it became a problem for me. She came to me for help when she needed help understanding, I helped her do the homework, and I had no problem with helping her. But I went from *helping* her with homework to me *doing* her homework because she was too busy doing everything else that was not important.

This is when it became a problem for me. My sister needed to do the work herself because she was the one going to school to learn it not me! I made the mistake of doing her homework one time, after she begged me to do it because I did not want to do it and she knew it. She turned in the work I completed for her to the professor, she received an A+ grade for the work and the professor told her to keep up the good work. It was over for me after that!

My oldest sister quickly became less interested in doing her own homework to learn and she gave me her schoolbooks to do it for her. But she was so caught up having fun and partying that she began to miss class. She began to make up excuses for not going to class and her number one excuse was proclaiming to be tired. Then my oldest sister became less interested with school, she no longer cared about her classes, and she stopped going to school all together. I have been down this road with her before; she starts things and then she never sees it through to the end.

Years prior, my oldest sister wanted to be a correction officer, I helped her study to pass the exam, she passed the exam and then quit pursing her goal. Hey, I was cool with it, her quitting school this time only gave me more time to ride around outside on the four-wheeler and I was happy doing me.

But things between my oldest sister and her boyfriend were getting bad and going downhill. Well, they were blowing through the extra money fast, they gave themselves more bills, they wasted the money and had nothing to show for it. The money was mismanaged, her boyfriend was lying about paying the bills again, and things began to get repossessed again. Well, my sister had a motorcycle accident pulling into the garage one night hurting herself badly and turned her motorcycle back in after that incident. Then her car was repossessed, and her boyfriend's motorcycle because there were more bills to be paid than money being made.

Well, I figured something was wrong when her boyfriend complained at her for not parking the car in the garage at all times, and he parked it in the garage himself. My sister was upset about her car being repossessed again, her boyfriend continuing to lie about things and keeping things a secret from her.

My oldest sister decided to get a job, she was hired to work in a grocery store stocking shelves from night to morning. I helped out around the house with the kids; helping the kids with their homework and ensuring the kids did not go in the room to disturb their mom while she slept before going into work at night. She worked at night and he worked in the mornings.

Apparently, things were downhill now, my oldest sister met a young man at work, they were coworkers, and she began having a secret relationship with the young man. Yeah, my sister found the time to creep around, I was not aware of her relations on the side at the moment with the young man, and I thought she was going to work too.

Look, I believed my oldest sister when she said, "I am headed off to work, and I will see you when I get back home." She was lying to her boyfriend, to me, and the kids.

Well, things became sexual between my oldest sister and this young man. I do not know how long it was going on, but I guess my sister's conscious was eating at her and she spilled the beans as they say. She confessed to her boyfriend and told him she cheated on him. But she did not spill all the beans to him, she confessed enough about the infidelity to sooth her soul with a sprinkle of more lies and a cherry on top. After confessing to her boyfriend, it took him some time to decide if he still wanted to be in a relationship with her, but he forgave her and took her back. Her boyfriend proclaimed to still love her, and he still wanted to be with her, but work to better their relationship together.

I think her boyfriend was fooling himself, I do not think he quite processed what my oldest sister confessed to him, and he did not deal with his emotions.

One night, while my oldest sister was at work, I guess her boyfriend was sitting alone with his thoughts and his emotions. His thoughts ran wild, and his emotions got the best of him. He waited until late night hours—while I was sleeping—to put my sister's belongings outside on the curb to be thrown away with the trash in the morning. Yeah, he put *everything* in trash bags, her clothes, shoes, purses, bras and panties.

I remember watching her boyfriend look out the window as the garbage man picked up the trash, I looked out the window, I saw the garbage cans outside and black trash bags on the ground. But I did not think anything of it because he always put the trash out on the street on the trash pickup days anyway. I watched him look out the window that morning as the garbage truck pulled up to empty the trash cans inside the garbage truck and drive away. Once the garbage truck drove off, he went into the bedroom and closed the door. I continued to get ready for school, and he dropped me off to school that morning.

My oldest sister picked me up after school, and she talked to me about the things which transpired between the two of them that morning as we drove back to the house. She was upset and decided to move out of the house. But her boyfriend did not want her to move out, he begged her not to leave and he was upset with her decision. She decided to move back to Overtown, and had plans to move in with our brother in his two-bedroom apartment for the moment.

Once we arrived back to the house, her boyfriend was outside in the driveway waiting to start some mess and he began calling her all kinds of derogatory names like a whore, bitch, slut. My oldest sister wanted me to help her grab the little bit of her belongings he did not throw away, so she could pack her car and leave.

But her boyfriend proclaimed my oldest sister was not allowed in his house anymore, she does not live here anymore, and she cannot take anything out of the house because everything belonged to him. He threatened to call the police if my sister did not get off the property, but we went inside the house anyway to get her belongings. He called the police, and the cops showed up to the house. The cops gave them both a warning, her boyfriend tried to get the cops to arrest her, but I intervened to explain to the cops they were having a lover's quarrel. The cops threatened to arrest them both if they received another call to come back out to the house. The cops stayed to let my oldest sister get what she needed out of the house, and then the cops left.

The kids and I continued to live at the house with her boyfriend as we continued to attend school. I was used to them having lover's quarrels, this was nothing new to me.

After that situation took place, he was calling her phone to apologize, begging her to get back with him and to come back home. My oldest sister moved in with our brother, but she was still dealing with her boyfriend and her young lover too. But her living with our brother did not last long because my brother allowed his drug addict friends inside his place and my oldest sister almost had a health scare.

One day, she stepped on a needle walking into the bathroom, the needle penetrated through her foot slightly, but she disinfected her foot with some alcohol, and went to the hospital to get tested for any diseases. She took the needle along to be tested for HIV/AIDS, the needle tested positive for HIV/AIDS, but my oldest sister's test came back negative for the disease which was a relief.

After that situation, my oldest sister moved out of my brother's apartment, and moved in with one of her girl friends. Her girl friend lived in a house with her family, with an extra bedroom available and she extended the offer for my oldest sister to move in with her. My sister lived with her girl friend, her husband, and her two kids in the house.

I AM GOD'S CHILD

My oldest sister spent her days living a double life, she was juggling two lovers; her boyfriend and her young lover. She was still working at her job, in between time she stopped by the house to check in on the kids and me. She continued to put groceries in the house and to stock the refrigerator with food. She spent most of her time in the bedroom talking with her boyfriend if he was home when she stopped by the house.

But my oldest sister did not stay at the house for long, she was in and out. She was sneaking around with her young lover, but she was not honest with him about her relationship with her boyfriend. She was completely hiding her relationship with her young lover from her boyfriend; she did not answer her boyfriend's phone calls while being with her young lover, and sometimes she powered her cellphone off.

But her boyfriend was suspicious of her still cheating on him with the young lover. He tried to go through her cellphone and drove past her girl friend's house at night to see if her young lover's car was parked in the driveway. He did not want to be played like a fool again—my oldest sister had his nose wide open—he did whatever she wanted him to do, and he continuously begged her to come back home. But she *was* playing him for a fool, she was having her cake and ice cream eating it all up leaving nothing on the plate.

Once again, I was caught in between their messy relationship, and it was not by choice. I tried my best to remain out of this drama, I knew of her young lover from talks with her, and she wanted me to meet him, but I was resistant.

Sometimes my oldest sister had me answer her cellphone to lie for her when her young lover called the cellphone, and she was at the house around her boyfriend at the moment. Sometimes her boyfriend tried to question me about my sister's activities, but I kept my mouth shut and I definitely did *not* want to involve myself in their business. Sometimes my sister tried to question me about her boyfriend's activities around the house, she wanted me to be a spy for her, but I was not with that mess. I was mad with my sister for involving me, I hated lying for her and being involved in her deceit. She was playing a dangerous game, I knew it. I wanted no involvement because I did not want to be a disloyal person and I did not want to get hurt being caught up in her mess. Honestly, my sister was toying with her boyfriend, but she needed him because he was her money source, and she was having fun with her young lover, but her kids were more important if you ask me.

My sister was persistent about me meeting her young lover, she begged me until I finally said yes. Her boyfriend had no idea I was going to meet her young lover. He knew I was going to hang out with my oldest sister, and we were going to see a movie together. I did not want to be caught in between their drama and I felt wrong about the whole thing. That night my oldest sister picked me up from the house, we drove over to her young lover's parents' house where he lived, and we hopped into his car to drive to the movie theater.

Honestly, I was quiet during the car ride, I felt awkward, and my oldest sister was asking me questions to get me to have a conversation with her young lover. I do not remember the movie we saw that night; I was ready to get back to the house, I was hoping the night was going to end without her boyfriend finding out and without an incident taking place.

But after we arrived back to her young lover's parents' house and switched back to her car, during the ride to take me back home, my oldest sister informed me about her suspicion of her boyfriend being with another woman. Apparently, her boyfriend stopped answering his cellphone since my oldest sister picked me up from the house earlier that day, she was calling his cellphone, but getting no answer and it was going straight to voicemail. My sister was speeding to get back to the house that night, and she kept calling her boyfriend's cellphone, but there was still no answer and it went straight to the voicemail.

As we got closer to the house, I started feeling nervous. My nerves *really* kicked in once she turned the corner onto our block and turned off the car headlights. We approached the house, her boyfriend's car was missing, there was an unfamiliar car parked in the driveway I never saw before and all of the lights in the house were off.

My oldest sister pulled into the driveway, she beat me getting out of the car, she opened the front door with her house key and walked inside the house. As I walked up to the front door, a woman ran out of the house right past me, she hopped in her car and drove off.

The front door was left wide open, I walked inside after my oldest sister, and she was arguing in the bedroom with her boyfriend. She walked in on her boyfriend laying down on the bed with this other woman still fully clothed and her boyfriend was drunk. Well, he proclaimed to have done this out of spite, and he wanted to get back at her. He proclaimed to have known we were out with her young lover, I think he might have followed us that day, he planned for her to catch him intentionally and the kids were in their bedrooms sleeping while everything was taking place.

My oldest sister tried to beat up her boyfriend, she picked up things to throw as he talked trashed fueling the situation and she broke pieces of furniture, shattering glass mirrors. I tried to stop her from acting crazy, but she was not listening to me. I tried to get in between the two of them because her boyfriend was trying to avoid her. But I moved out of the way to let my oldest sister carry on because I almost got punched and hit by an object she threw at her boyfriend. He ran around to the other side of the house, trying to get into the kids' room to wake them up to make her stop. She finally stopped fighting her boyfriend, she left the house, and her boyfriend called the police to report the incident, and he tried to get the cops to arrest her again.

A couple of days later, my oldest sister and her boyfriend were right back to communicating with one another. They were back to working on their relationship again, she began spending the night over at the house some nights, and for the weekends. They still had many issues to work out in their personal relationship, but she was still deceiving him and creeping around with her young lover behind her boyfriend's back.

After a while, my oldest sister decided to get back together with her boyfriend, and she moved back into the house with us because he was growing impatient and she had to decide if she was going to be with him or not. She proclaimed to have broken things off with her younger lover from what she told me. They began talking about moving again, looking at newer homes and bigger homes than before.

I thought to myself, "Here we go again."

Every time my oldest sister and her boyfriend's issues surface in their personal relationship they consider moving as a fresh start, somehow assuming it is going to fix their problems. They were two unhappy people together in a relationship, their issues were not resolved, and both of them needed to work on themselves individually, because both of them were crazy if you ask me. And they needed Jesus!

We moved into the new house over the summer, it was before the start of the new school year, and it was finally going to be my senior year of high school. I loved my new bedroom; it was like I had my own mini apartment, and I was happy to have my own privacy again. This time I picked out my own bed and bedroom set for my room. My bedroom was like a mini master bedroom suite, and I had a balcony door with access to the balcony that I shared with the master bedroom upstairs. My bedroom had a living room area, I had an office area with a custom built in computer desk and custom built in bookshelves. I had my own bathroom, and a custom built walk-in closet, although I did not have many belongings to fill my closet.

I decided I wanted to get a part-time job. I was ready to work to start making my own money. I had the discussion with my oldest sister and her boyfriend about me getting a part-time job while continuing to attend school during my senior year of high school. I figured I could do it. I could get a job working at one of the fast-food restaurant establishments or grocery store in the neighborhood near the house. I was ready to start working to make money to buy myself things, I did not want to keep depending on others to take care of me and I was ready to save money to get a car because I was ready to drive. I sat down to discuss my plans with my oldest sister and her boyfriend because I needed their permission, and I needed their help.

They did not want me to work, they wanted me to continue focusing on school. Their rejection of my plans only delayed them; they cannot stop me from working once I graduate high school. I just had to wait patiently and then I will be able to do what I wanted to do. I wanted to have some independence and I wanted to have control of my life. Meanwhile, I had to wait a little longer, I had to continue putting up with babysitting the kids and keeping the house clean.

My oldest sister found another job, and this time she worked with special needs people as a live-in caretaker. The job required her to be a live-in caretaker for the special needs people who were placed in a home with other special needs people whose family could not care for them. She worked three days to four days straight and then she was off for one or two days depending on her work schedule.

One day, my oldest sister took me to work with her and I was able to see firsthand what it was she did at work. It was an experience I will not forget, my oldest sister seemed to have liked doing her job, but her face's expression had *unhappy* written on it, and I gave her words of encouragement toward bettering her life until she figures out what is next for her.

Her boyfriend was up for a promotion at his job, he was happy, and he was going to be making more money than he earned now. Everything appeared to be going good between them in their relationship. They seemed happy, it looked like they were fine, and they were headed in the right direction.

My oldest sister was out shopping most of the time buying clothes and shoes to build back up her wardrobe after her boyfriend threw her things away in the trash prior. They were showing the house off to their friends and they were going out clubbing every Friday and Saturday night with their friends. I spent my days home with the kids, babysitting and keeping the house clean.

I hated cleaning this house, it was too big, and I did not think it was fair to make it my responsibility to clean up the house by myself. My oldest sister and her boyfriend were barely home, they spent most of their time away from the house busy doing everything else. The two of them were wrapped up in their own little worlds of partying, shopping, doing their own thing and playing their game of charades like they were in love and happy with one another. As a matter of fact, my sister's boyfriend came to apologize to me about them neglecting their responsibilities at the house, them leaving me home in the house with the kids all day and they promised to do better.

• • •

It was the start of the new school year; I attended Cooper City high school for my senior year of high school and again I was attending a different school for the fourth time. I was new to the school, and I did not know anyone. I was nervous and I did not know what to expect on my first day. I was in the school office sitting down in the waiting area to receive my class schedules and to be shown around the school by the principal.

There was another young lady sitting down in the area and she was new to the school also. Her name was Wendy, she was a senior also, and recently transferred to the school. We were both sitting down on the couch next to each other and neither one of us spoke a word to each other. I was looking around the office at my surroundings, I was bored, and I was waiting in that office for a long time. We happened to glance at one another at the same time.

So, I said "Hello" to her, she spoke back and said "Hello". I introduced myself to her, I reached out my hand and I told her, "My name is Samone."

She extended her hand, she told me her name is Wendy, and said, "It is nice to meet me you," as we shook each other's hands.

Wendy and I instantly clicked with one another, and we sat there having a random conversation as if we had already known each other. We both happened to share two classes together and we had the same lunch period together. We ate our lunches together in the school cafeteria enjoying each other's company.

I developed friendships with other classmates of mine in other classes; this was a completely different experience for me at this school. It was a predominantly white school—up until this moment I never attended a white school—and I was not used to being around so many white people at one time in my life. I could count on my fingers the number of black students or other minorities attending the school, myself included. I was the only black girl in most of my classes, I never knew the blackness of my skin could make me stand out so much, the white kids looked at me weird, and it was a new experience for me. But I stayed to myself, I was quiet in class, and I minded my own business. I shared one class with another black girl and her name was Shanice.

Shanice was a senior in school, she introduced herself to me the first day of class and said, "Honey we, as black girls, must stick together in this school."

We sat right next to each other in class, and she was a nice person too. Shanice also introduced me to some of the other black students who attended the school, and she had a part-time job working at one of the fast-food establishments in the neighborhood.

I met another young lady by the name of Melanie in my science class and it was a pleasure getting to know her. Melanie was a sophomore in high school, and it felt like I already knew her. Melanie was such a sweetheart, she was kind to me, and we were joined at the hip when we were in class together. She was a pretty girl; she had a lovely smile, and she was a smart girl. I loved her positivity, and her energy was contagious. We sat right next to each other in class, she loved to laugh, she laughed at almost everything I said, and called me funny, but I liked her spirit.

We ate lunch together sometimes, we exchanged telephone numbers and I invited her over to my house to hang out as we did our science class project together upstairs in my room. If I did not show up to school Melanie called to check in on me, and she was a good friend to me. We cried and we hugged one another on the last day of class. Melanie cried, thus making me cry and we hugged each other goodbye. I was going to miss her, and we lost contact with one another afterwards.

I met my girl friend named Christine; she was also a senior in high school, and she had plans of studying to become a doctor. We exchanged telephone numbers and we spent time hanging out with each other outside of school.

Honestly speaking I did not really care much about school; it was my senior year and as far as I was concerned, I was almost done with high school. I was absent a lot and my mind was not into school. I did not like going, so when my alarm went off to wake me up in the morning I stayed in bed and looked up at ceiling trying to decide if I wanted to go that day. I caught the school bus in the mornings. I had to walk outside of the gated community and then a couple of blocks down the street to the bus stop.

Sometimes, my oldest sister came into my room to check and see if I got up to go to school in the mornings. Sometimes, she let me stay home, other times she made get up to go to school and dropped me off, no matter how late it was, because I was absent too many days from school.

My absences and my tardiness to class had become a problem. The principal had a sit down with me and my oldest sister to let us know I can no longer arrive late to school, and I cannot miss any more days of school. I needed to be in school to be able to learn my classwork and bring my grades up or I was not going to graduate high school with my senior class.

Anyway, I started handling my business, I went to sleep at a certain time every night and I woke up in the mornings when my alarm went off to wake me up for school.

One morning when my alarm went off, I remember laying in the bed awake and a bad feeling came over me and something kept telling me to stay home. I knew I *had* to get up and go to school, but I laid in bed

I AM GOD'S CHILD

wrestling with my mind on making the decision to get up to go or not. I kept getting a bad feeling and something kept telling me to stay home. So, I laid there in the bed for about thirty minutes looking up at the ceiling, then my oldest sister walked into my bedroom, and she was shocked to know I was still home because she thought I was at school. She made me get up to get dressed and drove me to school.

I had no choice but to go to school, there was no excuse I could have come up with to stay home that day because I was not supposed to miss any more days from school. I was late to school that morning, I missed my first period class, and I was tardy although I was not supposed to be late to school. My oldest sister rushed to take me to school then to get back home to her boyfriend and my nephew. They were both home from work together that day. Before I left the house that morning, my oldest sister was braiding her boyfriend's hair and my nephew was sitting at the table eating his breakfast.

I remember being in school that day, sitting in class and my spirit felt worried all throughout the day while I was there. I wanted school to hurry up and let out so I could get back home. I remember walking home from school after getting off of the bus, and walking through the housing community. As I approached the house, my four-year-old nephew came running up to me, I saw the police cars in the driveway and my nephew kept saying, "Daddy choked mommy."

I knew it was bad when I saw the patrol cars in the driveway, and when my nephew said what he said to me I was *really* worried now. I walked up to the house, the cops asked for my name, my age, and my relationship to the homeowner.

The cops proceeded to inform me of the altercation which transpired while I was at school, I was shocked to hear the bad news. Everything happened so unexpectedly. I was in shock; I was in disbelief as I was standing there listening to the things that transpired between my oldest sister and her boyfriend. In that moment I *knew* why I felt that bad feeling in the morning and I was mad with myself for not staying home because I wanted to be there to help my sister. I called my mom to inform her of what happened, my mom came to the house to speak with the cops and then we went to the hospital to visit my oldest sister.

Apparently, my oldest sister's boyfriend decided to snoop around looking for her cellphone—which was hidden in the closet—while she was in the bathroom taking a shower. He found the cellphone, scrolled through it getting the contact number of her young lover, and he left the house to call the phone number using a pay phone down the street.

My oldest sister had no clue what her boyfriend was doing and why he left the house while she was in the shower.

Her young lover answered his cellphone when her boyfriend called. They spoke, and her young lover informed her boyfriend of their personal relationship, along with other personal things she did with him. Her young lover also informed her boyfriend of a recent lie, a one-week work trip my oldest sister recently took out of town was indeed a trip out of town with him, and they spent a couple of days in town hanging out at his place.

My oldest sister had her boyfriend, the kids, and me believing she was out of town working, but it was a lie she told us. *Wow!*

The whole time she lied about ending her relationship with her young lover, and was misleading her boyfriend because they were supposedly working to make their relationship better again. They had a lover's quarrel prior to this incident and recently made up once she forgave him.

Well, this news her young lover was telling her boyfriend made him furious, a switch went off in her boyfriend's head and that phone call led up to the events that transpired next.

After the phone call, my sister's boyfriend drove back to the house, his anger was boiling, along with his thoughts and he was in kill mode once he arrived back at the house. He unleashed a fury on her like never before, and my nephew was home with them that day.

My nephew was downstairs eating his breakfast and watching cartoons. My oldest sister was upstairs in my bedroom, her boyfriend went upstairs to the bedroom, and completely lost it attacking her.

At first sight, her boyfriend punched her in the face, and he began physically beating her. She did not understand why her boyfriend was attacking her, she did not fight him back, and she did not get a chance to defend herself because everything happened so fast.

Her boyfriend knocked her across the back of the head with the VCR, wrapped the cable wire around her neck, and began strangling her.

My nephew heard the commotion, so he walked upstairs to see what was going on, and he saw his dad strangling his mother with her feet lifted up off the ground. My nephew immediately screamed for his daddy to stop choking his mother, her boyfriend released his grip of the wire wrapped around my oldest sister's neck, and her body hit the floor as she gasped for oxygen. While she laid there on the floor, my oldest sister's boyfriend continued to punch and kick her after ultimately breaking her right kneecap.

Her boyfriend threatened to kill her. He took my nephew back downstairs to watch cartoons, and he grabbed a knife out of the kitchen to make good on his threat to kill her by stabbing her to death. Her boyfriend said, "I am going to get a knife and I am going to kill you bitch!"

My oldest sister had to think fast, she crawled to my balcony door, opened it and screamed for help.

I AM GOD'S CHILD

I have to admit, how glad I am that I left the balcony door unlocked that day because I normally lock the top lock and take the key out of the door.

When my sister screamed for help out on the balcony, the neighbors next door heard her scream for help as her boyfriend dragged her back inside the house. They called the police for help!

Her boyfriend ran back upstairs once he heard her shouting for help and he pulled her back inside. Instead of stabbing her, her boyfriend began choking her with his bare hands around her throat until there was no pulse.

The police arrived at the house after being called by the next-door neighbors, responding to the 9-1-1 call, the police knocked on the front door and her boyfriend answered it.

The cops immediately recognized her boyfriend's bloody shirt, he pretended to have a minor injury, but they saw he had no injuries. The cops handcuffed her boyfriend, then searched the house to see if anyone else was inside, they found my nephew and then discovered my oldest sister's lifeless body upstairs on the floor beaten horribly.

The paramedics arrived at the scene and performed CPR on my sister, trying to resuscitate her. The paramedic did not give up on her, and successfully resuscitated her. Once she had a pulse, they rushed her to the hospital. My oldest sister survived that day, she lived to see her boyfriend taken to jail.

We arrived at the hospital to visit my sister and saw the severity of her injuries sustained from the incident.

The paramedic who saved her life was there to visit her; he came back to make sure she was still alive. He sat by her bedside informing her of how they arrived at the scene, finding her body with no pulse, he performed CPR on her for five minutes. He was not willing to let her die, and not willing to call a time of death on her. The paramedic did not stop performing CPR until he felt the smallest pulse and that was all he needed to keep her alive. He was happy to know she was alive. My sister cried hearing the news, and she thanked the paramedic for helping save her life that day.

The kids were not allowed to see their mom, but I was allowed to go inside the room to visit my sister. I thought I could handle seeing her. My oldest sister kept asking to see me, and I waited outside the room sitting down in a chair as I tried to prepare myself and calm my nerves down. I sat there waiting for my mom to tell me when I could go into the room, but I opened the door to peek inside and what I saw hurt my heart.

Immediately, I was angry, my heart ached, I wanted to burst into tears, and I changed my mind about going inside the room to see her.

My oldest sister was unrecognizable, her face was completely swollen up, one of her eyes was barely open and she was crying tears. I exited the hospital, I did not want everyone to see me crying, I walked outside to cry, pacing back and forth talking to myself.

I was upset. I was mad at my oldest sister. I was mad at her boyfriend for what he did physically to her. The thought of her being dead really hurt my heart. I hated her boyfriend, and I decided I was no longer speaking to him at that moment. I was mad at my oldest sister for lying, and I was mad at her young lover for opening his mouth. I mean what did he *think* was going to happen after exposing those secrets to her boyfriend?

My sister's face was swollen, her eyes were beaten shut, and she suffered a busted eye pupil. Along with two broken ribs, a broken right leg with a torn ACL and she needed rehab to learn to walk again. She was hospitalized for a while, and it was going to take some time for her to recover before she was able to come home. Her boyfriend was locked up in jail and facing some serious charges with murder being one of the charges.

Well, we needed help now, my mom could not take off from work, the kids and I still had to go to school. I did not have a drivers license and I was not able to drive the car. Alicia was in town on a school break, and she decided to help out until the end of her break. One of Alicia's girl friends came along with her, they packed their bags to come stay at the house lending us a helping hand. I went home that night and I cleaned up the mess in my room from the incident. I broke down crying as I tried to clean up the blood stains on the carpet in my room.

While my oldest sister was recovering in the hospital, her boyfriend was locked up in jail, he continuously called the house to speak with the kids and me. I let the kids get on the phone to speak with him, but I did not get on the phone to speak with him because I was mad. The house phone constantly rang during the day, my oldest sister called the house phone, her boyfriend called the house phone, her boyfriend's employer called the house notifying him about a job promotion, but he lost the promotion and his job because he was sitting behind bars. The landlord called the house because the mortgage was due along with other bills and there was no money to pay them.

Alicia and her girl friend Tiffany helped out with the kids a lot. They babysat my nephew—the youngest one—they dropped the kids off to school in the mornings and picked them up after school. Sometimes they dropped me off to school in the mornings and picked me up after school.

But then Alicia's school break was over and she had to go back to college. A couple of weeks went by, but my oldest sister was still in the hospital recovering, her body still needed to heal, and she could not walk yet. My mom asked Tiffany if she could stay a little longer to help us out until my oldest sister got out of the hospital and she did.

I was acquainted with Tiffany, she was from Overtown, born and raised like me. We attended the same elementary school, we were not friends, but we knew of each other, and we met a couple of times in the past hanging out with Alicia in the neighborhood.

Tiffany slept in the guest bedroom downstairs, she got along with me and the kids fine. In the mornings, Tiffany helped me get the kids ready for school, she dropped us off to school, and she picked us up after school. She spent the rest of the day babysitting my four-year-old nephew until I got out of school to help out. Tiffany helped the kids with their homework, she helped me clean up the house, and do the laundry. As time went on the two of us got closer and became friends. I began to trust her, I let her come sleep upstairs in my bedroom with me because the guest room had no bed and sleeping on the couch in the living room was hurting her back.

A couple of weeks had passed by and I still had not been to the hospital to visit my oldest sister since the day of the incident. I looked at her blood stains on the carpet. I walked past it every day and looking at it angered me because this really happened, it was not a bad dream. I went to the store to buy carpet stain remover; I sprayed and scrubbed the blood stains until they were gone. I did not show my emotions, but I was angry, and I was mad with myself also. I was mad with myself for not staying home that day, I thought to myself this would not have happened if I stayed home or maybe I could have helped my sister. But I think everything happened the way it was supposed to happen, and who knows, if I did stay home things could have been worse, I could have been hurt or killed.

I decided to go with my mom to visit my sister at the hospital and get it over with. But to my surprise, once I walked into the hospital room there was her younger lover sitting in a chair next to her bed side. I was upset, I walked outside the hospital room and stood out in the hallway. I did not understand why her young lover was here and why my oldest sister was talking to him! I did not have anything nice to say to him, so I did not say anything at all, and I did not go back into the hospital room until he left. I was mad my oldest sister was talking to him again, although he did not physically beat her his part in this ordeal sparked what almost cost my oldest sister her life completely.

My oldest sister *died*, and the paramedics had to resuscitate her! I thought she was not taking the situation seriously. But he came to apologize to her, and she forgave him. I wanted to break down crying looking at her injuries as she laid there on the hospital bed, the only way I could keep from crying was to avoid looking at her directly. I could not handle seeing her in such bad condition. Hearing about her injuries was different than seeing the extent of her injuries up close personally. I did not go back to the hospital to visit my oldest sister again after that visit and it angered me to see her young lover at the hospital.

As the days went by, time was of the essence, Tiffany needed to get back home to her family, the bills and other priorities needed to be handled financially. My sister could not afford to stay in the hospital any longer, both of her ribs were still healing, and the good news is she was able to walk a little bit with the support of crutches. But she was barely able to see out of her busted eye's pupil—it was still healing—and she had to go home to finish healing up on her own.

My oldest sister was released from the hospital and Tiffany went home to her family. My sister was on bed rest for a little bit; she was not able to bend and lift yet. It was rough for her because the kids wanted to hug her, but she could not bend down to pick up my four-year-old nephew. I kept the house clean, and I help tend to the kids so she could get some rest to heal up. It was easier said than done and I did my best to help out in any way possible including helping aid her whenever she asked for my help.

In the mornings, I woke up to get the kids ready for school, I drove the car to drop the kids off to school and my oldest sister drove with one good eye using the crutches to press the car pedals to pick them up after school. My oldest sister stayed home with my nephew, she picked the kids up from school and I caught the school bus home because my school let out later than the kids'.

My sister was in pain, but she found the strength to physically rehab herself, she endured the pain, and she began to heal up. As time went on, she began walking without the crutches, though her ribs and her pupil were still healing up.

Eventually my oldest sister fully recovered from her injuries, and the vision in her eye was restored. Her boyfriend constantly called the house phone, he was still locked up in jail awaiting his trial and the two of them communicated over the telephone. They talked every day, throughout the day even though they were not supposed to be communicating with one another.

But we had another problem on our hands, we were getting house visits from the Department of Children and Families randomly since the start of the trial. They made house visits to question myself and the kids to ensure our living environment was safe because of the domestic violence incident that happened. My oldest sister was at risk of possibly having her kids taken away from her, but everything worked out fine, we were free and clear of that situation. Her boyfriend was facing some serious charges, he was at risk of being sentenced to serve many years of jail time, and he needed her not to press charges against him. My sister did not plan on pressing charges against her boyfriend, but she was subpoenaed to court to take the stand to speak of the events which happened on that day.

In the meantime, while her boyfriend sat behind bars, the bills were past due and there was no money. But my sister was able to keep the lights and the water on in the house for the moment. Her boyfriend was busy worrying about what she was doing on the outside and trying to keep tabs on her by calling the house daily. He begged and apologized to my oldest sister over the phone. He still wanted to be with her after everything that had happened; the infidelity and the lies.

You know what I did? I finally picked up the phone to speak with him, I accepted his apology, and I forgave him. I was tired of being mad, I did not want to be mad anymore. Listen, I had no problems with her boyfriend, we got along with each other, and I consider him to be like a brother to me. I was mad that he let his anger get the best of him that day and physically doing what he did. Her boyfriend had the right to be angry, but he could have handled the situation differently to where it did not result to him being locked up for killing her.

I love my oldest sister, but I realized she was a no-good woman. I realized I was taking this way too serious, this had nothing to do with me, and I was involving myself in their personal business. So, I removed myself from their business and I went back to minding my own business. I realized my sister did not learn her lesson from all of this, she did not learn anything, and this was a game for her. But I knew she was headed down a path of self-destruction, and I was witnessing self-sabotage.

My oldest sister turned to the bottle; she began drinking every day and night. At night, she went out driving around town, and to dirty little hole-in-the-wall clubs to meet men. She brought the men back to the house—a different guy every night. A few of them slept overnight, but left early in the morning before the kids woke up. A couple of times I had to help her sneak the men down the hall past the kid's bedroom, and out of the house.

Yeah, my oldest sister did not want her boyfriend to find out she was still out in the streets being a whore and bringing men back to the house. He still did not trust her, he had suspicions and sometimes questioned the kids—especially my four-year-old nephew—to find out things. She continued to play this victim role with her boyfriend, I kept my mouth shut and I minded my own business. These same kind of activities and behavior is what landed her in this predicament now. She spent her time throughout the day, upstairs in the bed sleeping, until nighttime and she was back at it again, doing what she did.

Well three months went past, and her boyfriend was still locked up behind bars. The landlord evicted us—we were served the eviction papers by the sheriff—and we had two weeks to get out of the house. The car at the time was our only transportation, but the car note was also past due, the car's tag was expired, and the repo man was looking for the car to repossess it. We packed up all of our belongings, my oldest sister had to figure out what the next move was going to be, and where were we going to live. There was not much time, we had two weeks to vacate the property, and we needed a roof over our heads.

At the last moment, my oldest sister decided to move back into the home we previously lived in prior to moving into the house we were being evicted from. Her boyfriend sold the home to a couple who were friends with them, but something happened because of some shady business and the family never had the chance to move into the house. The couple was in the process of remodeling it to their liking by painting the walls and changing the tile on the floors.

After my oldest sister sat down to have a personal conversation with the couple explaining she was not involved in her boyfriend's shady affairs, the couple gave her the keys to the house, and we were able to live there temporarily. We went without lights and water in the house for a little bit until my oldest sister was able to get everything turned on, but we improvised.

My sister was still involved with her young lover, so we went over to his place to hang out during the day, we took a shower there, and we went back home at night. We kept our belongings packed in boxes because the house was still a mess with the half-done renovations, and we lived like this temporarily, but I kept the house clean as best as I could. Some adjustments had to be made due to the circumstances, and we had to rough it out, but we survived it. Once the lights and the water were turned on things were a little bit easier.

We were not supposed to be living in the house, no one was supposed to be living there because it belonged to the bank, and our days were limited living there.

I know you may be thinking, why I did not go live with my parents, but I was *not* going to leave my oldest sister and the kids' side knowing they needed my help.

The kids and I did not attend school often for a couple of days during the weeks. We lived in a different area now, we had to travel further to school in the mornings, and sometimes there was no gas in the car or money to put gas in the car. My oldest sister took a risk every time driving the car, she was at risk of being pulled over by the cops for an expired tag, and having the car repossessed. She drove cautiously, we had to duck and dodge the cops while driving on the road.

One day, as we were getting ready to leave the house, I looked out the living room window, there were two police patrol cars outside in the driveway, along with a tow truck and they were there to repossess the car. The house was surrounded by cops and the repo man as they walked around the house looking through the window trying to see if anyone was inside. We immediately secured the latches on the garage door to make sure they were not able to lift it to take the car. Then my oldest sister, the kids, and me snuck out of the house through the back-patio door without being noticed.

We ran through the backyard around the canal to cut through one of the neighbor's backyard and we ran a couple of more blocks down the back street toward the park. We were able to get away, the police and the repo man were still at the house looking around hoping to repo the car that day. As we were walking down the back street, our next-door neighbors pulled up in the car on the side of us to let us know we were not spotted, and they were still at the house looking around. We politely thanked our neighbor and declined the offer for a ride. My oldest sister called up her young lover to come pick us up and we waited at the park until he arrived to get us.

That day we had to do what we had to do to survive, and I was with my sister all the way to the end. I looked into her eyes that day as she wanted to cry tears and she held them back because she did not want the kids to see her crying. She had a look of shame, embarrassment, and nervousness on her face. I told my oldest sister not to worry about it, the kids were fine, and we had to do what we had to do that day.

So be it! I was not embarrassed, and the car was still parked in the garage which was all that mattered at the moment.

We lived in the house for three months during the winter holiday season, and we moved out the following year. After a while, surprisingly my sister's boyfriend was released from jail, and he was put on probation with an ankle monitor. Her boyfriend lived with his young brother and his girlfriend at their place while out on probation. We went over to visit her boyfriend a few times after he was released from jail, but we were still living in the foreclosed house at the time, and he was out of jail trying to get back up on his feet again.

My oldest sister and her boyfriend were still communicating with one another although they were not supposed to, but you know how that goes. Her boyfriend immediately began working, he found a job doing printing like before, and he saved up the money to move us out of that house. Her boyfriend made promises to us: my oldest sister, the kids and me. He kept his promise—he promised to get us out of that house and into a better living environment. Being a man of his word, her boyfriend moved us into a three-bedroom condo apartment closer to our schools, he was still on probation, he was not supposed to be near my oldest sister, so he did not move into the apartment with us. He paid the rent and the bills in the apartment monthly.

The drama continued at the new apartment and my oldest sister started the same shenanigans again. Tiffany came over to visit us and she spent the night, but ended up living with us. It was cool, I did not have a problem with her, and soon after her friend Cara lived with us temporarily too.

Tiffany and Cara were best friends, but called each other sisters. I became acquainted with Cara, she was a cool person, and we got along fine with each other. The good thing was everybody got along with each other, we all shared a room together, my niece, me, Tiffany, and Cara.

Tiffany and Cara were young ladies, but they were a little older than me by two years, I think. They were young lady's living life, not knowing what they wanted to do with their lives, not caring about the direction of their lives and just living for the day. Both of them were single and still dating. Neither one of them had a job at the moment, but they hustled for money by doing hair, and kept their cell phone bills paid. They helped out around the apartment with cooking, cleaning, and they helped out with the kids. They helped out with the driving duties, driving the kids and I to school in the mornings, along with picking us up after school.

My oldest sister continued to sleep around with her young lover secretly behind her boyfriend's back, and she slept around with random guys she met and brought over to the apartment. She continued leading her boyfriend on, and pretending as if she wanted to be with him. She was using her boyfriend for financial support and shelter over our heads. But he was no fool this time, he did not trust her, and he drove through the parking lot of the apartment complex looking to see if her young lover's vehicle was parked anywhere. When he spotted her young lover's vehicle in the parking lot, he called my sister's cellphone to see if she would answer, and sometimes her boyfriend knocked on the front door to bust her, the excuse was 'he came to visit his son'.

The situation between my oldest sister and her boyfriend was ridiculous, I felt bad for the kids, because they involved the kids in their messy drama too. They both asked the kids questions to find out what the other has been doing, especially the child they shared together, and my oldest sister had the kids lie to her boyfriend about her young lover being at the apartment or around them. Her boyfriend was doing whatever possible to make her happy and trying to make up for what he did to her, some nights he took all of us out to eat at a restaurant as a family. She did not allow him to come inside the apartment when he came over to visit his son or the kids, most of the time he took his son for a car ride to buy him some food and question the child about his mother's actions or whereabouts.

My oldest sister went to her boyfriend for help, she depended on him, she wanted him to pay her bills and to take care of her, but she did not want to be *with* him. She continued to waste her time going out meeting guys, hanging out with her friends and drinking most of the time. She spent a lot of time hanging out with her young lover and his family at their house and going on family outings with them. While the kids and I stayed home she went out doing whatever in the streets.

Sometimes her young lover—along with his friends—came over to the apartment to hang out with us because some of his friends were dating Tiffany and Cara. Sometimes I spent time hanging out with them. My sister tried to hook me up with one of his friends, but I preferred not to date them, and I could not stand it when they tried to force me to date his friend.

Well, I was slowly coming out of my shell, I was a virgin, I was single, and I dated guys, but nothing serious.

My sister's boyfriend knew she was still creeping around with her young lover, and he wanted to catch her red handed himself. Once she was busted by her boyfriend with her young lover at the apartment, and her boyfriend decided to stop paying the rent along with the rest of the bills. She used the kids against her boyfriend to get him to continue paying the rent because he loved all the kids too much to not keep a roof over their heads. He has been in the kids' lives since they were little, he helped take care of them, he helped raise them and they called him dad.

I had more important things on my mind than thinking about a boy, having sex was not important to me. I was not trying to be in a relationship, and I most definitely was not trying to end up pregnant as a teenager to become another statistic. I had other important plans for my life, I envisioned a different direction for me, and I was busy making sure I graduated high school.

Guess what? It was graduation time!

I passed all of my classes and I was graduating with my senior high school class. It was getting closer and closer to graduation day. Well, I enjoyed myself at grad bash, and I attended my high school prom, although I arrived ten minutes before prom was over.

My graduation day finally arrived, and I was happy when I woke up that morning. I made it on time to my graduation ceremony. Although my family arrived late they managed to make it on time to see me walk across the stage to receive my high school diploma and graduate. My dad and my brother stayed home to watch the basketball game on television, but the rest of my family showed up to support me.

REBECCA S. SMITH

MY YOUNG ADULTHOOD

Well, I did it! I am a high school graduate, and now it is time for me to make some money to take care of myself.

I did not have any work experience; I needed a job and I needed money. So, I called my oldest sister's boyfriend to ask for his help, he came through for me the next day with a job interview at a printing press company working in the bindery. My oldest sister drove me to my job interview, I lied on my job application about having work experience and I finessed my way around the matter during the interview process that day. I told the interviewer; I was a quick learner and a fast worker.

The interviewer walked me around the building showing me the machines and the press-room. I had no experience whatsoever in printing or working in the bindery and I did not know how to work one single machine in that building. But I was willing to learn, I knew I could do the job and I was optimistic about being hired. I left the interview, and I waited for the call back because the job had to do a background check on me and verify my information.

I received the call back, I was hired for the job, and I began working the next day. Two days after graduating high school, I had a job paying minimum wage and it was the start to a new beginning for me. I depended on my oldest sister for transportation to get me back and forth from work at the time.

Well, you know the saying, "Once you turn eighteen and graduate high school you are grown." That was my mentality, I checked finding a job off of my list of goals and next up on my list was saving up enough money to get a car. I worked eight hours a day, forty hours a week and I was getting paid bi-weekly. I worked Monday through Friday and I was off on the weekends. I woke up every morning and I went to work to earn my money.

Some mornings were a hassle for me waking up early to get ready for work and making it to work on time. It was a hassle waking my oldest sister up in the mornings to drop me off to work, we had to stop for gas on the way because she was always driving all of the gas out of the car from the night prior.

When I was at work, I did my job correctly and I worked at a fast pace. I learned how to do everything in the bindery, and I worked my way into the press-room. While working in the bindery, I learned how to assemble a book, I learned how to take loose printed pages and bind them together into a book. To assemble a book is a process and it takes many steps to do it. Working in the bindery requires you to stand up on your feet for hours doing the job and it was never a good thing to get caught sitting down on a stool by the owner of the company.

There were three of us women working in the bindery, my supervisor who was a woman, an elderly woman, and me. It was our job to insert musical CD's into a CD pouch we stuck on the back of books we packed into boxes stacked on a pallet to be put up on the shelf in inventory to be sold. We assembled musical band books; the printed musical sheets of music came off of the press for us to assemble the books to be put into inventory. To assemble the bands required standing on your feet, proof checking the musical sheets for any errors, the process of setting up the musical sheets horizontally on the worktable and then the process of pulling the band. To pull a band, you must pull a number of musical sheets necessary at one time using your fingers with a little bit of fingertip moistener to grip the sheets of paper, walking from one end of the table stacking each band in a pile on top of the table as you go and then inserting each band into a cover to be put on the shelves for inventory.

The orders for the books and the bands were for different amounts, some orders ranged from hundreds to thousands, tens of thousands and sometimes hundreds of thousands of books. There was a time frame for each job to be completed, sometimes the orders had to be completed the same day, two days, and maybe even longer depending how fast we worked to finish the job.

It was not long before I caught the attention of my supervisor and the attention of the stitchery operator supervisor in the press-room. With my work performance, I quickly became the best worker in the bindery. Sometimes I worked so fast completing jobs way before the deadline, my supervisor had to tell me to slow down and take my time. Some days at work were slower than others, everyone in the bindery and everyone in the press-room had to find something to do until there was work for everyone to do. Instead of us going home, everyone found something to do like mopping the floors around the work areas and cleaning off the machines in the press-room. When there was no work to do in the bindery, my supervisor sent me into the press-room to work on the folder machine. The folder was the machine used to fold the musical sheets, I learned how to load the paper on to the machine, and I worked at the end of the folder collecting the sheets of paper stacking them in bundles.

The opportunity to work in the press-room came about eight months later, the stitchery operator supervisor was looking for a replacement for a guy he fired, the guy could not keep up with machine and the guy came to work drunk a couple of times—not able to do his job.

The stitchery operator supervisor offered me the chance to work at the end of the stitching machine alongside him and another worker. I accepted the opportunity, I worked on the machine for a week as a trial basis run to decide and see if I wanted to accept the new position change or not. I accepted the new position working in the press-room on the stitching machine, it came with a dollar pay raise and with more pay raises reviews every year.

I am not going to lie, working on the stitching machine the first week kicked my butt. Every day I came home from work, I went straight to take a shower then went straight to bed.

The stitching machine assembled the music books. The machine has six pocket feeders for you to load with the folded musical sheets of paper, and another pocket for the book covers, as it dropped down from the pocket onto the assembly line. The machine allows you to control its speed as it stitches and trims the books. At the end of the machine the books dropped out into bundle stacks and then pushed out the end of the machine.

This is where I came in, I worked at the end of the stitching machine. It was my job to make sure the books were trimmed correctly without any errors, looking out for any errors on the book covers or inside the books as the holder dropped them out, then I packed the books into boxes and I stacked the boxes onto a pallet to be put in inventory.

The stitching machine was not a problem for me, I did more than keep up with the speeds of the machine as we completed the orders of assembling musical books. As the machine assembled the books, I had to kept an eye out for paper jams near the cutter, and I had to continuously change the recycle bins filled with the paper trimmings to prevent paper jams. Along with checking to make sure the pocket feeders dropped the folded pages, I made sure the wire stitch went through the center of the books all at one time.

There were three of us working on the stitching machine, my supervisor, an older woman, and me. We worked together as a team to run the machine completing musical book orders for thousands, tens of thousands, and hundreds of thousands to be put in inventory. My supervisor praised my work performance, and I over exceeded his expectations of me working on the stitching machine. My supervisor claimed he never had anyone work with him who was able to keep up with the machine like me, and I did it better than most guys he worked with in the past. When I accepted the position, I took it as a challenge, and I mastered doing it in my own way. I am a detailed person; I pay attention to the small things, and I worked hard every day at work. I was not afraid to learn how to operate any of the other machines in the press-room. I learned how to operate the forklift and I received my certification to operate the forklift.

• • •

Meanwhile, back at home things were taking a change and everyone was getting ready to go their separate ways.

Cara left to go live with her family up the road trying to figure out what she was going to do with her life. My oldest sister's apartment lease expired, and she was not going to renew the lease. We had to move out and find another place to live. Tiffany packed up her belongings and moved back to Overtown with her family.

My oldest sister began playing nice with her boyfriend; she needed her boyfriend's help and financial support. She still juggled her personal time between her boyfriend, and her young lover. Her boyfriend helped her get a house this time, the house belonged to my oldest sister and the house was in her name. Her boyfriend had a friend who was a real estate investor with many investment properties, and he sold one of his rental properties to my oldest sister as a favor to her boyfriend. It was my sister's first time being a homeowner, the house had four bedrooms, two bathrooms with a spacious yard and there was a lake in the backyard.

The shenanigans and drama quickly continued at this house. My sister's boyfriend was off of probation now, he did not have a place of his own yet and he wanted to move into the house with us. My sister did not want to let him move into the house, but she wanted her boyfriend to pay the mortgage until she was able to find a job. She did not want a relationship with him anymore. Her boyfriend was spending money on her, and he only did it to be with her again. My sister did not want her boyfriend to think she was getting back together with him because he helped her, but he wanted to lay his head where he was spending money. In the end my sister decided to let her boyfriend move into the house because she needed him to pay her mortgage, and she knew her boyfriend was trying to find a way back in. But her decision to let him move into the house came with some rules and stipulations for him.

She made it clear to her boyfriend it was *her* house, the two of them were *not* back together, she was *not* having sex with him, and he could stay with her until he found his own place. My sister thought everything was going to be *that* easy, she thought it was going to be peaches and cream.

In the meantime, I was happy to have my own room and my own privacy again. My sister helped me paint and decorate my room. The kids had their own rooms, the boys shared a room together and my oldest sister decorated the kids' rooms nicely for them.

My oldest sister and her boyfriend slept in her master bedroom together. I was not wasting my time worrying about them and what they had going on. I was busy working at my job five days of the week, paying my cellphone bill and trying to save up some money to get my own car.

But my oldest sister began having problems with her boyfriend *again*, their issues started to affect my mood and the energy around the house. She searched for a job, but she was still driving around in the car with an expired tag and the repo man was still looking for the car. Her boyfriend wanted her to give the car back, and promised to get her another car to drive. But she did not want to give the car back, she did not trust him to keep his word, and she did not want to be without transportation.

She believed he wanted her to depend on him, she was supposedly trying to break free of him and make it on her own. She knew her boyfriend's help came with control and stipulations for her too.

My sister and I continued to drive around in the car, ducking and dodging the police while driving on the road. I used the car for transportation to work, my sister dropped me off and picked me up at work.

My oldest sister and her boyfriend's living arrangement was starting to become a problem for both of them. He wanted to have sex with her, and he wanted to get back together with her in a relationship like they were before. But my sister found out he lied to her about some things pertaining to the house; he was stealing from her, and she put him out of the house. I do not know how she found out about his shady actions, but like they say, "What you do in the dark, will come to the light."

Supposedly, her boyfriend kept the cash from the closing on the house, he never told her about the money, and kept it for himself. Then my sister found pawn shop receipts he tried to hide. He took the movie discs out of the cases along the DVD rack and sold them to the pawn shop for money to put gas in his car. Then my sister found out *his* new car was in *her* name; he forged her signature on the paperwork and pretended the car belonged to him. But she took the car from him, and gave it back to the dealership.

Lastly, my sister found out he lied about paying the house mortgage, she was behind three months on her mortgage, and had no money to pay the past due payments.

I spent most of my time in my room to myself minding my own

business, I was enjoying my privacy and the little bit of peace I had to myself. Tiffany and I still kept in contact, and we talked on the phone from time to time.

I saved up one thousand dollars to put as a down payment for a car. I was ready to get me some wheels, but I did not have my driver license although I was driving already. I had my restricted drivers license, but not a full drivers license. So, I went to the drivers license place to take my test to get my license so I could get myself a vehicle.

Well, my first car was a used 2001 four door charcoal gray Ford Taurus, and it felt so *good* to drive my car home the night I got it! I was happy and I was proud of my accomplishment. I made a goal; I accomplished that goal and I checked it off of my list. I said I was going to do something, and I took the necessary steps to do what needed to be done in order for me to have my own car. I drove myself to work early the next morning, I paid my own car note and car insurance because it was my responsibility.

I was not selfish with my new car. The car my oldest sister was driving was repossessed. She had no car to drive, the kids needed to get dropped off and picked up from school. So, I let my sister drop me off to work in the mornings, she had the car during the day and picked me up from work in the evenings. She found a job working as a telemarketer, but the job did not last long. So she went back to work at the grocery store again as an overnight stocker, but that job did not last long either.

My oldest sister drove around in the car all day doing nothing, and she still managed to pick me up from work late most of the time. But one day, while I was at work, I received a phone call from my niece telling me something was wrong with my sister, the kids were scared, and they called me. My sister was down on her knees crying, and she did not want to get up off the floor. She had a mental breakdown, she felt like giving up and she did not want to carry on with her life anymore. The kids were crying, and they was scared because they did not understand what was happening to their mom.

I tried to get my sister to pick up the phone and talk to me. She did not pick up the phone and she continued crying. I heard her in the background of the phone crying, she was crying like a person who just lost someone they loved. I heard the kids crying in the background too, and the kids asking their mother is she ok.

I was at work; I could not get in my car and leave work because my car was at the house with them. I called my mom's cellphone to let her know something was wrong with my oldest sister and I needed someone to come pick me up from work. My mom did not have a vehicle, she called my auntie Nia for her help and the both of them picked me up from work in my aunt's car. When we arrived at the house, we walked into the bedroom where they were on the floor kneeling down crying.

My oldest sister was down on her knees at the edge of the bed with her face down in the bed, the kids were beside her crying too and hugging her. She refused to get up off the floor as my mom and auntie tried to make her stand up. My auntie Nia walked throughout the house praying with her holy oil rebuking the spirit of the devil and casting out the wicked spirits in the name of Jesus! My mom and I remained in the room as we talked to my oldest sister trying to convince her not to give up on life.

She refused to get up as she continued crying tears, she said, "I am tired, I do not want to live anymore."

Tears ran down my face, and it broke my heart to hear those words come out of my oldest sister's mouth. I reminded her she is loved, I love her; she cannot give up and I refuse to let her give up on her life. She did not want to stand up and rise up on her feet. I grabbed her right arm, and my auntie grabbed her left arm and my oldest sister leaned on our shoulders as we helped her walk throughout the house.

Auntie Nia began praying, shouting out loud telling my oldest sister to repeat after her, calling the devil a liar, calling on God until my sister's spirit was lifted. But she still struggled to cope throughout the days, it was not long before she was back to her old ways again and the same shenanigans.

My oldest sister began drinking again every day and night to cope with her life's circumstances. She partied at night, came home drunk with a different man at night. She slept around with random men, and her young lover too. She brought random men around her kids, she had sexual encounters in return for money or favors and it was nothing to her. But she forgot about her three kids looking up to her, and they were watching everything she did.

Then my sister allowed one of her girl friends to move in with us momentarily, she was a childhood friend, and their kids grew up together. My sister and her girl friend were two birds of the same feather that flocked together. Her friend was a single mother of three daughters, she worked to support her and her kids.

They both left their kids at the house unsupervised to go out clubbing at little dirty hole-in-the-wall clubs at night. When they were not out clubbing, they still left all the kids home unsupervised to go meet up with random guys to party or whatever it is they were doing together. They drank liquor or wine until they were drunk or wasted with a hangover the next morning.

To my surprise, I woke up one Saturday morning to find my oldest sister asleep inside the house in her bedroom drunk, and her friend was drunk outside sleeping in the driveway inside of her own car. She was asleep in the passenger seat of her car, with the window rolled down and her right leg hanging out of the car with her panties down to her ankle. Her girl friend was drunk. The two of them went out clubbing Friday night and came back home drunk in the morning. Her girl friend was a person who could not handle her liquor, she became hostile, angry, and wanted to fight everybody when she was drunk.

• • •

My living experience in the house at the time was stressful, depressing, disrespectful, and unpleasant for me. I was naïve to a lot of things; I was trying to better my life, I was focused on my goals and working to make my money. I had no peace in my life, and I had no peace of mind at the time. I thought I could trust the people around me; I trusted the people I surrounded myself with, and I thought they were loyal to me.

I thought wrong. I was a naïve person. I was not paying attention to the people around me, it took me a while to open my eyes and to realize how I was being played like a fool. I was surrounded by chaos, turmoil, thieves, deceit, jealousy, envy, and no good using wicked people with alternative motives.

My sister and I were bumping heads and clashing with one another about my car. She had control issues. She was very disrespectful toward me, and my privacy. She took it upon herself to allow her young lover, random guys, and other random people to drive my car without my permission. She continuously drove out the gas in my car, and she expected *me* to replace the gas that she drove out. She drove around in my car with her friends smoking weed, driving drunk, and left my car dirty with trash in it for me to clean up the mess.

I was not too keen with my sister's friend living with us, she had no hospitality, she was not a clean sanitary person, and she did not have good hygiene. At times I came home to my oldest sister's girl friend in my bedroom, laying comfortably on my bed with her face on my pillows watching television in my room without my permission to be in my room. I told her to stay out of my room and I told my sister to tell her friend to stay out of my room—since it was her house guest—because it was an invasion of my privacy and disrespectful to me.

My oldest sister did nothing and she continued to allow her girl friend to totally disrespect my privacy. I had to become impolite with her friend to let her know to stay out of my room. She did things I found to be disgusting and rude. She did rude things like eating off of my plate of food with my utensil without my permission. It did not stop with the food either, her friend put her lips on my cup to take a sip from it without my permission. I felt like her friend did things like that to me intentionally. I no longer wanted my food or drink once she put her lips on anything. I did not trust her; I do not know where her lips have been and what she puts in her mouth! I was not going to put my lips on anything she put her lips on.

In the meantime, Tiffany was back living with us again, I shared my room with her, and we were getting along as roommates. We were growing closer together as friends, Tiffany introduced me to some of her friends and her family. Although Tiffany lived with us, she traveled back and forth from our house to her apartment in Overtown.

Tiffany's grandmother retired from work, purchased and moved into a house out of town. Her grandmother left the apartment to her and her two brothers, but they were responsible for paying the rent, along with the utility bills. Tiffany did not have a job; she made money every now and then doing hair as a hustle for money from time to time. Tiffany introduced me to some of her girl friends from high school. I became acquainted with her friends, hanging out with them and going out clubbing together sometimes.

I thought I could trust Tiffany, I trusted her, I thought she had my back, and I thought she was my friend. I was naïve to Tiffany using me and stealing money from me. Tiffany was the type of thief who steals from you and then helps you look for whatever she stole from you. I know because she did it to me and she got me a couple of times like this.

I always suspected Tiffany of stealing from me, but I did not want to believe it, and I wanted to catch her red-handed stealing from me, so I could punch her in the face. But I was not able to catch her red-handed, and Tiffany continued to steal from me as long as I allowed her to be around me, like a fool, to do it. There were many times forty dollars, sixty dollars, eighty dollars and a hundred dollars came up stolen out of my wallet. I searched for my money thinking I misplaced it; maybe it fell out of my pocket, or I lost the money.

I allowed Tiffany to drive my car also, we partied together, and we rode out together. We worked together helping each other out. Tiffany helped me put gas in my car, she helped keep my car clean and she did not allow anyone to drive my car without my permission. Tiffany received food stamps every month to feed herself, she shared her food stamps with me and helped feed me when I had no money for food. When Tiffany had no money and she needed food to eat I paid to feed both of us. I confided in Tiffany, and vice versa with Tiffany confiding in me. We laughed, and we joked around with each other. Tiffany was a person of cleanliness such as myself, we did not have any problems when it came to cleaning up the room, being sanitary, and our body hygiene as girls.

I had my car for six months now, I paid three hundred and twenty dollars a month for my car payment. I paid my own car note and my insurance myself. I kept my car clean, and I kept up with the maintenance on my car. I was able to afford paying my car note, my car insurance, my cellphone bill, and have extra money in my pocket after paying bills because of my pay raise at work. Things were going good for me, and I took pride in my independence because I do not like depending on other people.

My parents did not have a vehicle at the moment, they were walking and catching the bus to get to where they needed to go. I always took it upon myself to pick my mom up from work or the bus terminal and I dropped her off home after work. I wanted to help my parents, I did something impulsive that I did not think all the way through, and I decided to get another car. I was going to give my parents the car I was driving and let them take over the car note payments. I talked to my parents about my plan and what I decided to do.

My mom said, "No." My mom did not want the car, and she did not want to pay anymore car payments.

My dad said, "Yes." The car note payment was reasonable for my dad to afford. I gave the car over to my dad, it was his car, and he was free to do with the car as he pleased. We agreed once my dad paid off the car, I would sign the title over to my dad, and the car would legally be in his name. My dad gave me the money every month on time to pay the car note. I kept my word as promised, I paid the car payment every month, and I gave my dad the receipt every time as proof. I was trying to help ease things for my parents and I decided to help the best way I could with transportation for them.

I did not want to continue worrying about my mom walking to the bus stop alone in the morning while it was still dark outside, my mom carried a purse, along with other bags on her shoulders. I was worried someone might try to rob my mom and hurt her or possibly take her life for the bags she was carrying on her shoulders that are not worth taking her life. I was worried someone might try to rape and kill my mom. I was still praying to God; I prayed for God's protection over my mom, for her well-being and her safety.

My next car was a brand new 2007 Honda Accord coupe, my second oldest sister was my co-signer, and I thanked her for helping me because she did not have to do that for me. My car payment was almost five hundred a month, and my car insurance rate was higher. I paid my car note, my car insurance, and my cellphone bill every month. I made sure I went to work, and I worked all my hours because I could not afford for my paycheck to be short. To be honest, I was living paycheck to paycheck, I needed all of my money and I could not afford to come up short on my paycheck. I still needed to take care of myself, I had to feed myself, I had to clothe myself, and I needed money for gas in my car to get to work during the week. I prioritized my money, and I had to budget my money.

My money was tight, I had to stretch my money and make it work until my next pay week which was every two weeks. I tried to put my extra cash to the side and save up some money to get ahead of my bills. It was impossible for me to save money being surrounded by two blood sucking leeches—and thieves might I add—like my oldest sister and Tiffany.

I made a bad decision when I gave my oldest sister the spare key to my car because I was trying to help her out. Well, the plan was for her to use the car to take the kids to school, pick them up from school and to search for a job to make some money to handle her finances.

My oldest sister always had somewhere to go in the car, and it was never her going to a job interview. She drove around in my car day and night with her friends pretending like my car was hers and burning out all of the gas. The gas *I* went to the gas station for, and *I* paid for out of *my* pockets with *my* money. I kept my car on a half of tank of gas, and I filled my gas tank up occasionally. It only took about fifty dollars to fill my car gas tank up, and thirty dollars to fill the gas tank up halfway. But as soon as I put gas in my car, my sister had somewhere to go to drive out the gas with no money to replace the gas she burned out. If or when my oldest sister did have money for gas it was maybe ten dollars, eight dollars or five dollars. It was little amounts, and it was *never* enough to replace the thirty dollars or fifty dollars worth of gas I paid to put in my car for work the entire week.

But there were plenty of other issues I had with my oldest sister, she used the loose coins I left in the car to pay for the tolls in the morning when I drove on the turnpike going to work and coming back home. If I left a couple of loose bills in the arm rest of the car, my oldest sister spent my money without replacing it, and she took it without my permission. I am talking about thirty dollars, twenty dollars, ten dollars, five dollars, and the one-dollar bills. I was upset with her, she was being a user, and it was not her money to spend or touch because she did not put the money there, *I* did.

My oldest sister behaved as if I was obligated to put up with her disrespect, but I did *not* have to put up with *any* of it and I did not have to help her. Yeah, I was living in my oldest sister's house, but I paid bills under her roof, she was driving my vehicle for transportation, and I helped her out in other ways continuously only because she was my family. But my oldest sister was a grown woman with three kids, she was not handling her responsibilities and her priorities like she should have, instead of playing a hopeless victim looking for a pity party.

I was eighteen years old, working, I had my own car, I took care of myself, and I did not have any kids. I looked at this way, I am the younger

I AM GOD'S CHILD

sister, the youngest of all my siblings, and if I can get up off my butt to work hard, then so can my oldest sister.

She had no respect, and no regard to come back home with my car when I had somewhere to go in my car. She left in my car driving around in the streets, she did not answer my phone calls, and she powered her cellphone off because she knew I was calling for her to bring me back my car.

I was upset, my oldest sister *knew* I was upset, and I was going to snap on her when she came back home. Many times my oldest sister lied to my face trying to get me to believe the lame excuses she tried to feed me, but I knew it was lies coming out of her mouth with that smirk on her face. She could not handle the small task of picking me up from work on time, plenty of times I sat outside on the steps in front of my workplace, after work waiting thirty minutes, to an hour for my oldest sister to pick me up.

Some mornings, my sister was too drunk from the night prior leading up to morning, so Tiffany dropped me off to work, then went back to the house to get the kids ready and drop them off at school.

My oldest sister did not respect my privacy, she had no respect for me, my belongings, or my car. To me, I considered her to be an ungrateful and unappreciative person.

She constantly went into my bedroom when I was not home, she sprayed on my perfume, she took my clothes and my shoes without my permission. I did not have many clothes or shoes, but I had enough, it was mine and I was appreciative for what I did have. She did not ask me to borrow my belongings because she knew my answer was going to be no when she asked to borrow them. When I asked my oldest sister to borrow *her* belongings the answer was no, she only allowed me to borrow her belongings once they were worn out and she did not want it anymore. But when I bought a new outfit or a new pair of shoes she was right there asking to borrow them. When I told her no, she still went behind my back anyway to take them and wear my stuff anyway.

If I had dared to go into my sister's closet to borrow any of her clothes or shoes without her permission, it would have been a *big* problem and a *big* deal!

My oldest sister did not take care of my belongings she took, she dogged out my shoes, my sneakers were scuffed, they were dirty, and smelled like toe jam after she put her feet in them. She stretched out my clothes, and they were stained and dirty when she gave them back to me.

But I had enough of her shenanigans, I was fed up with her, she tried me for the last time, and I exploded like a ticking time bomb.

One day, I let my oldest sister use the car at the last minute, but Tiffany and I had plans to go somewhere, so we were dropped off to the event. My sister had four hours to handle her business and then come back to pick us up from the event. She was going to meet up with a friend of hers who was a Realtor, he was supposed to be showing her a property listing and my second oldest sister tagged along too. My oldest sister arrived *four* hours *late* to pick us up from the event, and I was furious on the inside while I waited for her to pick us up that night.

It was nighttime, Tiffany and I were the only two people left waiting outside on the street. All of the people were gone, the school was closed, and all of the lights were turned off. We were standing outside in the streets in the dark late night, alongside the street curb by ourselves waiting and I kept calling my oldest sister's cellphone. But she was not answering, and then the phone started going straight to voicemail.

She finally arrived to pick us up, and immediately proclaimed her cellphone battery was dead. But I did not believe her lies, I was not hearing anything she had to say to me, and we had a big argument in the car on the ride back home. I was fed up with her shenanigans, and I told her to give me back the spare key to my car. I took them from her, and she no longer had the privilege to get in my car to drive.

I let Tiffany drop me off to work in the mornings, the kids still needed to be dropped off and picked up after school. Tiffany picked me up on time from work, after picking the kids up from school, something my oldest sister could not do.

My oldest sister was upset with me, and we were not talking to each other. She decided to vent to our mom about how she felt about me snapping on her the other day and taking my spare car key away from her. I was not surprised when I received a phone call from my mom. My sister made it seem as if *I* wronged *her*.

According to my mom, I was wrong for allowing Tiffany the privilege to drive my car because she is not my family, my sister was jealous and felt like I was putting Tiffany before her. My mom said I should not trust Tiffany over my sister, but I did not trust my sister either. My oldest sister was really in her feelings, and she told my mom all kinds of lies about me that my mom believed.

I had to laugh, to keep from being mad and perhaps losing my cool over the phone with my mom because I could not believe this mess my mom had the nerve to say to me, which she knew nothing about. According to my mom I was supposed to be fine with my sister driving my car drunk, with her allowing others to drive my car, the car I pay for every month and deal with her disrespect because she was my oldest sister.

No, I do not think so! I do not care. Not anymore.

She was *not* going to drive my car or get my car keys back. It is not ok for your family to treat you like crap, but my mom was trying to convince me otherwise and I was not hearing it.

I AM GOD'S CHILD

I was nineteen years old; I was a young lady, I worked hard for everything I had, and I was having fun while still trying to figure out life. I made the decision to trust Tiffany with driving my car while I was at work, and I took full responsibility for anything that happened to my car when I gave her my car keys. This was another learning lesson for me, and I learned the hard way I cannot trust nor help everyone.

• • •

I put my trust in the wrong people, I had to learn to protect my heart. All I did was try to help those I love, and I trusted. I wanted to see everybody happy and doing good in life. I love my oldest sister, I trusted her, and I tried to help her the best way I could. When I was there trying to help her, she was not handling her priorities, and she did not take the opportunity seriously. She proved to me she was irresponsible; I could not trust her, she did not respect me, and she is supposed to be my family. I had to laugh over the phone to keep myself from being angry even more. My mom tried to pull that family card on me, she tried to guilt trip me by making me feel like I did something wrong, and it was hurtful to me.

I considered Tiffany to be my friend, and I thought I could trust her. How was I to know Tiffany was a fake friend? I did not recognize Tiffany's jealousy, or envy toward me, and her secretly running a competition with me, but I was never racing or competing with her. I was too busy handling my business and minding my own business instead of paying attention to what she had going on. I was being genuine with Tiffany, and she was deceiving me too. I was naïve, I gave from my heart without expecting anything in return, and did not see Tiffany for the user, the thief, and the leech she is. I consider a user to be a leech, a blood sucking leech that clings on to you, sucking your blood and then leaving after getting what they want from you.

Tiffany did not have a job, she had a job once, and it lasted two weeks. At the time, she worked at the football stadium at one of the concession stands part-time, after receiving her first paycheck she quit and said it is not enough money for her to continuing working there. Like I said, Tiffany's hustle was doing hair for money, but she did not do hair daily, and she did not have many hair clientele.

Tiffany and I were not around each other all the time. She was grown, I minded my own business, and at the end of the day we lived our own separate lives. It was Tiffany's responsibility to handle her own business, and handle her own priorities, not mine.

See, I woke up every morning to go to work to earn my money to pay my bills and to take care of myself. When I was not working, I spent the rest of my time throughout the day doing what I wanted to do, and I enjoyed my time alone. Tiffany was a cool person to hang out with, she was a nice person aside from her being a thief and deceitful. Sometimes Tiffany spent time away with her other friends, her family, and her boyfriend. At times, she was gone for days, and for weeks. I enjoyed having time alone to myself, I did not intervene in her business, and I let her enjoy having that personal time to herself. I preferred to chill-out at home. Tiffany called me a party-pooper or boring. She invited me to hang out with her and to tag along on outings, but I knew it was because I had a car. Sometimes I accepted the invite to tag along, and sometimes I rejected the offer. Sometimes Cara came down to visit from time to time, and all of us partied together. Tiffany spent her time throughout the day doing what she wanted to do and living her life.

In the meantime, my oldest sister got herself into some trouble, and she was arrested for trying to steal from a retail clothing store. This situation was not looking too good for her, she was arrested in the past for the same thing multiple times, and she was locked up awaiting trial. My oldest sister's charges were serious, and she was facing possibly serving multiple years locked up in jail. There was no money to hire a lawyer, but somehow my mom managed to hire an attorney for her case.

I put collect calling on my cellphone, so my oldest sister can call from jail to speak to me and the kids. I had to step up to handle more responsibility around the house and care for the kids while waiting to see what her outcome was going to be. But I did not do it alone, and Tiffany continued to help me out, along with my oldest sister's boyfriend.

Well, my routine was going to work, coming back home to tend to the kids, and keeping the house clean. Tiffany continued to take the kids to school in the mornings and she picked them up after school. But from time to time, my oldest sister's boyfriend helped out with dropping the kids off and picking them up from school. He continuously stopped by the house to visit the kids, checking in with us to make sure things were ok. The kids constantly called their dad to buy them fast food and he came right over to take them to get it because it was all they wanted to eat.

Tiffany and I kept the house clean. We washed the laundry; we did the grocery shopping for the house with my oldest sister's food stamps monthly, and sometimes we cooked dinner for the kids. I cooked dinner, but the kids only wanted fast food, and I was not going to spend my money buying that every day. The kids were used to eating fast foods because it was what their mom feed them, but not me. It was either eat the dinner we cooked or eat the food in the refrigerator we bought for them to heat up in the microwave themselves.

As the days passed while my oldest sister sat in jail, we received the foreclosure papers for the house in the mail from the bank, and a sixty-day notice to vacate the property. This was another problem, and more added pressure. But I took it one day at a time, I packed up my oldest sister's belongings, and I started packing things up around the house day by day. Surprisingly, my sister was able to go before a judge, the judge considered her time served and she was released from jail before we had to move out of the house. Being released from jail came as a surprise to her, and to everyone else.

Then one day things went from bad to worse for me, and then soon after disaster followed right behind.

I woke up late for work, rushing to get ready and out of the house. I woke Tiffany up to drop me off to work, and I was behind the steering wheel driving my car that morning. I had a car accident as I was reversing out of the yard, and my car was damaged in the back. It was my fault; I made the mistake of miscalculating the distance and speed the other vehicle was traveling. As the other vehicle was approaching, I reversed out of the yard, I pulled out in front of the other vehicle and the driver slammed into the back of my car.

The back of my car was completely damaged; the trunk, the rear bumper, and my right taillight. The driver of the other vehicle was fine, and the guy had no injuries either. Tiffany and I had no injuries. Most importantly I was happy everybody was ok, and still alive. But Tiffany had a little bit of soreness in her neck from the whiplash of the impact from the car crash and she decided to go to the hospital. I was upset with myself; I was really hard on myself for making a big mistake like this and putting other people's lives in jeopardy.

Honestly, I had no choice but to continue driving my car with the damage from the wreck until I was able to save up the money to get my car fixed myself. I still went to work that morning, my oldest sister dropped me off, and Tiffany went to the hospital for the pain in her neck from the whiplash. I still had to make my money, and I needed all my money because I did not know how I was going to get myself out of this jam. I was not prepared for what happened next, and it was a blow to the stomach that knocked the wind out of me.

A couple of weeks later, near the end of my work shift, I got a call. Tiffany called my cellphone, I answered assuming she was calling to let me know she was outside in the parking lot already waiting for me to get off. That is what I *thought*, but Tiffany was calling to inform me she was involved in a car accident at the moment, and I could not believe it. Tiffany called me from the scene of the accident, she proclaimed the accident was not her fault. She was riding the tail of the other vehicle, assuming the driver was going to speed up to catch the traffic light, but the driver hit the brakes and she slammed into the back of that car.

Well, my car was no longer driveable, and I had my car towed to the house. I did not know how bad the damage was, and I was really hoping it was not as bad as it seemed to be.

I told Tiffany not to worry about the situation, and I called someone to pick me up from work. I remember coming home that day, as we pulled into the driveway, I looked at the damage done to my car from the wreck and my heart was crushed. I was devastated, I was heartbroken, and I did not know what my next move was going to be after this situation. Tiffany was not at the house when I arrived home, she went to stay at her auntie's house for the entire week, I did not speak to her, and I did not receive one phone call from her that whole week. I spent the weekend home in bed crying, and I did not want to do anything.

Our photographer neighbor who lived across the street, tried his best to cheer me up, and he surprised me with home cooked meals of my favorite food dishes that weekend. Then my neighbor and I had a personal talk, to sum it all up he basically encouraged me to keep on pushing until I land back on my feet again because he knows I am a go-getter. But I had to get over this ordeal, what is done is done and it was my decision to allow Tiffany to drive my car. I took accountability, I accepted the full responsibility and consequences for my decisions because it was my car.

I had a talk with my mom over the phone, she gave me a pep talk and she reminded me that I have to keep pushing forward. Now, I had to rely on my family for their help with transportation for me to get back and forth from work until I was able to get back up on my feet again. My mom suggested I stop being too prideful to ask for help, and my mom took it upon herself to notify the entire family about my situation. I noticed my oldest sister around the house gloating, with a smirk on her face, and laughing in my face whenever we made eye contact.

My oldest sister approached me one time to say, "Where is your friend at now?" She laughed in my face and then she walked off.

But I did not let it bother me, I could have said something slick back to her, I see me being down brought my sister satisfaction and I recognize her envy toward me. But at this point in my life, I had to swallow my pride, I had to put my pride to the side along with my ego and I had to humble myself.

By the grace of God, I received help from my family, I had a way to get to work and a way back home every day. I caught a ride with my second oldest sister for a week, she dropped me off to work and picked me up after work. Afterwards, my dad extended his helping hand by lending us his car for a while and he caught the bus to work.

Then my oldest sister was able to get a vehicle with the help of her boyfriend and then I relied on her for transportation to work. I woke up every morning to go to work, and I came back home after work. I had to deal with my oldest sister's spitefulness, it came with her help, and I dealt with it. I was not going to ask my oldest sister to drive her car, I knew if I asked to drive her car, the answer was going to be no. But I asked my oldest sister on purpose to drive her car to see how she was going to react, and she reacted exactly how I expected her to act. My oldest sister was still mad at me, for taking my car keys away from her and not allowing her to drive my car anymore before this wreck happened. She felt as though I wronged her, and she acted like I did her wrong.

But I did *not* wrong my oldest sister, I was helping her, I shared my vehicle with her, but she was not grateful, appreciative, or respectful toward me or my property. But once I put my foot down, and I let my oldest sister know I will no longer tolerate her bull crap anymore, she was upset. She did not allow me to drive her car, one time I asked to drive her car down the street to the corner store, and the answer was no. It was cool, but it was not cool, and I took it on the chin like a champion. I expected my oldest sister to behave like this, she was being spiteful and vengeful.

Yeah, my oldest sister behaved funky with her car toward me, she did not want me to drive it, but she always wanted me to pay to put gas in it. She only let me get behind the wheel of her car *once*, and the only reason she allowed me to drive it was because it needed gas. I had to continuously pay to put gas in the car in the mornings on my way to work, and once I put gas in the car, she drove it all out. It did not matter, if I filled the gas tank up, or filled it up halfway, she drove the gas out, and then told me it needed gas again.

Honestly, all I cared about was making sure I got to work to make my money and saving up to get my own car again, so I do not have to depend on others.

As for my emotions at the time, I was still hurting on the inside, but I did not show it, and I was depressed a little bit. It was really God who kept me during those days, I prayed to God, and I talked to God especially when I started to feel defeated or doomed.

As Dr. Maya Angelou once said before, "We may encounter many defeats, but we must not be defeated."

I prayed myself to sleep at night for strength, and I prayed to God for a peace of mind. Well, Tiffany finally came back to the house after she began missing me since the car accident and she apologized to me. I accepted her apology, and again I told her not to worry about paying for the damages done to my car because it was my decision to allow her to drive my car, she had no money anyway to pay for damages.

The time had come—much earlier than expected—for everyone to go their separate ways, because the bank forced us to move out of the house sooner than expected.

We moved out of the house near the winter at holiday time. Tiffany packed up her belongings and she moved back to her auntie's house. My oldest sister, the kids, and I packed our belongings up and we moved in with my parents. My oldest sister rented a storage unit to store the rest of her and the kid's belongings because there was not enough space at my parents' house.

• • •

Here we go again, I was back to living under one roof with my entire immediate family again, it was a full house, and it was filled with chaos.

There was a difference this time around living with my family, I was not a kid anymore, I was grown now, and everyone else was also older, including the kids; they were not little babies anymore. But two things remained the same living under my mom's roof; there was no order, and no discipline! This was the continuation nineteen years later picking up from when we were little girls being raised under our mom's roof, with those never talked about horrible family secrets from the past, and here we are pretending like we are this big happy family that all love one another.

My family was in turmoil and my family was dysfunctional—as you can see for yourself. Everybody in my family was still struggling to survive, including me and I had a job working to earn money. But I knew with everybody living together again, this time around was going to be more drama filled and so the drama began.

I shared a bedroom with my oldest sister; we slept on a full-size bed together and the kids slept in the living room on the couches. My wrecked car was parked outside in the driveway with a car cover on it, and I decided to give the car back to the dealership as a voluntary repo. I apologized to my second oldest sister because she was my co-signer for the car, I was able to get the car because of her help and now the car was wrecked, due to my bad decisions. It was going to cost thousands of dollars to fix my car, I could not afford to get my car fixed while continuing to pay the car note at the same time and I decided to cut my losses with the car.

The house was crowded, there were eight of us living under the same roof among one another trying to co-exist with all different personalities, egos, attitudes, and habits. It was my mom, my dad, my oldest brother, my oldest sister, my niece, my two nephews, and me all living together in one house.

My second oldest sister and my niece moved out of the house into a new place. My oldest sister's boyfriend moved into my parents' house when my oldest sister put him out of her house, but he moved out to make room for us to move into the house. She was still fooling around with him, and they still had nothing but drama. They had it going on again, they were two crazy fools.

While my oldest sister was busy fooling around with other guys, her boyfriend was busy fooling around with another woman also, and the drama began. When my oldest sister found out, she stole her boyfriend's car, she destroyed his car, and threw away all of his belongings in a trash dumpster. After all was said and done her boyfriend still wanted to be in a relationship with her again. But things did not work out between the two of them, and they called it quits.

Both of them moved on and began new relationships with other people. But the drama did not end there between the two of them. Now, they argued about the child, about money and everything else. But I stayed out of their business, I did not want any involvement in their drama, and I minded my own business, although they tried to get me involved in it.

Then more of my oldest sister ex-boyfriend's lies and secrets began to surface into the light. This was not good news for anyone living in the house because the house was in foreclosure, we were served with the paperwork and now our living situation here became unstable.

My oldest sister's ex-boyfriend was taking the money my parents paid him for rent monthly, but he did not use the money to pay the mortgage. Instead, he used the money to take care of himself.

If those papers were not served at the front doorstep, I do not think her ex-boyfriend would have confessed about the house being in foreclosure, and he would have continued to keep it a secret. He confessed the truth when approached about the situation, but at the end of the day there was nothing anyone could do to save the house because nobody had the large amount of money needed at the time.

Here we go again, from one situation, into another situation and the uncertainty of not knowing when we had to be out of the house. Honestly, nobody had any money, and if the bank would have told us we had to be out immediately, then we might have been homeless. The plan moving forward, we were going to continue living in the house until we *had* to move out, and everyone saved up their money to get a place of their own until then. Here I am trying to save money to get another car, and now I need to save money to find another place to live. Honestly, I did not earn enough money working at my job to afford a car, and a place of my own.

The winter season and holiday time was here. But I was unhappy, I was depressed and stressed out. Living in the house with my family was unpleasant and stressful at times for me. I still did not have a car, and I depended on my family for transportation. I was in a bit of a funk emotionally and I did not want to be bothered. My goal was to get a car to get back on the road and that was my focus at the time. I *thought* when faced with a dilemma like our situation at the time my family would start prioritizing better, saving their money and being responsible.

Nope, not my family!

My family did not take this situation seriously. I expected different from them, and they continued to do the same things they been doing, which was nothing and wasting time.

Growing up around my family taught me to be a survivor, I had a plan to reach my goal, I am not a person who sits around waiting on other people and depending on others to do for me when I can do it for myself.

In the meantime, my oldest sister continued to do what she did best during rough times like this; she spent time away from her kids and away from the house most of the time. She went off looking for an escape as usual, she was hanging out with her friends clubbing, getting drunk and searching for another man to take care of her. Yeah, she left the kids at the house all day long for everyone else to tend to, while she was out in the streets doing whatever.

I do not know what my oldest sister was doing with her time away, but I know she was not searching for a job, and she did not come back home with any money. But she was bringing a different guy over to the house, introducing them to everyone, and crying broke to her children when they asked for money to buy something. She did not have any money to provide for her children financially, and these guys she brought around only spent money on *her*.

My oldest sister came back to the house showing off the material things one of the guys gifted her with, and she proudly boasted about it, but I saw a problem with it. The kids needed new clothes, socks, underwear and shoes too. The kids were wearing the same clothes they outgrew, the same raggedy old mismatched socks, and old dirty shoes. But my oldest sister had new clothes, new shoes, and her hair and nails were done.

Anyway, I spent my time going to work, and coming home because I needed my job to make my money. All I cared about was getting to work, my oldest sister was my transportation and me depending on her was becoming a problem.

• • •

In the meantime, I met a guy one night making a run to the corner store for some snacks in my oldest sister's car, and we exchanged telephone numbers. I was single, I had other guy friends I talked to also, but nothing serious, only conversation from time to time.

That night as I walked out of the corner store with my snacks going to the car, another car pulled up in the parking lot, and this guy stepped out of the car with his son to go inside the corner store. The child ran past me into the store to get snacks of course, but the guy stood there next to his car watching me as I walked passed him.

He stopped me as we made eye contact with one another. I thought he was handsome, but I smiled at him as I kept walking pass him toward the car and he tried to get me to stop to talk to him. He stood there watching me walk away, I turned around to look back at him and he smiled back at me. He said, "What's up?" I smiled back at him, I said nothing to him, and I got inside of the car. I overheard him say, "It's like that?" Then he turned away and he walked inside the store to be with his son.

I did not drive off immediately, I decided to wait before I drove off, and instead I sat inside of the car looking at the guy inside of the corner store with his son.

Well, I will admit I found the guy to be attractive, I thought he was sexy, and I liked his smile. I watched him look outside the store window at the car to see if I pulled out yet, as his son grabbed snacks, and I sat in the car smiling watching him. I thought to myself, "What if I never see this guy again? Why not talk to him and—worst-case scenario—if I do not like him, then I will stop talking to him." I waited in the car listening to music, as he walked out of the store with his son he approached my car and he proceeded to tap on the passenger side window to speak to me again.

He was a gentleman, he asked for my telephone number, we exchanged numbers, and he asked to call me later on that night. Then I drove off and I went back home.

Sure, enough later on that night, he called my cellphone like he said, and I answered the call. His name is Shawn, as we talked on the phone for hours that night, it was instant chemistry between the two of us, and we had a great conversation as we talked.

After meeting that night, we were in constant communication with each other, we talked to each other daily, and during the night as we fell asleep on the phone talking to one another sometimes. Shawn spent many nights coming over to my house to visit me, we spent time talking to one another and we enjoyed each other's company.

Shawn worked with his hands fixing sport motorcycles, he worked in the mornings like me, and we text each other good morning every day on the way to work. Shawn was a single dad, and he co-parented with the mother of his child as they raised their child together. Shawn spent his time throughout the day working, spending time with his son, and in between time we spent time on the phone talking to each other. We were friends getting to know one another, I enjoyed the nights he came over to visit me, we stayed up late-night chilling outside talking about all sorts of things laughing and joking with one another. Shawn took his time to get to know me as a person, he never tried to pressure me about sex, and I was going along with his flow. We were dating each other, but we were not exclusively dating or together in a relationship, I was still a single lady, and he was still a single man.

Well, once the winter holiday season was over, I was able to put my plan into motion and get myself another car. It was the beginning of the new year, it was income tax season, and I had plans to handle my priorities with my money. I called my oldest sister's ex-boyfriend again and I asked him to help me find a car. I was able to get another car with his help and his connections.

This time I got a 2007 Infinity G35 coupe, and it was such a nice-looking car. I was happy, I had a car again, I was back on the road, and I did not have to depend on my family for transportation anymore. I thanked God, I was grateful, and I was able to bounce back! My new car brought about jealousy, and envy from my family. My family showed fake love to me, but I became the center of attention, and I was simply trying to mind my own business. My family thought I had more money than I did, and everybody had their hands out wanting something from me. They asked me for money, or they wanted me to buy them something, and they asked to drive my car instead of everyone being focused on handling their priorities and saving their money to find another place to live because it could be any day now when the bank tell us we have to get out of this house.

I was constantly fighting or arguing with my family, and I had no peace of mind living with my family. They say blood is thicker than water, and as family we are supposed to be there for one another. They say family is going to fight one another, but as family it is important that we love, be kind, and forgive one another. There was no love, loyalty or respect, no forgiveness but there was definitely a lot of spite, vengeance, grudges, and fighting with my family.

My mom and my oldest sister were in constant disagreement about my oldest sister neglecting her kids. You know at the time I was unhappy; I was dealing with a lot of family drama, and I was doing my best to survive. I argued with my oldest sister about disciplining and chastising her kids. The kids were disobedient, rude, and disrespectful at times to my mom. The kids did not want to listen to my mom, they did not want to help clean the house, and they did not like to do as they were told by their elders.

Well, I am auntie Samone, I do *not* tolerate disrespect from kids, and I did not tolerate the kids disrespecting their elders, their grandmother, especially my mom! I disciplined and I chastised the kids when I was home if they were misbehaving. The kids did not like it when I disciplined or chastised them because they knew I meant business and I definitely did not tolerate disrespecting my mom in front of me because it was not going to end well for them.

The kids called their mom on the phone, and they complained to her about me because I disciplined them. I did not let them have their way, and they did not want to listen to me. My oldest sister was not around to keep up with her kids and she was not around to spend time with them. But she gave her kids permission to go against my word, and my parents' word when they were not allowed to do something or go somewhere. The kids called their mom to get permission from her to go and do as they pleased after they were already told no.

My oldest sister once said to the kids in front of me, "I am your mother, not Samone. I am the one who takes care of you, I tell you what to do and you listen to me."

I am the kid's auntie, I have been helping raise these kids since they were babies, and I was a kid back then. But the kids knocked on my bedroom door, they came to me when they were hungry or needed something and I was there for them. I loved the kids too, as their auntie I was doing my part with helping raise the kids by teaching them right from wrong, teaching the kids about principles, morals, values, and integrity when it comes to life.

I had many arguments and confrontations with my drug addict brother. My brother was the definition of lazy, he stayed home all-day long eating food, getting high, sleeping, and pooping like a dog. He lived off of his disability check and his food stamps every month. He spent his disability money on drugs, and tricking with women buying sex. He liked to live in filth, and he lived like a bum. He did not take showers, brush his teeth, and he wore the same stank dirty clothes and dirty shoes for months.

Most of the arguments and confrontations I had with my brother were about his hygiene because I could not tolerate his odor in the house. The rest of my family tolerated my bother's filthy hygiene, I could not tolerate it and look the other way pretending as if everything were ok. I am his sister, he is my brother, and what kind of sister would I be if I did not say something to him about this problem? I argued with him whenever he was being mean to the kids, disrespectful to my mom, and being greedy with food. He is a confrontational person, but I did not care, and I did not back down from him during our confrontations.

Well, my brother is a Mr-Know-It-All crackhead, he really thinks he knows it all, but I know it is the drugs talking. He does not like to be approached about anything pertaining to his hygiene or taking a shower. He gets defensive and then he becomes confrontational. Whenever I approached my brother to have a talk or conversation with him in the best manner possible, it still led to a confrontation and me being the bad guy because I decided to say something to him. Oh, my brother gets upset with me, he gets outrageous shouting derogatory words at me, and then he threatens to physically fight me. Then I get upset too, I exchange hurtful words with him, I dared him to touch me because I was not afraid of him. My brother is mean, he is grouchy mainly when he has no money for drugs to get high, and no food to eat.

At times there was no food in the house for the kids to eat, but my brother had food. He would not share any food with the kids, and he sat at the kitchen table to eat his food in the kids' faces. But he came to me for help when he had no money, and no food stamps for food to eat. And I helped him at times. If I had money on me, I gave him money out of my pocket for him to get something to eat. Sometimes I gave my brother the plate of food I was eating, when he walked up to me saying he was hungry and rubbing his belly. But when the time came for my brother to return the favor, when I needed help or food to eat and when I asked him for help the answer was *no*.

As for my parents, I do not know what kind of relationship to call this mess, but they were still with the shenanigans, and nothing really changed besides the fact they were older now.

My parents still had the same relationship issues, both of my parents cheated on one another, and pretended as if they were in love with each other. My dad proposed to my mom three times, and each time she said no. The last thing they needed to be was married, I do not know why my parents were still together and I could clearly see these are two people that were not happy. My parents were not in love with one another, and they did not make each other happy. They were still fighting; my dad still came home trying to beat my mom when he was drunk and high. My dad still drove home drunk at night coming from Overtown after hanging out with his buddies, he continued to live carelessly and recklessly. My dad continued his drug use, sniffing cocaine, popping pills, smoking weed, and whatever other drug he used.

My dad and my brother were smoking partners, they smoked dirty joints at home together in the house. I stayed home to protect my mom, I had altercations with my dad a couple of times, and it does not make me proud to admit this either. Because my dad came home drunk at night waking up the whole house with his episodes, and sometimes he messed with the kids, which upset me more because he woke the kids up out of their sleep. My aunt Diane once said to me, "God is your mom's protector, and no one can protect her better than him."

• • •

I AM GOD'S CHILD

In the meantime, I remained in contact with Tiffany, and we were still friends. Silly me, I considered a foe to be a friend, and I naively continued to have Tiffany in my presence.

When I was without a car, Tiffany still came over to the house sometimes to hang out with me and my family at times spending the night. But you know what? I have to admit I did not learn my lesson the first time around, and I learned my lesson the hard way this time around. I did not stick to the script of what I told myself, which was stay to myself, and no one drives my car, but me. And you know what? I did not take the time to ask myself why was I friends with Tiffany? I do not know why I considered Tiffany to be my friend anyway, I should not have let her in my presence, and I should have questioned her motives for being around because she was not a real friend. I knew I could not trust her because I felt like she was stealing from me.

No, I *knew* she was stealing from me, but I could not catch her, and she was slithery like a snake. But a real friend will not steal from you, and I should have cut her off completely. Beware of thieves, you can trust a thief to be a thief, but do not trust a thief, a thief is a liar, and a thief will kill you to keep their secret hidden.

Well, I stuck to the script in the beginning, when I first had my car, no one drove my car but me, and I did not care who was mad about it because it was *my* car. When someone asked to drive my car, the answer was no, and no one touched my car keys but me. I drove myself back and forth to work, it felt good too.

Everyone was mad with me, my sisters, my dad and Tiffany. My sisters and my dad complained to my mom because I did not let them drive my car. Then my mom came to me, trying to make me feel bad acting as if I was being a mean person for being stern with them, and now I was the bad guy to my family. Honestly, I was stern with my family because I did not trust them to be responsible driving my car, and I did not complain when they acted funky toward me with their car when I was down.

My dad wanted to drive my car to hangout in Overtown with his buddies, drive his other women around in my car and drive drunk behind the wheel of my car. My oldest sister wanted to drive my car around in the streets doing nothing and dog my car out driving recklessly. My family acted as if I was obligated to let them drive my car, like whatever is mine belongings to them, and they were entitled to what is mine.

I spent most of my time going to work and coming home. But from time to time, after work I went over to Tiffany's auntie's house to hang out with her and her family. Sometimes we went back to my house to hangout, and other times we found other places to go. But I still made it my responsibility to pick my mom up from work every day and take her home no matter what I was doing throughout the day.

I lost contact with my old friends, I spent time hanging out with Tiffany and her friends in Overtown. I made time to visit my second oldest sister; spending time at her place, going with her to visit my nephew at his dads' house, and I went to his football games to support him. Every chance I had to visit my nephew with my second oldest sister, I went to see him because it was not very often, I had the chance to spend time getting to know him.

But back at home, my oldest sister found a new boyfriend, she moved in with him and left her kids living at the house with us. Once she moved in with her new boyfriend and his family, she spent most of her time away from her kids. This was nothing new. She was already leaving the kids home while she was out spending time with her boyfriend and neglecting her kids if you ask me. For my oldest sister it was all about pleasing her boyfriend and making him happy because she depended on him to take care of her, the kids were not included.

Then another problem arrived, the water was turned off due to a lien against the house, and we were without water now. Well, the water utility remained turned off, everybody cried broke, and my family did not want to put our money together to get the water turned back on. So, I began to spend more time away from the house, and away from my family.

But in my time of need Tiffany's auntie was gracious enough to open up her home to me, allowing me to come take a shower at her house many days and nights. Her auntie completely opened up her home to me, allowing me to take showers, feeding me meals, and she allowed me to spend nights sleeping at her house. As long as Tiffany and I made it to her auntie's house before a certain time at night, before she locked up her house to go to bed. I was thankful and grateful for Tiffany's auntie's help because she did not have to help me.

I did not want to wear out my welcome at her auntie house, so some days and nights we went over to my second oldest sister's apartment to take a shower. I considered Tiffany to be my friend, and we looked out for each other. I did not want to wear out my welcome at my second oldest sister's place either, and at one-point Tiffany's friend opened up her doors to me. Tiffany and I spent time staying with her girl friend. I slept on her friend's couch, she fed me and allowed me to take showers at her house. I began to allow Tiffany to drive my car again. At one point I let her use my car for transportation when she attended community college, instead of attending class she used my car to chase behind her boyfriend trying to keep up with him and his whereabouts because of his infidelity. Luckily, she did *not* get into a car accident while driving my car and wreck out again.

While I spent time away from the house for a couple of months, I still went to work every day to earn my money to pay my bills and to take care of myself. I only went home when I needed to get some clothes, shoes, and some of my personal belongings. My parents called to check on me from time to time, and to inquire about me coming home. I was stressed out mentally, I was worrying, I was in my head too much thinking all the time, and at night I found it hard to sleep because I could not stop my mind from racing. I had many restless nights, and emotionally I was unhappy, but I never showed it.

Some days I called my grandmother Rebecca in South Carolina to speak with her about family issues, and my personal issues. I prayed to God for guidance, and I prayed to God for peace of mind because I was having really bad migraines which blurred my vision sometimes. My grandmother always encouraged me to stand strong, to keep on pushing with life no matter the difficulty of circumstances and the uncertainty of situations because God is with me. I enjoyed my phone conversations with her, I enjoyed laughing and joking with her. I missed my grandmother, I missed being able to be near her physically, and I did my best to stay in contact with her often.

I began having issues with Tiffany pertaining to my car, her girl friends, her lies, her thievery, and we were bumping heads with one another.

Tiffany began to get besides herself, it rubbed me the wrong way when home girl began to feel like she was entitled to drive my car like it was hers, but the last time I checked it was *my* car. I knew Tiffany was the one stealing from me although I never caught her red handed, I was surrounded by users, people I could not trust, and it weighed heavy on my spirit.

You know I have to admit I was being naïve, and I was not listening to God. I was having man problems; Shawn and I were not seeing eye to eye. Shawn and I only spent time talking over the phone, and we barely spent time with each other personally like we used too.

I began to recognize I was being used by Tiffany for my car, and she was still stealing from me. I had a personal conversation with my dad, he convinced me to come back home, and my family turned the water back on illegally although it was not the main reason I came home. Everybody around me wanted to use me, everybody wanted something from me, and I just wanted to be left alone. I decided to distance myself from everyone. I took my dad's advice; I stayed away from Tiffany, I went to work, and I came home to rest.

Of course, Tiffany felt some kind of way when I distanced myself from her, I did not call or speak with her, and it only took about a week before she called my phone. Yeah, Tiffany was stuck at her auntie's house with no money, no car to get around in and that was the reason for the phone call. Like a fool, I decided to repair my friendship with Tiffany, and I began to hang out with her again.

One night we were on our way to Tiffany's auntie's house, and I let her drive the car that night. The cops pulled us over because she failed to come to a complete stop at the stop sign. When the cops ran Tiffany's name through their police system, there was a warrant for her arrest, she was arrested that night and booked at the county jail.

Well, Tiffany called me from jail hoping her case would get dismissed or she would get bond. Tiffany's case was not dismissed, the judge granted her bond, but she had no money to make bail. This was not Tiffany's first time being arrested or jailed, but her family did not know it, and she did not want them to know. Tiffany has been jailed previously for getting caught stealing from retail stores, and I was there to help her out. But this time, Tiffany decided to tell her family about this situation, and she did not receive any help from them. Tiffany's boyfriend had no money to offer to help her with this situation and I did not have any money to offer either. So, Tiffany had to sit in jail, but I was there to help her out in other ways. I showed up to Tiffany's court dates, and I kept in contact with her public defender about her case. I put collect calling on my phone so she could call me from jail, and I showed up to visit her every week on visitation days.

Meanwhile, Tiffany sat in jail, and I continued on about my business as usual. I went to work to make my money and pay my bills. Honestly, while Tiffany was locked up none of my money came up missing, and it was refreshing to be to myself again. While Tiffany sat in jail for a couple of months, one of her main concerns was her boyfriend, trying to keep tabs on him, and he only visited her once.

Listen, I minded my business and I keep my lips *closed* when it came to her personal business with her man. None of Tiffany's so-called friends were there to help her, but I was there to help because I felt bad for her, and she had no help. Luckily, Tiffany was released from jail, after I was able to make sure the public defender showed up to her court date—and let me tell you it was not easy. After Tiffany's release from jail, she was back to doing the same things again, and it did not take her long to steal from me again once I let her in my presence.

After everything I did to help this girl, she stole money from me *again*, and I knew it was her because none of my money ever came up missing while she was locked up, like I said before. And it was not long before Tiffany popped up pregnant from her boyfriend after only being out of jail a couple of weeks.

I decided to distance myself from Tiffany again, I talked to her over the phone, and I barely went to visit her at her auntie's house. I spent my time working, being at home with my family, being by myself and spending time with my boyfriend.

I AM GOD'S CHILD

• • •

I was in an exclusive relationship with Shawn now, I decided to be with him, and I cut off all communication between my other guy friends. Shawn and I dated for ten months before we made our relationship official. This was my first serious relationship, and Shawn was my first serious boyfriend. We spent more time together personally getting to know one another, we had great chemistry together, and we never had a first date together. Shawn was like my best friend, I trusted him, I wanted to be with him, and I lost my virginity to him.

Although our relationship was not perfect, his love displayed for me was genuine, and I did not have any trust or infidelity issues with him. Both of us had a lot going on in our personal lives with family, the major problem in our relationship was timing, and both of us had to make the time for one another to help our relationship grow.

I was patient when it came to us seeing each other and spending time with one another because he had a child to raise too. I respected the personal time Shawn spent with his son alone, and the nights he did not come to see me because he stayed home to be with his son. Shawn was acquainted with my family, but he lived with his family, and he drove a long distance to visit me every time.

Now, this is the part of my life where things are beginning to change for me, because I have a boyfriend and my friendship with Tiffany changed.

Tiffany called me complaining about the distance between us, and the time I spent with my boyfriend because I was not hanging out with her anymore. But I never complained or cared about the time Tiffany spent with her boyfriend when I was single, and I did not have a boyfriend. But I was tired of Tiffany's thievery, she was stuck at her auntie's house, but she only wanted to get back around me to use my car and steal from me. The last time Tiffany was around me; she stole sixty dollars I stashed away in my nightstand drawer next to my bed inside of an envelope. She denied stealing my money when I questioned her about it and pretended to help me look for the money. I knew I could not trust Tiffany, but against my better judgment I allowed her in my presence again.

Silly me, I know, *I know*. I was being a fool. I had compassion in my heart, and I felt bad for Tiffany at the time during her pregnancy. Tiffany was having a hard time deciding if she was going to have the baby or get an abortion, and her boyfriend at the time did not want her to have the baby. Tiffany's boyfriend was trying to convince her to have an abortion, her boyfriend said he was not ready for another child, he already had two children, and he was struggling trying to take care of them.

It was not a happy time for Tiffany during her pregnancy, she was living from pillow to post sleeping at her auntie's house, at her cousin's house, and at my house. Well, Tiffany's family does not believe in aborting children, and she knew her family would not support her getting one. Tiffany asked for my opinion one day, she asked me what I thought she should decide to do?

Listen, it was not my decision to make, it is not my life, it is hers and I was not going to make that decision for her. Like I said to Tiffany, "I can't make this decision for you, and I am not going to tell you if you should or should not go through with the pregnancy because at the end of the day the decision is totally up to you. I am not going to advise you to have a child because that child will not be my responsibility and I do not have any money to give you to help take care of your child. But right now, I know you do not have a job or any money to financially support you along with a child. You do not have a stable place to live, where are you and the baby going to live once you do give birth? Having a child is a big responsibility, and once you have a child you cannot give it back."

Well, Tiffany decided to go through with the pregnancy and to keep the baby. As a friend, I did not ask Tiffany any questions to get up in her business, and I let her sleep at my house with no questions asked. But problems began when Tiffany stole money from me again, and from my second oldest sister. Tiffany thought I was going to let her leech off of me, she thought it was my responsibility to let her use my car for transportation to get around and go to her doctor visits, instead of her boyfriend's.

No, I let Tiffany know that is not my problem, nor my responsibility and she was going to have to find a way to handle her business because my help stopped at a certain limit.

As for me, my personal business and my boyfriend. This was not Shawn's first serious relationship, his previous relationship was with his child's mother, and that relationship did not work out for him. Shawn dealt with problems from the mother of his child, although they were no longer together. I have never met the mother of his child; I have never spoken to her and I have never interfered with the co-parenting of their child. I let Shawn handle that part of his life because it involves his child.

The mother of his child had some jealousy, control, and anger issues pertaining to Shawn's love life. It appeared she was having a hard time moving on and accepting the fact Shawn did not want to be with her.

I have never met Shawn's son, it was not by choice either, the main reason was because of the mother of his child at the time, and I did not want to cause any problems for him. She had a problem with Shawn having his son around me once she found out he had a girlfriend, and she threatened to keep his son away from him.

I knew how much Shawn love his son, he loved spending time with him, and being a father to him. The mother of his child tried to use their child as a pawn against Shawn, whenever she wanted more money from him. If she did not get the money she kept his son away from him.

During my relationship with Shawn there were a couple of times, when the mother of his child called the cops, lying to get him arrested and locked up in jail. But she was a liar, and each case against Shawn was dismissed because of her lies. I used to think Shawn was over exaggerating when he talked about some of the things he went through with her, the kind of person she is, and the crazy things she does. Until I saw some things for myself. I was there to support Shawn as his woman, and as a friend through tough times.

You know some people do not believe God has a sense of humor. That is funny to me because I think God has quite the sense of humor, he is the master of laughter. God is my master, I am his creation, and God *has* to have a sense of humor if he made *me*. I can tell you that right now!

It is funny to me now, but I remember when I was praying to God asking him to send me my soulmate and telling God I do not want to be with a man who has kids already because I did not want to deal with any baby-mama-drama. It is funny how God works, and I said this to God way before I met Shawn. As I said before, it is not your way, and it is not your plan when you are dealing with God. Your life belongs to God, it is God's way, and it is God's plan as you travel along your journey in life to fulfill your life's purpose.

Unexpectedly one day, while at home I received a phone call from Shawn telling me to come pick him up down the street from my house. I immediately grabbed my car keys to drive down the street to pick him up as instructed, and to find out what was going on. As I pulled up to Shawn, from the look on his face I knew something was wrong, he was not driving his car and I knew it was not good news. I was shocked to hear Shawn almost lost his life after someone just tried to shoot and kill him. A person Shawn gave a ride to opened fire on him after exiting the vehicle, firing shots at his car while his son was inside the car with him, he wrecked the car stepping on the gas pedal to get away, he then grabbed his son, and they ran for their lives.

Shawn ran with his son, hopping over fences running through people's backyards, and he did not stop running until they were safely far away as possible. Shawn called the mother of his child to come pick up his son, and then I received that phone call from him. That day, Shawn left his car at the accident scene, all of his personal belongings had been in the trunk of the car, but were stolen from it. All of Shawn's clothes, shoes, and jewelry were stolen from his car after the accident. Shawn was living out of his car because he could not trust the family members he lived with, they were a bunch of users, thieves, and liars.

That night Shawn stayed at my house with me. The next morning before I went to work, I dropped him off to the police station, and I waited for him to call me. The police did not arrest Shawn, and he was not charged with anything. By the grace of God, Shawn and his son were both lucky to still be alive. My heart was hurting for Shawn, I felt bad for him, and I stayed by his side to support him. Shawn was terribly upset, and he was upset that his child's life was put in danger.

You know, it is such a shame when you cannot trust your own family, and they treat you like you are not family. We are quick to say we are family, then treat them like crap, but treat a stranger better. It is such a shame when you cannot count on your family to help you, and the only person you can count on is yourself. But as soon as you start doing good, family wants to come around you with their hands out. It is such a shame when your own family becomes jealous or envious and they hate you!

But you can count on family, *right*?

I extended my hand to Shawn with him down on his luck right now, and with nobody to count on besides himself. I volunteered my services to help him, while he figured out his next move because his car was wrecked from the crash. I trusted Shawn, and without any hesitation I wanted to help him because that is just the type of person that I am.

Shawn caught the bus to get around until he was able to get his car fixed or able to get another vehicle, and I offered to let him use my car for transportation to get to work, along with handling his personal priorities. In the mornings Shawn drove my car to visit his son, he spent time with him by walking with him to school. It was the only way he was able to see his child because of the child's mother. She wanted more money in order for Shawn to spend time with his son, she was jealous, and she was upset he drove my car to visit his son. She was a stripper at the time, she only cared about getting money from Shawn, and at the time it was money he did not have to give her because he needed the money to get back on his feet. Shawn accepted my helping hand, I cared about him, and I was happy to help him out the best way I possibly could.

I took it upon myself to have a one-on-one talk with my mom pertaining to Shawn's situation, I asked my mom if it was ok for my boyfriend to move in with us because his living environment with his family was toxic. The travel distance was too far away, far away from his son, and his job and he needed another place to live.

Although my living situation was no better, Shawn still accepted my help. I explained Shawn's situation to my mom at the time, and my mom allowed Shawn to move in with us.

Let me just say for the record, this part of my life journey is where I began a new adventure filled with more highs and more lows with my family and my personal relationship.

I was *not* prepared for what was coming my way, I must say.

• • •

You know, God does not answer our prayers the *way* we want him to, and God does not answer our prayers *when* we want it done. But can you recognize when God's blessing is right in front of you? Can you recognize when God is talking to you? Are you a disobedient child doing the things you want to do your way? Are you listening to God? I know it might seem like I am doing too much for Shawn, maybe I am moving too fast by allowing him to move into the house with me and my family. My family thought I was being young and dumb for Shawn because he was older than me, although they never said it to my face.

I *was* young, but I was *not* dumb. It was my life to live, and I felt in my heart I was doing the right thing.

My family thought Shawn was using me, they thought I should not be with him, and I should be with somebody else. Well, if my family knew me like they claim to know me, they should have trusted my decision to be with Shawn, instead of wanting me to be with another guy because they did not like him for no reason.

See, I take pride in my independence, I took pride in relying only upon myself, and not being dependent on other people. I was not looking for a rich guy with a lot of money, I do not chase money and money is not everything to me! It is not all about what someone can do for you financially in a relationship if you are looking for *love* and not chasing a guy with money. I have seen where chasing after money gets you, I can tell you right now it is not pretty, it is definitely not all peaches and cream, if you know what I mean.

I never dated a guy based off of the amount of money he was making or how much money he spent on me, and I was not about to start thinking that way now because of what my family thought I should do. I was not with Shawn for money, I had my own money, and I took care of myself. Shawn was not using me, he is a good man who treats me with kindness, respect, love, and he protects me.

But most importantly, Shawn is a *loyal* man; he is loyal to me, and I love that about him. Shawn was the one person in my life during this time I could trust, I could count on him to have my back, and his love is genuine. This man has helped me before in my time of need without me asking for his helping hand, with no problems or complaints, and to be honest with you it made *him* happy to be able to help *me*.

REBECCA S. SMITH

When the A/C unit in the house stopped working nobody in the house wanted to give money to help get it fixed, and everybody in the house had to deal with the heat instead. All I had was a fan to use for the heat, but Shawn still came to visit me, and he sweated it out with me.

One day, Shawn surprised me showing up to my house with a new window air conditioner to put in my room, so I did not have to sit in a hot house anymore, and he setup the air conditioner in the window. Sometimes, Shawn brought me food to eat on days when I had none, he changed the brakes on my car, and he helped me with so much more by doing all he could, when he could help me. Shawn was not a perfect man by any means, and he has flaws like we all do. But I knew his flaws and I knew how to deal with them. I am not a perfect woman myself and I have my flaws too. But at the end of the day, we worked through our issues in our relationship, and we wanted to be with one another.

Well, the first thing Shawn and I did was change the locks on my bedroom door. Yes, we put a dead bolt lock on the door, so my family members could not go into my room to steal anything when we were not home—because they were thieves too.

They all snooped through my room, my oldest sister was still taking my belongings, my clothes, shoes, and they took whatever else they could take of mine. I caught my crackhead brother snooping through my room, going through my drawers, stealing my movies off of the DVD rack, but leaving the movie cases, and stealing the money I left in my drawer.

Yeah, my family was being slick. They thought I was a dummy, but all of it came to an end once we changed the locks on the bedroom door. My family was low key mad at me, but I did not care how they felt—*they* were the ones stealing from *me* anyway.

Shawn was aware of the living situation pertaining to the house, he knew how my relationship was with my family from the talks we had together, and he already saw my dad in action before; having one of his drunken episodes coming home trying to beat my mom. Shawn moved in with nothing but the clothes on his back, and a few more of his belongings in a black trash bag. And to my surprise the most important possession to him in that trash bag was a *Bible*. It was a *Bible* given to Shawn from his mother when he was a kid, and he has kept it with him ever since then.

I learned something new about Shawn, he believes in God, and he prays. I was happy to know this about him, I have known this man for about two years, and I just learned this about him.

Shawn and I were a team; we worked together. It became a *we* mindset, not a *mine* and *yours* type of relationship! Well, I cared about my man, I did not have much for myself or much money, but I went to the store to buy him boxers, socks, undershirts, deodorant, and the other necessities he needed. I let Shawn drop me off to work in the mornings, then he drove the car to his uncle's motorcycle shop to fix bikes.

Shawn is a hustler, he had many other ways of making money, and he is not a man who sits around doing nothing. Shawn works with his hands—he is *good* at working with his hands—and he is good at fixing things.

One of the ways Shawn made money was reinvesting his own money in buying used motorcycles then restoring or rebuilding the bike, with added customizations and then selling it for a profit. He decided to use the money he had saved up to get his car fixed, then continue to figure out things as he goes from there. Shawn wanted his own vehicle to move around how he wanted to, to do the things he did on a daily basis handling his business and making his money.

Well, things were going good in our relationship aside from the baby-mama-drama, and Shawn missing his son because he was not able to be with him like he wanted too. He was not happy, and he did not smile much, but I tried my best to make sure I kept his spirits up throughout this rough time. When we were at the house, Shawn stayed in the room to himself most of the time, because he did not trust being around anybody besides me or his younger brother at the time. Shawn spoke to my family, but he stayed to himself, and I was cool with it because I understood how he felt. He was a guest living in someone else's house, and these people already did not like him.

My family did not have to tell me they did not like my boyfriend because their actions showed me everything I needed to know. All of a sudden, my family decided to hangout in the living room all the time, all waiting to see my man come out of the room to stare at him awkwardly and trying to make him feel uncomfortable. Especially, my two sisters who were trying to be all up in my business and being nosy anyway. I am not perfect like I said before, and yes, I was shacking up with my boyfriend at my parents' house. No, we were not married, neither was marriage a topic of discussion at the time, and I know some people may not agree with my situation. Hey, it is, what it is.

That year, Shawn spent the holiday season with me and my family. But early on Christmas morning, Shawn left to be with his son and surprise him with a gift. He bought his son the gaming console he wanted for Christmas. We shopped around looking for it until we found a store with one in stock. But Shawn also went to give his son a haircut, and to spend time with him playing the game because he was happy to just be with his son.

Well, Shawn drove my car to visit his son, but he parked my car around the corner and then walked down the street to his child's grandmother's house where his son lived because the mother of his child had a problem with him showing up in my car.

On Christmas day, the mother of his child decided to intervene with the time Shawn was spending with his son by complaining to him about money, then getting confrontational, causing a big commotion and then calling the cops trying to get him arrested in front of his son. Shawn was doing the best he could at the moment, trying to be a father to his son, and trying to raise his son with a person who spewed hatred toward him.

The mother of his child said to the father of her child, "I wish you'd die or get locked up again and go back to jail."

How do you co-parent or raise a child with a person like this? This sounds like hate to me; those are hateful words to say to someone and to wish on another person's life, if you ask me.

But the drama did not end there with the mother of his child. She sent text messages to his cellphone late night hours while we were in bed sleeping and pictures of her supposed boyfriend. We looked at the text messages, we laughed about it and we went back to sleep.

The drama continued. While the mother of his child was stripping one night at the club her car was broken into in the parking lot of the club, and this girl told the police Shawn did it and for the police to come arrest him. The girl lied to the police, we were home all day and night that day. She became mad when the police never came to question Shawn after she named him as a suspect and he was not arrested. She lied, then she called Shawn's mother to tell her a lie about him stealing her car, and his mother called him fussing. I had to vouch for Shawn to his mother and explain to her that the mother of his child was lying for no reason. But this girl was not done stirring up trouble, trying to bring Shawn misery, she wanted him to suffer, she wanted him to hurt bad and she knew *exactly* what to do to hurt him to the core of his heart next time.

The mother of his child plotted and planned the entire time to do something drastic. Let me just say for the record the following year was a test to our relationship, we hit a rough patch that year and we had to fight through it together.

One morning Shawn went to visit his son, to walk him to school as usual, and to his surprise the grandmother informed him his son no longer lived at her house.

What? Yeah, the mother of his child packed up everything and she moved away with his son. Where did they go? The grandmother informed Shawn she was given instructions by her daughter not to give him the address to his son's whereabouts or her daughter's new telephone number to reach his son because the phone number was changed. Shawn was upset after being told something like this, and it did not sit well with him of course. But to make a long story short, the mother of his child took his eight-year-old son and she moved out of town somewhere without letting this man know anything!

The days turned into weeks, the weeks turned into months, and the months turned into years since Shawn last saw his son that Christmas day.

Well things went downhill fast from there to bad, to bad again, and then to worse for us. Shawn used his money to get his car fixed, which turned out to be a bad decision and the money went to waste because the car began having *other* numerous problems that needed fixing after being repaired from the accident. Once Shawn's car broke down after he got it fixed, I called my uncle Cliff to inspect the car, and he told us it was best to not waste any more money on it. Shawn took a loss, and he voluntarily gave the car back to the dealership.

Then Shawn's uncle's motorcycle shop closed down, and he was out of a cash paying job. Transportation was not a problem; we had my car to get around and we shared my car. Money was not a problem; I did not complain or trip about money to Shawn and I still went to work. As I said before Shawn is not lazy, he did not sit home doing nothing and he is a hustler. Shawn used his hands to make money by fixing other people's motorcycle bikes from personal ads, and other people he knew personally with motorcycle bikes. At the moment Shawn restored two motorcycle bikes he customized himself and he was busy trying to sell those bikes too.

But working on motorcycles was not consistent work, nor was it enough stable cash for Shawn at the moment. He was able to get a job working at another motorcycle shop, he worked there for two months and things were looking up for him. Shawn was happy working at this motorcycle shop, he liked working on motorcycles and he liked doing his job. I was happy for my man, he needed this job, and he needed the cash.

Now, with that being said, Shawn is an ex-convict—as a teenager he did some things in his past—and after serving two years in jail getting hired for a job was hard to come by because of his past criminal record. So there was one problem; one of the co-owners of the shop was a racist man and he did not like Shawn. Shawn was hired for the job by the other co-owner, and the guy did not have a problem with him. But the racist man took it upon himself every day to do something to make Shawn mad or to make him tick to get rid of him.

One particular day, the racist man succeeded at making Shawn lose his cool. Things did not get physical, but Shawn *threatened* to physically beat up the racist man and he was fired that day.

The funny thing is I did not know Shawn was fired from work that day, and he did not tell me until two weeks later. After being fired, Shawn continued to wake up in the mornings as if he was going to work, and I thought he was going to work.

After getting fired, Shawn was disappointed with himself, he thought I would be disappointed with him, and he did not want to disappoint me. That was the reason Shawn went looking for work every day, trying to find another job and a way to make some money. I was not disappointed with him; I was happy he decided to communicate with me, and he no longer had to pretend by wearing his work shirt.

I cared more about Shawn communicating with me, and finding a resolution to continue moving forward. I would rather know, than not know, I wanted Shawn to know I had his back, and he can count on me to support him in any situation. We were a team, we worked together, we had to stick together because it was just the two of us and we were all each other had!

Well, I still had my job working to make money, and I did not stress about the situation. The difference is, I no longer thought with a *mine* frame of mind, I thought *ours*, and he thought *ours* too. We had money, it was not much, but we budgeted our money to pay bills, to feed ourselves and to survive day to day.

Aside from those tough times, there was a lot on our plate, and living in the house among my family was not happy times for us.

As I said before, Shawn protected me, and he protected me from my family. My relationships with my family members were rocky, and Shawn did not allow my family to disrespect me. He did not interfere in arguments with my family, he did not talk bad about my family, and he never tried to turn me against my family. But when my brother or my dad decided to have one of their episodes flipping out, then Shawn came out of the bedroom to interfere and say something. Especially if someone was being disrespectful toward me, Shawn came out the bedroom to check whoever, letting them know he will not tolerate anyone being disrespectful toward me and he will not allow anyone to put their hands on me.

Shawn mostly stayed in the bedroom to himself thinking about his son and trying to figure out his next move. He was never disrespectful to my family, he tried to get along with them and he was respectful to everyone.

My family was not used to a man like Shawn, he was stern when speaking, he was straight forward, direct, not afraid to speak his mind and he was not afraid to come to my defense against my family when I needed him. He tried to build a connection with my family, and he learned firsthand exactly how my family is. Yes, there have been a couple of situations with my family that turned into physical altercations between Shawn, myself, and them a couple of times. It does not make me proud to admit this.

I did not want to fight with my family, and I did not want my boyfriend to fight with my family. I do not believe family should fight one another. You must teach family how to love one another, how to treat one another with respect, and how to get along with each other. But see, my family did not want to get along, my family only wanted to get along with me or be nice to me when they wanted something from me, and when they wanted me to do something for them.

Basically, my family were a bunch of users in my opinion, but I felt bad fighting with my siblings and my dad in front of the kids as their auntie displaying these types of actions. I tried my best to teach my nieces and my nephews how family should love one another, not fight each other!

In the beginning, Shawn did get along with my family, or so I thought. Then I think my family grew to not like him for whatever reasons they had in their minds, because he did nothing to deserve the hate he received from them. Shawn came out of his shell to talk, joke, and to laugh with my them.

He was respectful toward my parents aside from the family drama, and it appeared as though my parents liked him. Shawn loved my mom, he respected her, and he did anything she asked of him. My mom came to knock on my bedroom door asking Shawn to lift or move something around for her in the house and he did what she asked of him with no problem. Sometimes, my dad and Shawn sat outside having conversations while grilling food and drinking beer. Shawn tried to get along with my brother, aside from the drama that came along with him too, and he played with the kids. He took it upon himself to take out the trash, he helped clean up the house, and he mowed the lawn without being asked to do so. But my family still came with drama, disrespect, lies and hatred toward us.

Apparently, despite Shawn genuinely trying to get along with my family, they considered what he did for them to be like nothing. They decided not to have any respect for him because he was not rich with enough money for them. Secretly, my family did not like my boyfriend, and they pretended to like him when I was around.

How do I know? Well, there were times when I heard my family talking about us like dogs, making a mockery of Shawn being broke with pennies. My family laughed at me, my family slandered my name, they slandered my boyfriend's name, and they slandered my relationship.

My immediate family told lies about us to other family members, to neighbors, and to other people to sway their opinion of us. According to my immediate family, I was being a fool, I was being young and dumb because my boyfriend was older than me.

According to them, Shawn did not love me, he was controlling me, and he was only using me—if you let them tell it. Honestly, my immediate family did not know much about my personal relationship with Shawn. I learned they could not be trusted, and they ran off to tell what little bit of my business they knew to other people putting my business out in the streets. My relationship, my boyfriend and my personal business became the center of attention for my family.

A couple of months later, unexpectedly disaster struck for me, and I was laid off from work. I worked at this company for five years, straight out of high school, and now here I was being laid off from work out of nowhere!

You know, honestly, I did not know how to feel when my supervisor told me I was being laid off, and he was supposed to have fired me a week prior, but he could not bring himself to do it. Well, this was the first time I have ever been fired from a job, my emotions were all over the place, although I did not show it, and I was hurt at the moment.

It's funny how I was happy when I first started this job, and here I am feeling hurt after being laid off from this company. My feelings were hurt, I felt like I was wronged, I worked so hard for this company, and here I was being thrown out like a piece of trash. My supervisor told me I was one of the best workers he had ever worked with, he volunteered to write me a letter of recommendation for my next job, and said I could use his name for a job reference anytime.

You know my supervisor was trying to tell me I was being laid off earlier that morning when I came into work, but I was not listening, it was too nosy from the machines, and I could barely hear what he was saying to me. I worked all the way up to my first fifteen-minute break of the day, my supervisor had to literally sit me down during my break to tell me because he was not sure if I heard him telling me I was being laid off earlier that morning. I did not finish working the rest of the day, although my supervisor did give me the option to finish working, but I left and I went to the park for a while to clear my head before going home.

It was now my turn to go to Shawn to speak with him about my getting laid off from work; he was supportive, and he comforted me. At this point Shawn and I were both jobless with not much cash. To survive, I collected unemployment to pay bills and we budgeted our money to stay afloat. I continued to search for employment filling out various job applications online and I searched for a job by word of mouth.

Shawn continued to try to find work using his hands to get paid cash and he was able to find another job painting the highway walls for eighty dollars a day. One day, Shawn came home with paint all over him and a smile on his face. He was happy, and I was happy for him. As a man, it made Shawn proud to find his own way, his own job, and to make his own money. I learned to let a man be a man, to find his own way in life doing things his own way and learning on his own. Shawn was raised by his father to be his own man, and he learned a lot about being a man from watching his father growing up as a kid. I understood Shawn as a man has to find his purpose in life, he had to find his own way and I had to be patient with him.

During the tough times I faced ahead, I learned a lot about my immediate family. I thought I could count on them to help me. This is the part where family is supposed to be there to help one another, family is all we have *right*?

And my family let me down! Honestly, I did not expect what I received from my family because I loved them unconditionally, and no matter what I was there for them in their times of need.

My family was *happy* to see me down on my luck and struggling with my boyfriend. Yeah, somehow it brought my family joy, I think they thought me being down this time was going to break my spirit, and they thought I was going to give up. Well, I learned some people love to smile in your face and then kick you while you are down.

But that is something you must never do! You never laugh at a person when they are doing bad, and you never kick a person when they are down, because God can easily bring you down to your knees.

You know it was funny to me, I was being disrespected by my family, and it was not cool, but I just laughed it off. I had to laugh to keep myself from being mad or angry, and snapping at them like I usually did whenever I was mad. The truth is my family does not like to hear the truth. I am honest, I am straight forward, and I am outspoken with them, which they did not like about me.

It took a lot to make me mad, but I was short tempered. Once I snapped *everything* coming out of my mouth was cold hard facts and the truth. I was not disrespectful, I spoke my mind, but my mouth is a problem for some people because I am going to say what needs to be said, rather than what people want to hear me say, and some people do not like me simply because of my boldness to do so.

My immediate family labeled me as the rude, judgmental, harsh, selfish, and disrespectful family member. I felt like an outcast in my family, I was treated differently by my family, and by my mom growing up. My mom has always treated me differently from my siblings and I cannot not stand it at times. My mom cared more about being in my business, rather than what my other siblings were doing, and my mom wanted *me* to help everybody. I am the responsible one and I am the reliable one of all my siblings. But I was hated and used by my family.

As a child of God, as a woman, I was trying to keep my faith in God, and I was trying to stay strong. As a woman I stood strong side by side with my man against my family, I loved and trusted my man. My family was trying hard to break up my relationship with Shawn, and they did hateful things in hopes he would leave me because they were a lot to deal with.

Shawn was no fool, he was a strong man; he was strong mentally, and strong physically. Shawn genuinely loved me, he handled my family, and he was the right man for the task. Honestly, my family *was* a lot to deal with *for real*. I knew Shawn loved me, and he did not have to stick around to deal with all of this drama and chaos.

Well, as things were beginning to look up for us with Shawn working now, he already had a plan, and he was saving up cash from working painting the highway walls for a week now.

But a stroke of bad luck came again, Shawn was not able to continue working painting the highway walls after he became sick one night with a fever and he had to be taken to the hospital. He was supposed to work the same night he became sick, but he did not answer his cellphone that night when the guy called to come pick him up for work. Once Shawn recovered from having the fever, he called the guy's phone number, but the guy never answered the phone again.

We had a lot to deal with at the time, it was all happening so fast, and it was one thing after another. I was stressing out, and Shawn was stressing out thinking about how we were going to make some money. At the moment we were still surviving on my unemployment, money Shawn saved up, and money from him selling the motorcycles for less because we needed it. But our funds were running low, we barely had enough money for food to eat, and there was not enough money to continue paying our bills. We were managing to get by day to day, my unemployment money was soon coming to an end, and I was still searching for employment.

Shawn and I were both seeking employment, but both unsuccessful at finding jobs at the moment. We needed money to continue paying the car payment and the car insurance payment, our cellphone bills, food to eat, and gas for the car.

My family loved every bit of it, they smiled, and they laughed in my face. Oh, my family was some piece of work, they really showed me their true colors, and I do *not* mean it in a good way. It was amazing how my boyfriend was the primary target for my family, and they were focused on him not having a job. Yeah, they pretended as if they cared, and acting as if they wanted to help, but they were really coming in my face to gloat, *especially* my oldest sister.

I thought it was funny when my oldest sister got in my face to tell me about a job hiring or someone she knew who could help me get a job, and she needed a job herself. When my oldest sister came to me about a job, I told her, "Thank you, but no thank you, I am good." Then I let my oldest sister know her oldest son needs a job, our second oldest sister needs a job, and so does she.

I stopped talking to my mom about my personal business, and my personal relationship because she ran her mouth to tell my business. My mom cannot hold water, and I could not trust her. But at times my mom was around to talk to Shawn and me when we had arguments to teach us how to communicate better with one another, but she was also being nosy.

When my mom kept coming to me about jobs for Shawn, I had to tell her to stop coming to me about jobs for him, and I did not appreciate it because it made me feel like she was being a little bit shady. My mom only got in *my* face telling me about jobs, but she did not go to my other siblings about these jobs, and they *all* needed jobs too.

At the time, my oldest sister and her new boyfriend moved down the street from my mom's house into an efficiency in the back of someone's house, but her kids were still living at the house with us. Yeah, my oldest sister left her kids at the house to be among chaos, the kids were sleeping on the floor on a mattress in the bedroom and sleeping in the living room on the couch. My nephews slept in the room with my brother, my niece slept on the couch in the living room, and during the night I woke up out of my sleep to check on my niece to make sure my dad or my brother did not touch her because I did not trust them.

My oldest sister, along with my second oldest sister were both hanging out together in the streets having a fun time, also having sexual encounters with random guys they met. Although my oldest sister had a boyfriend whom she lived with, she still cheated on him with other men, and her boyfriend cheated on her.

Instead of my two sisters handling their priorities, focusing on raising their kids, and working to earn a paycheck, they left their kids at the house all day, while they ran the streets. The house became a fun house with no rules or authority.

Yeah, I called it the fun house, it was the playhouse for my nephew, my niece and their friends to do as they pleased. My oldest nephew sat outside on the side of the house smoking weed with his friends, making a bunch of noise and hanging out in front of the house all day doing nothing. His friends came over to eat and to spend the night when they disobeyed their parents, and my mom allowed it.

My oldest niece walked around the neighborhood hanging out with her clique of girl friends being fast and grown. Yeah, my oldest niece was a sneaky girl, but I kept my eyes on her, and she knew to hide what she was doing with her friends from me because I stayed on top of her, paying attention to what she was doing unlike her mother. My oldest niece was into boys now, she snuck off with her girl friends going to boys' houses, texting provocative pictures to boys, and she was having sex. But my oldest sister was too busy to notice until it was brought to her attention about what her kids were into during their personal time.

My oldest sister's youngest boy spent his time outside playing with the neighbors' kids next door, besides playing with his friends, he preferred to be with his father, and he called his father all the time to come get him because he was being neglected.

The kids were not doing good in school, my oldest nephew, and my oldest niece were both failing in school. They were absent from school a lot, missing too many days, they were not doing their classwork or homework. They were in jeopardy of flunking out of high school and they were placed in a 'last chance' school. The youngest boy was behind on his grades in school also, and not doing his homework.

But my family had their eyes on *me*, with their noses all up in my business, not paying attention to their *own* issues. Meanwhile, my second oldest sister's boyfriend was living at her apartment, sleeping in her bed, but my mom was paying the bills at her apartment. My second oldest sister needed a job, and so did her boyfriend, but nobody got in their faces talking about a job.

As for Shawn and me? Our relationship hit a rough patch as we continued to fall on hard times, dealing with our stress and personal issues individually in different ways. Sometimes, we argued although I was the one doing all the shouting, as Shawn calmly told me to stop shouting or to stop being loud for others to hear our business and my family loved it when we were unhappy or arguing. During this rough patch in our relationship, we were still immature in certain ways, we both had to do some growing up individually to grow together and to make it through this time together.

We had to work on communication in our relationship by talking things out, but also listening to each other. Shawn dealt with his stress, along with missing his son by getting drunk. I felt bad about him not being able to be with his son, but he was drinking liquor and beer to get drunk trying to cope with everything. Shawn's drinking habit to cope was becoming a problem for me, I did not have a problem with him drinking until it *became* a problem and we started arguing. It began with Shawn drinking on the weekends, then him drinking every day, and it was not good because he was drinking too much. Although Shawn tried to hide the fact he was drinking excessively from me, I still found the liquor bottles he hid underneath the bed or in his drawer, and I found the beer cans he hid in the car underneath the car seat.

Although I did not go looking for anything, I knew he was drinking because I could smell the liquor or the beer on his breath. Whenever I found one of the liquor bottles Shawn stashed, I left it where it was, and I brought it to his attention I found the liquor bottle. I did not like what I was seeing from him, the change of behavior, along with the up and down mood swings which angered me sometimes. It reminded me of my dad and dealing with his alcoholism growing up.

My man lost sight of his focus, lost sight of what he was doing, I could not sit back quietly ignoring what was happening right in front of me and let him continue in a downward spiral. But here I was in a similar situation like my mom, minus all the abuse, and my man was beginning to drink himself away, getting drunk daily.

The man I love was having drunken moments of embarrassment, and I had to decide what I was going to do about this situation. I was beginning to question my relationship; I was not sure if our relation was going to survive, and I was contemplating being in this relationship if he continued to get drunk. But I could no longer sit back watching Shawn continue on like this, and I had to have a serious conversation with him about him getting drunk whether he wanted to hear what I had to say or not.

I, myself, had to take a look in the mirror. I am flawed too. I had an attitude problem and when I was upset it was not a pretty sight to see. It does not make me proud saying this, but I struggled with controlling my anger, my emotions, and sometimes it caused problems in my relationship.

I was like a firecracker, and once my fuse was lit I yelled instead of talking. But when I was really mad, I would completely shut down by ignoring Shawn and not speaking to him until I calmed myself down. Well, I did not have self-control when I was upset, I reacted, and I said things without thinking about what I did or what I said at the moment. This was my first serious relationship; I was still immature, and at times, in certain situations, I acted childish.

You know how you want to have your way all the time? You believe that you are *right*, he is *wrong*, it is not *your* fault, and *he* is to blame. Moments when you are still naïve, when you are young. This was a side of me I displayed when I was mad or upset and I decided to change it.

I had to grow up from being a young lady in my relationship, and I had to learn to become a woman. My man was patient with me, I had to learn how to talk *to* him and not talk *at* him because that is what I was doing. I was not expressing my feelings or emotions correctly to him, and I decided to change, to help rebuild the communication in my relationship. The problem was both of us held things inside ourselves, instead of talking and communicating with each other.

I was stressing out because our money was tight, the bills came every month, and we were barely scrapping by to keep up. I needed a job; I was searching for a job, and I wanted to work, but I had no luck finding work. My unemployment money was coming to an end, I was struggling to keep up with my car payments along with the car insurance payments and I did not want my car to get repossessed.

At the time, we were also sleeping on a mattress on the bedroom floor, my mom unknowingly brought bed bugs home after helping someone clean out their apartment and I ended up having bed bugs in my room. Well, I threw out all of my bedroom furniture to be rid of the bed bugs completely and the only thing we had to sleep on was a mattress on the floor until we were financially able to afford a new bed set to get up off the floor.

We were down on our luck; I swallowed my pride and borrowed money from my oldest sister to pay my car insurance once, and I regretted asking her for help. Sure enough I was supposed to give my oldest sister the money back at an expected date, but I did not have the money at the expected time to give it back to her, when I thought I was going to be able to give it back. It immediately became a problem when I did not have the money to give back to my oldest sister and I did not expect the treatment I received afterwards from her.

You know, my oldest sister hounded me every day, she called my phone every day for a week straight to let me know her boyfriend wants his two hundred dollars back and he wants to know when to be expecting his money. I thought I borrowed the money from my oldest sister, but *she* borrowed the money from *him*, and I did not know this until now.

My oldest sister called me every night to ask me if I had her boyfriend's money, late night hours too. I felt disrespected, and I could not believe her behavior. Every night she called I let her know I do not have the money yet, and I was telling her the Gods honest truth.

Honestly I did not have the money to pay her back, I did not know exactly when I would have it, but I told her when I got the money, I would be sure to give it back to her boyfriend first thing. Then one night my oldest sister called my phone at midnight to tell me her boyfriend wants his money back *right now*. He loaned her the money to help me out, and he did not have to do that, so I needed to give her man his money back *now*.

So I politely said to her, "I thank you again for loaning me the money, and you did not have to help me. But I do not have your money right now, I do not know exactly when I will have the money to give it back, and you have to wait. If I do not have the money, then I do not have it, and there is nothing I can do about it right now."

Well, my oldest sister hung up the phone in my face, she stopped speaking to me, and she treated me like I was not her family. I was already stressing, I was depressed, my hair was falling out, and at the time I did not know where my next meal was going to from. I literally had *no* money, I was broke, and living day to day trying to survive each moment. See, I was raised to never count the things you do for people and to never bring up what you do for somebody else. I do not count the things I do for other people, and I have never kicked a person when they were down.

We were completely broke, our funds were depleted, and my car was repossessed. I knew the repo man was coming, I was hiding my car at my second oldest sister's house, and I was trying to buy more time to come up with some money. But there was nothing I could do to stop the car from being repossessed and I only had five more payments left to make on the car before I owned it. All I needed was one hundred fifty dollars to make the car payment that month, but I already owed my oldest sister money, and I could not borrow any money from the rest of my family.

Once my car was taken away, I felt devastated, I was angry, and I cried like a baby. I felt so many emotions at once until I just felt anger, and I did not understand why everything was taken away from me. I asked God why is this happening to me? I was heartbroken, I became angry with God, and I did not understand why I was being punished. What was I doing wrong?

I literally hit rock bottom, and I was back at square one starting all over again. I was angry with my man. He promised me this would not happen, but he was not able to keep his word. I was angry with my family, I could not believe I had no help; the mistreatment, and the disrespect I received while I was down at my lowest point. No matter how much I argued or how much I fought with my family, I was still there to help *them* as best as I could, and I helped everybody out regardless.

Yeah, everything was good with my family when I was a do girl letting them drive my car, letting them borrow my belongings, and when I was helping them out giving them my money.

Umm… Let's take a jog down memory lane for a moment and let me refresh a couple of memories, if I may, since others seem to be forgetful about some of the *many* times I was there to help them.

Once my oldest sister did not have the money to pay her storage fee, she was at risk of forfeiting her belongings, the kid's belongings too, and she needed one hundred fifty dollars that same day to pay her storage unit fee. When I came home from work that day, she was in the bedroom crying and I gave her all of the money I had after paying all my bills, which was the exact amount of money she needed to pay the storage fee. I genuinely helped out my oldest sister, I did it from my heart and I told her she do not have to pay me back the money.

When my dad had a job interview, I gave him the keys to my car to drive to the interview because he had no car, and he was supposed to come right back home. Well, I do not know if my dad lied to me or if he told me the truth about going on a job interview, but he was gone with my car all day long and he came back home at four in the morning drunk as a skunk. I was upset. My dad had the audacity to power his cellphone off, and he drove drunk behind the wheel of my car. While driving drunk, my dad could have had a car accident, he could have hurt or killed someone driving drunk—including himself. What if something did happen to my car, what was I going to drive for transportation? Who was going to pay to fix my car? Who was going to buy me another car? My dad did not apologize to me for his carelessness and his recklessness. Oh, but once my dad was sober, he thanked me for letting him use my car, and then asked me not to be mad with him. Then my dad was bold enough to tell me his reason for powering off his cellphone was because he was hanging out in Overtown with my car for a little while and he was not ready to come back home.

When my second oldest sister was down on her luck struggling to pay her bills, I did not have any money to give to help her, but I did help her get a job working temporarily for the same printing company as I did to help with her financial problems. My sister had no transportation at the time, not a problem, I was her transportation to work and from work every day.

When my mom or my oldest sister came to me about my second oldest sister needing help, I helped out the best way I possibly could, and I never asked for anything back in return. I babysat for my second oldest sister anytime she needed me too, and I did it because I genuinely wanted to help her from my heart. My second oldest sister had a boyfriend at the time, her boyfriend was living with her, and he was not helping her pay bills, but it did not stop me from helping her.

I helped my drug addict brother out, even though I fought with him, although he disrespected me many times to my face time after time calling me out my name, calling me everything but the child of God. I still gave my brother money to get food to eat after he blew all of his money tricking with women for sex and on drugs. I gave my brother food to eat when he saw me eating food, as he rubbed his stomach and told me he was hungry.

But when I needed food to eat, and I asked my brother for food or to borrow money to get some food the answer was no. Plenty of times he ate food in my face when my stomach was hurting, and I needed to eat.

When *I* told *him* no, he got mad at me and expressed his hate by calling me out my name. But I humbly accepted it every time he told me no, and I was left to fend for myself. Sometimes, I begged him just to borrow five dollars or ten dollars, and the answer was still no.

Although my mom did not like my boyfriend, it still did not stop Shawn from treating her with the utmost respect. He still walked my mom to the bus stop early in the mornings, when we no longer had a vehicle, to ensure she safely got on the bus to make it to work.

Honestly, my mom was the person I went to for help, and I felt comfortable enough to ask her for help when I could not help myself. I did what I had to do to help myself before I asked for my mom's help, and I only asked for help when it was my *last* resort.

But my mom's help came with a price. It came with her wanting control. She wanted me to do everything at her beck and call. Every time my mom has helped me, I have thanked her, I tell her I appreciate her and everything she does for me. I cleaned up the house so my mom did not have to do it after being on her feet working all day. I made it my priority to always pick my mom up from work when I had a car, so she did not have to catch the bus and walk home. I made sure the house noise level was quiet, so she could get a good night's rest to be able to get up for work in the mornings. I ironed my mom's work uniforms, I put the covers over her, I turned off the television and the bedroom lights when she fell asleep at night after being too tired from work.

Now, here I am at this part of my journey where I am mad at God, I blamed God, and I stopped praying to God. Well, I had to take a look in the mirror, when God brought me down to my knees because I was wrong for being mad with God when he disciplined me for being disobedient and not listening to him! I am God's child, but I was being a disobedient child, I was not listening, and I was busy doing what I wanted to do along my journey. I was mad with God, my family, my boyfriend and myself. I was not taking accountability for my decisions or actions. I lost my faith in God, and I thought I was in control of my life. But God, had to remind me who he is, and who is in control.

I had to learn the hard way, so God stripped me of everything to open my eyes and to show me because I was not listening. God never left my side, but I thought God left me, and I was afraid I was alone now.

God had my attention now, after a reality check, my eyes were opened and I had to learn my lesson the hard way. So, I kneeled down on both my knees, as I cried tears I prayed to God, and I asked for God's forgiveness.

I cried like a baby one day in my room, I prayed to God for his forgiveness, his mercy, his guidance, his protection, for peace of mind, and for his love. I prayed to God, and I begged him to never leave my side because I need him! God has always been with me, God has been by my side from the beginning of my journey. He is *still* with me, and I am the one who turned my back on him.

What happened next?

Well, I can tell you right now after praying my life did not change at the snap of a finger, and it certainly did not change overnight. I took everything that was on my mind and on my heart and I gave it to God. I let it go, and I left it in God hands for his will to be done. Honestly speaking, I had to restore my faith in God again, and his faith in me. I had to believe in God with my heart, and I had to keep my faith in God to continue along my journey. Because I was so angry with God, and I stopped believing in God. I stopped believing God is who he says he is. I stopped believing in God's word to keep his promise to do what he says he will do, and I stopped believing God can do all things.

The hard work began restoring my faith with God when I started praying again. There is *power* in prayer; when you pray to the almighty

God, and when you talk to God. We need God's words to feed our spirit when it is weakened, to keep your faith in God, and to believe in God because it is he who keeps us regardless, as I said before.

Well, I had my soulmate by my side, praying for the both of us through this storm when I was not praying or talking to God because I was angry. We began praying together sometimes, our connection and our love grew stronger.

I am proud to say, I have a man who loves me, who prays for me, and through his faith with God, he has helped me to restore my relationship with God. But most importantly, I went to God for myself, and I myself prayed to God. I am not perfect, nobody is perfect, but I do pray, I do believe in God, and I trust in God with all my heart.

Reality set in for me, I had to work my way back up from rock bottom. I obeyed God, I listened to him, and I took action to do my part because God is not going to do everything for you. Every day along my journey I woke up and I recited my favorite *Bible* prayer to make it through the day.

> *"The Lord is my shepherd; I shall not want. He makes me lie down in green pastures: He leads me beside the still waters. He restores my soul: He leads me in the paths of righteousness for his name's sake. Yea, though I walk through the valley of the shadow of death, I will fear no evil: for thou art with me; Thy rod and thy staff they comfort me. Thou prepare a table before me in the presence of mine enemies: Thou anoint my head with oil; my cup runs over. Surely goodness and mercy shall follow me all the days of my life: And I will dwell in the house of the Lord forever." (Psalm 23)*

I continued to put my trust and my faith in God every day. I did not know how my days were going to go, I did not know what was going to happen and I did not know what the outcome would be! But I knew God was with me, and with God by my side I believed everything was going to be ok, although I could not see it. As I said before, my orders come from God, and I am his child.

• • •

As the time passed by and the days went on, things in my life began to shift. Things did not change drastically in a big way, it was more like baby steps, and I had to grow up all over again. I was like a child being reborn, I was learning how to crawl for the first time. I had to learn how to crawl before I could walk, and I had to learn how to walk before I could run.

As I continued doing my part, God was already working on things for me, all I had to do was listen and do as I was told. I have been down this road before, I know what it takes to get back up. You have to be mentally strong, you must have determination, focus, and a strong will to keep going on no matter what!

I live by the words Dr. Maya Angelou once said, *"We may encounter many defeats, but we must not be defeated."*

We were able to get another vehicle within two weeks—with our moms help. Shawn borrowed money from his mother, and I borrowed money from my mom with every intent to pay the money back.

We used the money as a down payment to buy a used car, and we paid the car payments ourselves. I was able to get a job delivering newspapers with help from my uncle Willie. I never delivered newspapers before, and it was not the ideal job I expected to be doing in my lifetime.

My delivery route did not pay much money, but it was enough money to support us from week to week, and we did not have to ask anyone for any help. Delivering newspapers required working late night hours every day and night with no days off.

Well, it was a good thing I had my own vehicle at the time because you *must* have reliable transportation to deliver newspapers every night. I was not ashamed to be delivering newspapers. I did not have a problem doing it, I needed a job to make my own money, and I did not like depending on my mom or putting more pressure on her.

I do not like to depend on other people, I do not like to ask other people for help, and I rather work to earn my own money anyway.

At the time, my second oldest sister gave birth to her third child, she was struggling too, she needed a job herself, she was depending on my mom and my mom was supporting her household.

But I was not delivering newspapers by myself, my man was right there by my side. Shawn was with me every night, no days off, and we delivered newspapers together. We were working the graveyard shift now, I was not used to working late night hours, but we adjusted, and we got through it together. Shawn and I worked every night from nightfall to sunrise delivering newspapers.

I prayed continuously for Shawn, I prayed his son was safe wherever he was with his mother, and I prayed for Shawn to see his son again.

Ultimately, Shawn decided to stop drinking and he stopped getting drunk. He regained his focus mentally, he began exercising; going to the gym to release his stress. I was glad to see him dealing with it in a better way, and our relationship began to get better.

There is more good news, and I can tell you God does answer prayers, but not how you may want him to.

Randomly, Shawn's cellphone rang one day, it was a telephone number he did not recognize, but he answered the call, and it was his son's voice on the other end of the telephone. After three years, the mother of his child allowed his son to finally call him, and it was such a happy moment. Shawn kept the same phone number hoping for this day to come and his prayers were answered, although it took three years.

Shawn and I actually had fun together delivering newspapers on the beach at night, and it was a humbling experience for me, in a good way. It opened my eyes up to see what some people, and some families were doing to survive financially, to feed themselves or their families out here in the world. I met many different people who delivered newspapers, some couples, some families, some individuals, but all of different ethnicities, ages, and different skin tones, from different walks of life and all trying to survive like me. For some of these people delivering newspapers was their second job, for others it was their only source of income like me at the time, and some of these people have been delivering newspapers every night for five plus years. For some families, the entire family was up at night delivering newspapers, each family member was responsible for doing their own delivery route from the mom, the dad, the sisters, and the brothers all together.

Well, my newspaper delivery route was in Broward county on Las Olas Beach. Throughout the area we delivered newspapers to nice big mansions, and to high rise penthouse apartment buildings. Before we drove around at night to make our delivers, we had to meet up at the warehouse to receive the newspapers.

At the warehouse we waited for the delivery trucks to arrive with the newspapers, then we arranged the pages, and inserted coupon packages to create the newspaper packets. Waiting for the newspapers bundles to arrive and creating the newspaper packets took about three hours depending on if the trucks arrived late or on time with the delivery.

It was also a task packing the newspapers inside of the car, and inside of the trunk. After packing all of the newspapers inside the car, we drove throughout the night delivering to our route on the beach until morning.

It was not a hard job, it was actually quite simple, it was about using strategy, moving fast, and using your time efficiently.

The guy doing the route before me, trained me to use his strategy to do the route correctly and in sufficient time. I was given a portable device to use—with the addresses uploaded on it—every night for my delivery route. I memorized all of the address locations, and we delivered to the same customers every night. We delivered newspapers to the high-rise apartment buildings first, with multiple floors since those were the biggest orders that required the most time because there were so many floors.

Then we delivered newspapers to the houses on the route last; the houses were the easiest and the quickest to get done because we tossed the papers on the driveway. Some customers on my route called to complain about me, some complained about wanting their newspaper placed neatly at the front door or tilted on the door so the paper could fall inside for the customer once they opened the door. Some called to complain about the noise, they could hear the footsteps when I delivered the newspaper to the front door at night, and they did not want to hear any noise. Some called to complain if their newspaper was not delivered to them at a certain time, and some complained about not receiving their newspaper at all, but their neighbors were the ones stealing the newspaper placed at the front door.

Some nights doing the delivery route were better than other nights, we had to deliver newspapers in the rain, and the customer called to complain if the newspaper was a little wet. We were out delivering newspapers for the holiday season, we delivered newspapers for Christmas, and bringing in the New Year. We delivered newspapers every night for a year. Once we finished our delivery route in the mornings, we went straight home, and we went to sleep because we were tired.

One thing I like to do is make sure I get my rest to regain my energy for work, but sleep was hard to come by with a house full of people making noise, slamming the front door, going in and out of the house all of the time. After a while, delivering newspapers became difficult as we began to have car problems; we had transmission problems, and the air conditioner did not work which made it difficult to see through the front windshield on rainy nights. When the delivery route pay was minimized it was no longer feasible for us to continue.

We stopped delivering newspapers. I was happy not delivering them anymore, and it did feel good to be in bed resting at night. It was the beginning of the new year now. It was back to square one in finding another job to earn some money.

Our living circumstances was still the same, but with help from my mom we managed to fix the car, and when Shawn won money playing lotto numbers we could buy groceries; some days we had nothing to eat. Back at home was a full house, filled with drama and chaos with everybody still struggling to survive.

Well, there is some good news, we reconnected with our cousin Cindy after fifteen years and she moved in with us. My second oldest sister, my niece and the newborn baby boy lived at the house with us. My cousin Cindy slept in the living room on the couch, along with my niece. My second oldest sister and the baby slept in the bedroom with my mom; she had her own place of residence, but lived at the house with us daily.

My oldest sister moved my niece, along with my younger nephew in with her and her boyfriend into their efficiency. But my oldest nephew continued living at the house with us, sleeping on a mattress on the floor in the bedroom with my brother.

My parents with their drama and shenanigans was the tip of the iceberg for the new year. My dad was kicked out of the house, after my mom caught him cheating *twice* with one of his women. My second oldest sister pressured my mom to put him out of the house, and he moved in with one of his other women.

I did not involve myself in my parents' personal matter, I minded my own business, I have been down this road too many times with them and I knew my mom was going to take him back again. *Ahh!*

My dad cheated on my mom *all the time*, this was not the first time she caught him cheating and she knew he was cheating on her. But I needed to focus on my priorities and deal with my issues. Hey, the way I see it is, if my mom wants to continue being played for a fool then, so be it.

Well, I thought my mom was going to take my dad back, but my second oldest sister made sure that did *not* happen. She witnessed the drama that ensued when my mom caught my dad cheating again and came home more upset that night than my mom. She packed his belongings and put them at the front door. My dad tried to sweet talk my mom into letting him move back into the house, but my second oldest sister moved in with us and set up shop in the room with my mom to make sure it did not happen.

My dad lived with another woman, and I did not speak to him for months. But my dad quickly found out the grass was not greener on the other side with his other woman, and he beat up this woman also. My dad still kept in contact with my mom trying to get back with her because this other woman did not want to put up with his bull crap like my mom did all these years.

But it was too late for my dad to come back anyway, as time expired for all of us living at that house. We finally received the letter from the bank notifying us the house was being auctioned off, the bank gave us ninety days to vacate the premises. We knew this day was coming, then the day arrived and nobody was prepared for it; nobody had any money saved up to find a place to live, including me.

Shawn and I did not have any money. We had no idea as to where we were going to live, and we did not know what we were going to do with our belongings. Everything for us was up in the air, we were unsure as to what we were going to do as the ninety-day time period was coming to an end.

As for the rest of my family, my mom definitely did not have any money to get a place, and neither did my drug addict brother. My second oldest sister was the only one with a place of her own although she was not staying there, instead she was living at my mom's house for months during all of this time.

The plan for my family moving forward? They were *all* going to move in with my second oldest sister and live at her house. My mom, my brother, my oldest nephew, my cousin Cindy, my oldest sister, my oldest niece and my younger nephew were bunched up at my second oldest sister's house.

Well, I helped pack up everything in the house, my mom put some of the furniture in a storage unit, and she took the rest of her belongings with her to my second oldest sister's house.

As for me, I traveled in a different direction from my family, I took a different path, and I began a new journey with my man. I wanted to start a new life, I have a man now, and I wanted my own privacy. I have never lived on my own, I lived with my family most of my life, and I wanted to be on my own. I knew going to live at my second oldest sister's house was *not* an option for us, we wanted our own place, we were a team, and we were sticking together no matter what. I did not want to live with my family again, there was no space at my sister's house with eight people living in a two-bedroom house, there was bad blood between my family and I anyway.

First of all, my family does not like my man, secondly, I never spoke with my second oldest sister to inquire about me even moving to her house, and I was most certainly not going to inquire about asking if my man could live at her house. Shawn came up with the idea of him going to sleep at a shelter and I go sleep at my second oldest sister's house with my family until we could get enough money to get our own place.

Umm... *No!*

That was a quick no. I did not have to think about it. He was trying to get me to listen to the idea to maybe consider it, but the answer was still no, and we were not separating, like I said before.

Hey, if push comes to shove I rather we slept in the car together parked outside my sister's front yard. I was serious, and I know I may sound a little crazy, but I am not. But I was praying to God that it did not come down to us splitting up and I knew we were going to be blessed.

My spirit was at ease, and I prayed to God because I needed a place of peace in my life.

So, Shawn decided to turn to his mom for help, he explained our living situation to her and his mother was able to help us financially get a place of our own quickly because time was ticking.

I thanked God for Shawn's mother's help at this time when we had nothing, and no one else to turn to for help. At the time, Shawn's mother was able to give us the money we needed to get a place, and we were able to find a place with a reasonable price for rent within a short amount of time. Every last single penny Shawn's mother has given to help us in our times of need, we intend to repay back plus so much more because she did so much more for us than we could have ever hoped for many times.

We needed a place that was affordable, nothing too big, a place that was big enough for the two of us to share, a clean space, and in a good area.

Well, we were able to find a nice efficiency, which met the criteria for what we were looking for when it came to a place for us to live. I praised God, and I thanked God for blessing us because this had God's name written all over it.

Once we received the keys to our new place, we packed up our belongings in our car, and we moved into our place together. This was the start to a new beginning for us, a new path in life, and I look forward to seeing what the future holds for us.

WALKING WITH GOD

I am *God's child!*
I *love God* and I *serve* only the lord.

I have been walking on my spiritual journey with God for thirty-three years now, and he has never left my side. Throughout my travels so far, it has been a long journey and a long road traveled. I had some delays, and some detours along the way.

I had my trials and my tribulations. I survived heartbreak, and I survived enemies' attacks. I have made mistakes, bad decisions, and had failures in life. I am a different person now, I learned the lessons from my mistakes, my bad decisions and my failures. I *listen* to God; I am wiser, and I seek wisdom. I am grateful, I am thankful, and I am humbled to still be alive traveling along my journey to complete my mission.

I was once a *disobedient* child. I am not perfect. As a father raises a child, I am raised by God, and *he is my father*. As a mother loves a child, I am guided by wisdom, and *she is my mother*. Being a child of God, being a disobedient child, and not listening to *my father* made him discipline me.

My test, and my spiritual awakening came calling for me. My test has been surviving my family and learning to survive on my own. I am surrounded by my enemies, and my eyes are beginning to open wide with clarity about the mission I must complete. I was not meant to survive, the devil is after my life, and many snakes lurk privily to attack me. But *God is my Protector*, and I *do not fear evil*.

I *will* complete my mission, and I intend to *cut the head off the snake!*

ABOUT THE AUTHOR

A testimony, the story of Rebecca S. Smith as she talks about her journey through life. Telling the story of her life journey growing up with her family, to becoming a woman, her faith in God, and seeking to find her purpose in life. Facing the trials and tribulations that comes with life after being born into a poor and dysfunctional family. From being the youngest child being neglected, to being a loner, and to learning self-worth through the love of God. From the love of God, to her spirituality, to finding love, and her strong will to not give up on life.

www.ingramcontent.com/pod-product-compliance
Lightning Source LLC
Chambersburg PA
CBHW051433290426
44109CB00016B/1542